HOW TO
WRITE
SONGS
on Guitar

Rikky Rooksby

"The next big thing is a good song."
BRIAN EPSTEIN (manager of The Beatles 1962–67)

HOW TO WRITE SONGS ON GUITAR
A guitar-playing and songwriting course

Rikky Rooksby

A BACKBEAT BOOK
This new second edition 2009
First edition 2000
Published by Backbeat Books
An Imprint of Hal Leonard Corporation
7777 West Bluemound Road,
Milwaukee, WI 53213
www.backbeatbooks.com

Devised and produced for Backbeat Books by
Outline Press Ltd
2A Union Court, 20-22 Union Road,
London SW4 6JP, England
www.jawbonepress.com

ISBN: 978-0-87930-942-8

A catalogue record for this book is available from the British Library.

DESIGN: Paul Cooper Design
EDITOR: John Morrish

Origination and print by Colorprint (Hong Kong)

09 10 11 12 13 5 4 3 2 1

CONTENTS

FOREWORD
TO THE SECOND EDITION

How To Write Songs On Guitar has become something of a phenomenon among songwriting books. First published in 2000, its sales have reached six figures. Clearly, there were many people who wrote songs on guitar and wanted a little extra guidance and inspiration, and others who wanted to write them but were not sure how to do it. *How To Write Songs On Guitar* (and the titles that followed it) is now to hand by many a guitar, multitracker, or computer.

This is a book for songwriters, guitarists, and people who write songs on the guitar. It is also for anyone fascinated by popular song, that magic medium in which little worlds of experience and feeling are evoked in a mere two or three minutes. It not only covers the craft of songwriting, it provides the basic chords to build songs. It also highlights how certain guitar techniques – such as altered tunings – have songwriting potential. Above all, *How To Write Songs On Guitar* was revolutionary in its citation of popular music since the mid-50s, as the index of artists and songs (here increased to over 1,800 titles and almost 700 recording artists) makes plain.

The content and character of *How To Write Songs On Guitar* was distilled from several decades of playing, teaching, and writing songs on guitar, and listening attentively to a range of music. I was always curious why songs sounded as they did, how they were constructed, and why they generated their emotion and atmosphere. This led me to develop a short-hand for describing how songs work – terms like 'turnaround', 'reverse polarity', 'stretching', 'displacement', 'tyranny of four' – and to formulate the Song Chords chart, which readers have since said is invaluable. There are other ways songwriting could be described, but *How To Write Songs On Guitar* will get you practical results. Some of its ideas were described in more detail in my later books.

For this second edition, *How To Write Songs On Guitar* has a new layout and some updating to take account of recent musical and technological changes. Section 3 in particular has citations for bands who have enjoyed success since the first edition. I hope this revision will please readers who have the original edition, and continue to inspire songwriters and spark would-be songwriters.

In 2000 I wrote, "The popular song, commercially distributed on vinyl, tape, and CD is a marvellous art form. For 50 years it has woven itself into the fabric of the lives of millions of people across the world." Since then it has also been delivered by digital download. As I write these words, a young man walks by, humming to himself, with the tell-tale white cable of an iPod dangling across his chest. Digital technology will now put in your pocket thousands of songs, whole chunks of the legacy of popular songwriting. There is plenty to learn from that legacy. And don't you want to add some songs of your own?

RIKKY ROOKSBY, Oxford, England, January 2009

THIS BOOK IS DEDICATED TO THE MEMORY OF MOTOWN BASSIST **JAMES JAMERSON** (1936-1983)

HOW TO USE THIS BOOK

If you are a beginner to writing songs on guitar I suggest you work through the book section by section, though don't feel you have to memorise all the chord shapes in Section 2 before going to Section 3. If you have been writing songs on guitar for a while, there's no reason not to dip into the book wherever you like, though Section 3 makes more sense if read from start to finish because the concepts laid out there are progressive, in that they work from simple to complex.

How To Write Songs On Guitar has 16 sections. Section 1 provides a quick overview of the way in which songs are written. Section 2 is the first bit of a two-part guitar chord dictionary. It has the basic chord types and shapes that dominate popular songwriting. Section 3 leads you step-by-step through the ways in which chords are linked to form the building blocks of a song. Here you can learn which chords fit in which keys, about turnarounds, three-chord tricks, and much more. Additional techniques to apply to these building blocks are provided in Section 4. The basic elements of song structure – verses and choruses – are discussed in Section 5. Sections 6, 7, and 8 deal with rhythm, melody, and lyrics, respectively.

By the mid-point of the book you have all the information to write songs with simple harmony. The second half of the book extends this knowledge. Section 9 is part two of the chord dictionary, with extended chords that give additional flavour to your harmony. Section 10 discusses the technique and effect of changing key within a song. Sections 11 and 12 focus on the role the guitar can play in your songwriting; this includes a brief tour of the wonderful world of altered tunings, for which some chord boxes are given to get you started. After writing a song you will want to record it, which is the focus of Section 13. *How To Write Songs On Guitar* finishes by looking outward into the world of popular music for inspirational examples. Section 14 is a gallery of memorable songs, analysed for what they have to teach about the songwriter's craft. Section 15 provides examples of famous songwriters reflecting on how they write personally, and Section 16 highlights some recommended albums that songwriters should know. The Indexes enable you to find song citations by artist or by title.

Please note that *How To Write Songs On Guitar* does not offer transcriptions of any of the 1,800 songs cited. References to the use of chords in well-known songs are only to illustrate what the progressions (or parts thereof) sound like. This book is a guide to writing your own songs, not to learning other people's. Nor are they always given in the original key. The majority of the examples in Section 3 are listed in C major so they can be compared with each other. *How To Write Songs On Guitar* leans toward classic artists of the period from about 1960 to the 1990s because their music will be familiar to a greater number of readers, and because many set high standards for songwriting.

To find out more on chord sequences, melody, guitar chords, and writing songs on keyboards (especially if you're a guitarist), go to *The Songwriting Sourcebook* (2003), *Chord Master* (2004), *Melody* (2005), *How To Write Songs On Keyboards* (2005), and *Lyrics* (2006). If you write riff-based songs, *Riffs* (2002) is the most encyclopaedic study ever published about them. To find out more about getting the most out of your songs in terms of their musical presentation and recording, have a look at *Arranging Songs* (2007). Information about these titles can be found at www.backbeatbooks.com and www.rikkyrooksby.com.

INTRODUCTION

Some say you can't learn to write songs from a book. It's a good example of a dangerous half-truth.

This view smugly implies that you can't really learn to do anything from a book, and the ghost of William Caxton wonders why he ever bothered getting out of bed. Consider this: would you be happy having brain surgery from a surgeon who had only read the books? No, me neither. But would you be happy having brain surgery from a surgeon who was entirely self-taught and thought there was no medical knowledge or craft to grasp before hitting the operating theatre?

Of course, to write songs you need a modicum of musical awareness. If you're reading these words you've probably got it. Innate musical awareness and intelligence is a flame – most people have it to some degree, and various influences with which they grow up can feed it. Musical knowledge is like a stream of oxygen that will make it burn brighter. That is what *How To Write Songs On Guitar* is about.

Like all great musicians, truly great songwriters are probably born, not made. No tutor, no book, no study course, can of itself guarantee writing songs with the potential to lodge themselves in the memory of a generation, or achieve critical as well as commercial acclaim. Only a fortunate few know what it is like to compose a song such as 'Good Vibrations', 'Strawberry Fields Forever', 'Walk On By', or 'Like A Rolling Stone'.

Popular songs (of whatever genre) are often viewed as disposable artefacts – enjoyed today and thrown away tomorrow. Many of them are. But decades on, the best songs aren't looking quite so disposable. In the 1960s it was assumed there would be an endless supply of groups to follow The Beatles and The Rolling Stones, until the record-buying public got bored with electric-guitar beat music. History hasn't worked out that way. It now seems that the songwriters, singers, groups and producers who wrote, performed, and recorded the finest popular music are not as common as once thought.

Craft

Even if not born a great songwriter, you can still learn to write good songs – songs that not only delight yourself and friends, but also please the ears of a music industry that needs songs for artists who don't write their own material. If you already write songs, there's always something new to be learned about the craft that will help you to improve or try a new avenue. No-one ever masters the craft of songwriting.

Songwriting is easy when you feel inspired yet, sadly, inspiration cannot be turned on whenever it's wanted, like a tap. All songwriters with any experience know the subjective difference between writing when inspired and having to write to meet a deadline. It can feel like the difference between sailing a boat with the wind in your sails and rowing the damn thing. There are certain tricks you can use and develop to encourage inspiration, by making yourself fertile ground for an idea. This usually means living life well, making sure your sensibilities are stimulated by new experiences. Songwriters should have a healthy interest in all the arts – not just music – because the arts are a great source of ideas (especially for lyrics). They encourage inspiration to approach by finding out what puts them in the mood to be inspired, perhaps by watching a film or listening to certain types of music they find affecting, or improvising and recording whatever comes out.

But a good songwriter should be able to write a song to order. Give me some indication of what you want (style, time, tempo, key, mood) and I can write the music for a song in 30 minutes (lyrics take longer). This can be done purely from craft and knowledge, even if there isn't any initial inspiration. I don't say you will write a great or even good song just from craft. But sometimes a song started in the spirit of trying to bolt one together without strong inspiration can transform itself and become truly inspired halfway through the process – much to the songwriter's amazement.

Unconscious and conscious elements

When a song is taking shape, it is a delicate entity. For many writers it starts as no more than a mood or a feeling rather than a musical idea. This feeling attaches itself to a chord, a chord sequence, a melody or a rhythm, or a word phrase. Suddenly what was ordinary is 'ensouled' in some way, like a charged battery. At this point a thousand possibilities hang about the nascent song. It could develop in many directions. As it is shaped, many subtler choices – some conscious, some unconscious – are made. These choices are part of the craft, and in this area knowledge about songwriting can make a vital difference to the finished song. As the choices are made, the possibilities decrease in number, but the song takes on a palpable identity.

Being a songwriter involves fulfilling a mixture of roles, and different writers identify with these roles in differing degrees. In one way, the songwriter acts as a midwife, bringing into existence something that subjectively feels as though it already has an existence of its own. This is why songwriters, when interviewed, often express the notion that in some way the song is not really theirs. They speak of trying not to get in the way, of listening for what the song really is, and of not imposing on it and forcing it to take on a form that will be alien to its basic energy or nature. In this way of looking at things, it is as though the songwriter is a medium or 'channel' for the song. For the song idea to fulfil its potential the songwriter has to discern what kind of song it wants to be. If this sounds too abstract, a concrete example would be the way finished songs can be arranged in a variety of musical styles. But early on in the process of writing a new song a songwriter discerns whether the composition is going to be a ballad or up-tempo, in a minor key or major key, whether acoustic or electric, in a rock style or reggae or soul or folk, etc.

In another way, the songwriter is someone who practises a craft, in the same way a sculptor takes a block of stone and carves it away until a form is realised. This also has its truth. Looked at from this angle, knowledge of songwriting technique is a positive thing because it enables you to surpass your limitations. It gives you a means to avoid writing the same song over and over.

You need an awareness of both these roles. The 'midwife' role will keep you in a frame of mind that is creatively receptive and prevent too much conscious interference, especially early on in the writing of a song; the 'sculptor' role will take a good inspiration and make it better. That's what this book is about.

The better informed you are, the better able you are to make these choices. This means that instead of doing something too obvious, you come up with a better idea. This is craft – craft that can be learned, and absorbed, so that its operation becomes intuitive. You bring it to bear before the song sets in the mould. That way you can avoid a fork in the compositional road that will result in the song idea being progressively weakened by a sequence of poor decisions. Most songwriters have had the experience of a song that arrived as a fantastic idea but slipped from their grasp, only to finish a pale imitation of the initial idea.

Making changes at a later stage can be difficult – and the more radical the change the greater the inertia to overcome. Changing a chord is one thing; deciding to cut two verses and a bridge, halve the tempo, and change the key of the last chorus is another! Listening to great cover versions is a good guide to the ways in which songs can be re-imagined at a later date. Think of Jimi Hendrix's 'All Along The Watchtower', Joe Cocker's 'With A Little Help From My Friends', Harry Nilsson's 'Without You', and Tori Amos's 'Smells Like Teen Spirit'. Compare Marvin Gaye's 'I Heard It Through The Grapevine' to the earlier version by Gladys Knight, or The Beatles' 'Something' with Shirley Bassey's, or the Guns N' Roses cover of The Skyliners' 'Since I Don't Have You'.

This book states, or implies, many musical rules. It is good craft to know them before you break them, but always remember:

Rule 1: There are no absolute rules. A great song may break a rule.

Rule 2: When rules dominate, formula results. Too much formula is the enemy of invention.

Mystery

At its core, all great music has a profoundly mysterious quality. This is taken as a truism in 'classical' music, especially for works such as the later symphonies of Finnish composer Jean Sibelius or the English composer Ralph Vaughan Williams. But to some degree it is also true of great popular songs – be they pop, rock, folk, blues, or soul. Obviously large-scale works such as a symphony, running for anything between 20 and 45 minutes, contain more music than a popular song. This is not just because of their extended duration, but in their very texture. There is simply more going on at the purely musical level, including in the complexity of architectural design and the development of ideas. By contrast, popular song is almost entirely about the statement of a musical idea. There is no time, desire, or expectation of development. Instead, the idea will be repeated. Most songs last between two and five minutes. Because of its relative harmonic simplicity and its avoidance of development, a popular song often stands or falls on the level of inspiration in its initial material, which is thus exposed.

Take, for example, a chord sequence such as G-D-Am, G-D-C. How many songwriters in 1971 sat with a guitar or at a piano playing those chords at some time or other? How many thousands actually finished songs in which those chords appear roughly in that order? How many made it to live performance or recording? Probably hundreds – yet only Bob Dylan wrote 'Knockin' On Heaven's Door'. And if you or I sit down to write a song on that sequence tomorrow, the mood our song captures will be different again. It is as if the chords of a song are like the guy-ropes that keep a balloon in place; they aren't the balloon itself. The balloon here is a symbol of the mysterious inner spirit of music. In the same way, 'The Tracks Of My Tears' may be a song that consists mostly of G, C and D, but its spirit goes beyond its harmonic content. In this way, the elements of a song can be classified as more or less central, depending on how special they are. The most individual element is the performance, then the sound of the arrangement, then words and melody, then harmony, then rhythm, then tempo.

Remember this facet of songwriting because it is a source of encouragement. Songwriters who have been writing for a while sometimes find it hard to write songs with simple harmonic sequences because they don't spark any ideas. As a result, they search for more unusual or more complicated sequences. Remembering that harmony is always re-invigorating itself reminds you that there are always great songs to be written with the simplest of means.

What kind of song?

For the purposes of this book, let's define the kind of song you're trying to write. Songs come in all shapes, sizes, forms, and styles, from the 12-minute extravaganza of a Meat Loaf hit to the two minutes of an Elvis tune from the 1950s. Artistically speaking, there is no such thing as a right or wrong form. If all songs were written to commercial formulas, we would all die of boredom. The dullest periods in the history of the singles chart were the ones where formulas dominated and eliminated the diversity of popular music.

For practical reasons, *How To Write Songs On Guitar* is based on a few assumptions; namely that you want to write songs:

■ that are not longer than about six minutes and averaging three to four minutes
■ that use a traditional verse/chorus format
■ that are approachable rather than avant-garde and will appeal to people who listen to a broad range of popular music
■ that use guitar as the main composing instrument. (If you want to supplement this with piano have a look at *How To Write Songs On Keyboard*.)

In the first edition of *How To Write Songs On Guitar*, something like 1,000 popular songs from the 1950s to the 1990s were cited as illustrations of specific techniques of songwriting. In this revised edition (2009) that number has been increased, with citations of artists and bands from the last decade, bringing the story up to date, as well as the inclusion of more classic tracks from earlier decades. A large number of these songs were hits on one or both sides of the Atlantic. I am not implying that they are all great songs, even if they were hits – some are, some aren't. I have tried to select songs that I think have longevity – otherwise future readers might not know enough of them. But this book's interest in these songs is structural and technical. From Dusty Springfield to Led Zeppelin, from The Four Tops to The Sex Pistols, from Madonna and Catatonia to Dido and Amy Winehouse, from Bob Marley to Oasis to The Raconteurs, there is an extraordinary range of artists. If a song wasn't a single, you'll probably find it either on a 'Best Of' compilation or a well-known album. The Beatles are notably well-represented, not only because they were an outstanding group but because many people are familiar with their work. A copy of my *The Beatles Complete Chordbook* (Wise, 2000) is invaluable from a songwriting point of view. If you don't find your favourite song or artist, don't get mad. After all, if I had attempted to consult the entire history of Western popular music in time for the deadline, this book would never have been finished.

Note: it is not the purpose of *How To Write Songs On Guitar* to teach you how to play these songs. They are alluded to only to illustrate a particular songwriting technique – usually about a chord progression (as in Section 3 and 4). This book is about writing your own songs, not learning other people's.

Have all the great songs been written?

Sometimes it can feel as though all the great songs have been written and all the best ideas used – but there are always great songs waiting to be written. If it helps, think of them as hovering in the ether. It is true that the musical forms of a particular period cannot again have quite the same impact as when they were first heard. But locate yourself at any year in pop history, look at the next year's charts, and think about the songs no-one had yet written. There were probably songwriters in the Brill Building in New York in 1962 chewing on their pencils, frustratedly staring at piano keys and blank manuscript paper, thinking that there were no more good tunes. Yet within a couple of years Lennon and McCartney, Holland-Dozier-Holland, Bacharach and David, and Asher and Wilson would be creating classic songs by the bagful. How come it took rock music 40 years to produce 'Smells Like Teen Spirit'? (And that a decade after it was widely believed that guitar rock was dead.) How was it that 'There She Goes' by The La's was written in 1989 instead of 1968? How come no-one wrote 'Why Does It Always Rain On Me' before Travis did in 1999? Why did no-one at Atlantic or Motown in the 70s write 'Rehab' before Amy Winehouse?

As this is a handbook of songwriting technique, don't feel that you must read it in sequence. Dip into different sections and play with ideas. There's no requirement to tackle the whole lot at once.

The challenge of today

Many feel that the period from (roughly) 1960 to 1980 (or 1963-79) was a 'golden era' for popular music, when more memorable songs were released, especially as singles, than in later periods. Is this true? Or is it merely rose-tinted memories of the music heard when young? Will those who grew up in the 1980s, 1990s, and 2000s feel the same way about the songs they hear? Young listeners all have the fact of youth in common. But earlier generations certainly heard the popular song under different historical and technological conditions. Today songs are downloaded digitally and never have physical form, passing straight to a computer or iPod. Mostly gone are the days of travelling to a shop where the air smelt of plastic sleeves and vinyl to buy a seven-inch single in a paper or picture sleeve, or a twelve-inch album with its massive visual presence. Gone are the days when popular music belonged primarily to the young rather than being the *lingua franca* of advertising.

Actually, there are objective factors that point to a decline in the quality of much commercial songwriting – that is, the music that fills the airwaves and the Top 40 and Top 100. Rap music drastically impoverished both the melodic and harmonic content of popular music, by largely setting aside the former, and hugely simplifying the latter. Both will, I think, in the long run, affect its longevity. Lyrically, popular song has grown insular and afraid to address the world, while at the same time more pretentious, confusing obscurity with profundity. When it comes to banality, what difference is there between the next record that tells you to "shake your body' and The Archies' 'Sugar Sugar' – except that the former will hide its vacuousness beneath a tough, metallic production, its volume level artificially raised so that in your CD player it will only sound loud?

If there is a decline in popular music, the causes are many. Some are diffuse and sociological; others are easier to locate. One obvious factor is the misuse of technology. Human beings are easy to tempt, and technology is seductive. When cost-cutting, a ticking clock, and laziness link up, it is not surprising if technology is made to serve these purposes in ways that are detrimental to music.

In the hands of the unmusical, digital technology too often dehumanises music. At times the charts have been full of 'virtual music' created entirely on computer – music that has never moved a molecule of air. Anything thus programmed has no expression at the point of execution, even if it has an in-built expression of design. Our minds are more sophisticated in hearing music than many believe; we register the difference. The triumph of the silicon chip over the human spirit is nowhere better heard than in the chopped-up sampling of a singer's voice, done so a single vocal phrase can be manipulated on a keyboard. Sampling replaces the old crime of plagiarism with a new, more thorough-going one: the stealing not only of an idea but the performance and real-time expression of that idea. Musicians' actual performances are thus coerced into new musical contexts without their permission. For example, instead of taking the time to find a great drum sound, why not sample a

1970s rock album? Suddenly, 50 other people go for the same sample. The ability to play an instrument is itself devalued.

Craft and musicianship are replaced by a cut-and-paste ethic: the montage is everything. Why bother to paint when you can combine bits of other artists' pictures? Recordings no longer capture the sound of a group of musicians, perhaps highly talented, playing together. The arrangement no longer benefits from the excitement that such recording generates and is swathed in sterile perfection. Click tracks and drum machines impose a rhythmic tyranny in which an unrelenting beat is perfectly in time. The groove is lost, and techniques such as the crudest sudden division of the beat into smaller units to create pneumatic-drill snare-rolls and a twist of EQ replace the continual invention of a good drummer. Rhythm is exalted over melody, harmony, time, tempo, and key changes. The success of a band like The White Stripes – with its deliberate lo-fi rawness – or The Hold Steady (in the USA) and Arctic Monkeys (in the UK) is an example of how listeners want something more honest.

More than anything else, today's popular music is sick with repetition. In the past, bad pop records overstayed their welcome by repeating a hook or a chorus for what seemed countless times. Now it's worse, because if a track is constructed out of loops on a computer hard drive each repetition is not a re-performing (with tiny human variables) but the *exact* recycling of a couple of bars of music. Why sing a chorus more than once when you can copy your performance onto the second and the third? It's cheaper and quicker, but another opportunity for expression is lost. Why record a I-VI-IV-V or a I-V-II progression when you can sample a couple of bars from 'Every Breath You Take' or 'Knockin' On Heaven's Door', copy them identically, sing something different over the top, and pass it off as a 'song'? What does 'Tears Dry On Their Own' say except that Amy Winehouse felt she couldn't at that moment write a song as good as the Gaye/Terrell version of 'Ain't No Mountain High Enough' which provides everything except her words and melody? Why create a mood yourself when, in an act of musical vampirism, you can suck one from a record that already exists in collective memory? Have writers and performers grown so cynical? Is this all they think a popular song can be? Do they believe in this soul-less vision? Or do they go home after every TV promotion and listen to Aretha Franklin, Bob Dylan, The Byrds, The Moody Blues, or Led Zeppelin with relief?

I think the popular song is capable of much more than this impoverished parody of itself. That's one reason why I wrote this book. From these pages I hope you will take new ideas and new inspiration.

SECTION 1
SONGWRITING METHODS

What's involved in writing a song? A song has four basic elements: words (the lyric) are sung to a tune (melody) that is supported by chords (harmony) and played to a certain combination of beat (rhythm) and tempo (speed).

> **a song = lyric + melody + harmony + rhythm**

In different styles of music the balance of importance between these elements changes. If you have been writing songs for a while, you may feel more adept at or interested in some of the four elements than others.

In 90s dance music the lyric is often reduced to a few lines, sampled and repeated; melody and harmony are also simplified, but rhythm is everything. Rap dispenses with melody and significant harmony but emphasises the lyric. MOR ('middle of the road') music stresses melody and a non-dissonant harmony but downplays rhythm. Rock and soul stress rhythm, though not necessarily at the expense of the other elements.

Even famous songwriters are often better at certain song elements than others. Bob Dylan's early music was harmonically conservative, using three or four chords, coming as it did out of the American folk tradition, and his style of singing is hardly conducive to bringing out the contours of a beautiful melody, yet the attitude of his vocal style and his lyrics revolutionised popular music.

Where should I start?

There is no set way of writing a song. You do not have to do things in any fixed order. Some writers prefer working in one method, while others find that songs arrive in many different ways. John Lennon liked to put a sheet of lyrics on a piano and then poke around on the keys, looking for a chord sequence to which he could sing those words. Paul McCartney has related how 'Yesterday' – one of the most covered of all songs – came to him in a dream. If you are lucky, sometimes a new song forms in your mind, with words, melody, chords and

ABBREVIATIONS
Roman numerals **I–VII** indicate chord relationships within a key.

m=minor

maj=major

SONG SECTIONS:

b bridge; **c** coda; **ch** chorus; **f** fade; **hk** hook; **i** intro; **pch** pre-chorus; **r** riff; **s** solo; **v** verse

Most of the chord-sequence examples are standardised for comparison into **C major** or **A minor**. The famous songs are therefore not always in the key of the original recordings.

rhythm, when you're not actually playing an instrument. So a song can be composed in any of the following ways:

1 Start with a lyric and then set it to music

Some people prefer this method because the lyric's subject may suggest certain things about the mood of the music. The rhythm of the words can evoke a tune. Some songwriters find it easier to have words to sing when constructing a melody instead of humming or using nonsense lyrics. To facilitate working this way keep a notebook of lyric ideas, even if they're unfinished, or even just titles. You need only one verse and a chorus to compose the basic structure and music of a song – extra verses can be written later, when the music itself might inspire them.

2 Start with a melody and then harmonise it

I call this 'top-down' songwriting. Much recent songwriting, notably from guitar bands, suggests to me that this has become a less common technique, and songs have suffered as a consequence. Too often melodies are constructed *after* the chord sequence, and as a result the melody can be constrained or neglected. In the mid-20th century, popular songwriters emphasised the melody at an early stage in composition. The beauty of this technique is that it encourages you to compose an effective tune. If a tune sounds good on its own – if it has an expressive quality, interesting intervals, some pleasing twists and turns, and a catchy 'hook' – it will sound even better accompanied and harmonised. Think of the shape of melodies such as Dusty Springfield's 'I Only Want To Be With You', or The Beatles' 'She Loves You', or Traffic's 'Paper Sun'; they are delightful even when sung unaccompanied.

3 Start with the harmony

Construct a pleasing chord sequence and then try to find a melody. I call this composing 'from the middle out'. Not surprisingly, this is a common approach, especially among guitarists. Strumming a chord sequence does not require much technique, and it allows the mind to play with words and melody. Chord sequences can be inspiring and often suggest an emotion or mood that can be distilled into a melody and a lyric.

The disadvantage of this approach is that a chord sequence can prevent the melody from developing a shape of its own because the sequence encourages the melody to go in certain directions. The danger is that the melody becomes an afterthought. For example, it is too easy to get a melody by singing a couple of steps up or down as the chords change, moving from a note that fits with one chord to one that fits with the next. The result is a highly linear or 'horizontal' tune squeezed into a narrow range of pitch – usually less than an octave – and often monotonous. R.E.M.'s 'Losing My Religion' is a case in point, and The Beatles' 'I Am The Walrus'. They might be great songs, but if so *in spite* of their melodies, not because of them. Male singer-songwriters/guitarists are prone to this because they are usually less willing or able to write a melody with a wide vocal range that they might find difficult to sing. Female songwriters often write melodies that have a wider span and more vertical 'jumps' because their voices can deliver them. Compare the 'vertical' melodies composed by Tori Amos or Kate Bush with some of Jackson Browne's or Bruce Springsteen's songs.

Another drawback of composing the chord sequence first is that it may artificially chop the melody into phrases only as long as the time spent on a chord. To get a sense of this, listen for songs where each melodic phrase starts on the second beat of the bar (or thereabouts) and ends just before the next chord change. The verse in Texas's 'Summer Son' is an example. This can indicate that the melody was composed after the chord progression: the writer is waiting for the chord change to help pitch the next melodic phrase against the new chord.

4 Start with a rhythm track

The rhythm track could be a type of strum, a drum pattern or sampled loop, and a tempo. I call this 'bottom-up' composing. If you are writing songs in any genre in which rhythm is a major component, then this makes sense as a creative procedure. Any music intended for dancing needs strong rhythm. One typical fault of singer-songwriter material composed on guitar is that it lacks rhythmic interest. This is a way to avoid that trap. If you haven't worked this way before, try singing against a drum rhythm to give your melodies greater rhythmic character. Try writing chord sequences with a drum machine or drum loops, an approach used by Kate Bush for her 1980s albums *The Dreaming* and *Hounds Of Love*. This can increase awareness of the role of rhythm in your songwriting. It's especially fertile if you think you write too many slow ballads!

For a further refinement of the 'bottom-up' approach, add a bassline to the drum track. The bass can reinforce the rhythm, and it will also suggest harmony. You will, however, be free to treat the bass notes as the foundation of major or minor chords or their inversions, since a single note in the bass can imply a number of different chords. (More about this later.)

If one of these four basic methods doesn't work for you, try another. Or, to stop yourself from writing the same kind of song over and over, deliberately choose a different method from the one you habitually employ.

Other strategies for songwriting

Here are some strategies you may find helpful:

1 Compose away from your instrument. This stops you falling back on familiar patterns rooted in physical movements on the instrument. A typical example is a songwriter who has only played the guitar a short time and can't hold down a barre chord, so writing a song in G major the chord of Bm (which usually has a barre) is missed out. Instead of looking for things within the instrument, imagine and shape music in your mind. When you have an idea firmly in place, then go to an instrument.

2 Pick up a different instrument. Guitarists tend to use the same chord sequences and keys because they are the easy ones to finger, or because they sound good on guitar. Compose on a keyboard instead. To work out simple chord sequences all you need is the ability to play major and minor triads.

3 Borrow a structure. This is a bit like keeping the scaffolding but changing the building inside. Take a song you like and write down its basic form. Remove the chords but keep the same structure, tempo and length. Then write a new song with new chords using the same structure.

4 Arbitrarily choose some limits – a key, a tempo, a time signature, a theme, a style – and write a song to fit. Experiment with different genres. Set yourself a challenge by writing a song:

- that is only two minutes long
- that starts with a chorus
- where the verse is in A and the chorus in F
- that is in any time signature other than 4/4
- that changes from 4/4 to 6/8 and back
- that has an odd number of bars in the verse or chorus
- that increases in tempo
- that does not have a turnaround (see later)
- where the structure is verse, verse, bridge, verse, and the 'hook' is in the verse
- that is a sad song with only major chords
- that has no minor chords
- that begins with some effective rhymes picked from a rhyming dictionary and used to generate a lyric.

5 Write in the style of a singer or band you admire. Many songwriters begin this way by default, writing songs that sound like their favourite music. But it is a useful exercise for more experienced writers, even when they have worked through the initial phase of strong influence by one particular artist or group. Often your own creative impulses steer the song away from the person you are supposed to be copying, and it turns out only an elaborate trick for sparking your own inspiration.

6 Read a book or magazine, see a film, go for a walk. Imagine and observe. Listen to conversations in cafes, on the bus, or in the shopping queue. Then put it down in a song.

7 Visualise a song. Sit in a silent room and close your eyes. Imagine a box of 45rpm singles, each one an unwritten classic. Choose one, look at the label, take it out of the sleeve. Put it on a turntable, lower the stylus onto the grooves, and listen to the crackle and the low-level rumble of the turntable. Keep your mind clear and allow the music to start. You may get a song from your memory. You may get something new – even if it's only a few bars, it could be enough to start you on a new song.

At the start of this section you read that a song consisted of lyric, melody, harmony and rhythm. The first of the four song components to examine is harmony, and this means discussing chords, what they do, and how guitarists use them.

SECTION 2
CHORD DICTIONARY PART 1

ABBREVIATIONS

Roman numerals **I–VII** indicate chord
relationships within a key.

m=minor

maj=major

SONG SECTIONS:

b bridge; **c** coda; **ch** chorus; **f** fade; **hk**
hook; **i** intro; **pch** pre-chorus; **r** riff;
s solo; **v** verse

Most of the chord-sequence examples are
standardised for comparison into
C major or **A minor**. The famous songs
are therefore not always in the key of the
original recordings.

In this section, we will look at the function of harmony in songs. Harmony is supplied by chords, and learning chords is how most people start on the guitar. One factor that makes the guitar popular as an accompaniment instrument is that it is relatively easy to learn some chord shapes, strum them and sing. Many professional performers have got by for years with little more than this. The basic chords presented here provide all the chords you need to start writing songs. Part two of the Chord Dictionary, in Section Nine, deals with more complex chords.

What is a chord?

A simple major or minor chord comprises three notes and is called a triad.

The four types of triad

| Notes | Degrees | SCALE | |
		Gaps	Name
C E G	1 3 5	2+1½	C major
C E♭ G	1 ♭3 5	1½+2	C minor
C E♭ G♭	1 ♭3 ♭5	1½+1½	C diminished
C E G♯	1 3 ♯5	2+2	C augmented

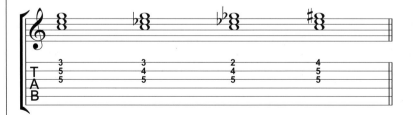

Of these four triad types, it is major and minor chords (the first two) that most concern the songwriter. The expressive major/minor fluctuation, along with the possibility of key changes, is one of the glories of the Western musical tradition.

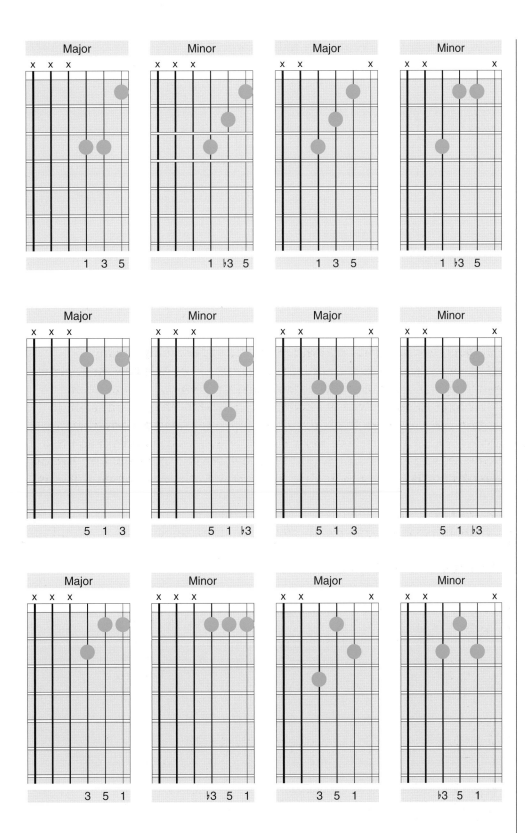

Major	Minor	Major	Minor
x x x	x x x	x x x	x x x
1 3 5	1 ♭3 5	1 3 5	1 ♭3 5

Major	Minor	Major	Minor
x x x	x x x	x x	x x
5 1 3	5 1 ♭3	5 1 3	5 1 ♭3

Major	Minor	Major	Minor
x x x	x x x	x x	x x
3 5 1	♭3 5 1	3 5 1	♭3 5 1

The diminished and augmented triads are less important, having specialised applications.

SECTION 2 | 17

How notes are duplicated in guitar chords

Most of the basic chord shapes that guitarists strum take the three notes of a major or minor triad and double or triple them to get a fuller sound:

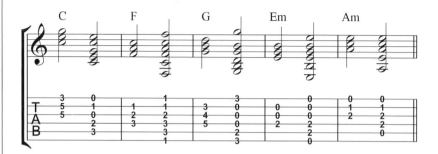

Contrasted A major shapes

A single chord like A major is capable of many voicings on the guitar:

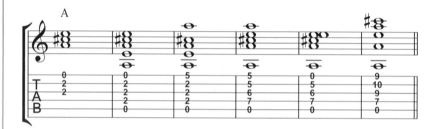

Major chords

Major chords are the most important chords in songwriting; everything else revolves around them. They are the most flexible for conveying the widest range of moods. By varying the setting and arrangement of how they are played, a huge variety of emotions can be expressed. Compared to minor chords, major chords are often said to sound positive, upbeat or happy. Even so, it is possible to express sadness with them, by devices such as slowing the tempo, and by choice of melody combined with lyric theme.

Major chord shapes

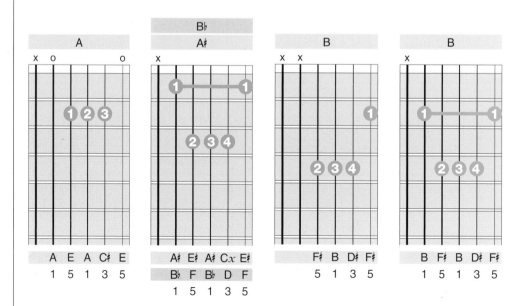

SECTION 2

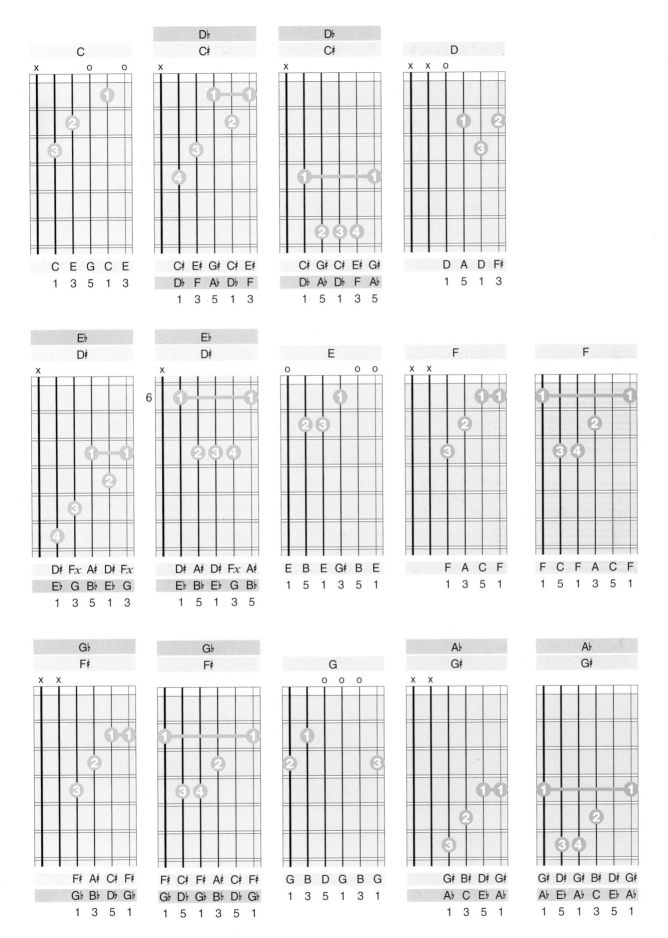

All guitar chords are subject to the broad category division of those that have open strings and those that don't. Open-string chords are more resonant than fully fretted chords. The chords of A, C, D, E, and G on the guitar have effective open-string shapes, and the other major chords are derived from these shapes. These are the five 'master shapes' as far as major chords go. If a chord has no open strings in it, with or without a barre, it is a movable shape and can be positioned up and down the fretboard.

Minor chords

Minor chords sound sad, unhappy, and melancholic. A song written entirely in minor chords will accentuate this (the opening minutes of Sufjan Stevens's 'The Seer's Tower' is an example, though he brings in major chords later in the song). A clump of minor chords in a song darkens the mood, as can be heard in the verse of ELO's 'Livin' Thing' where Fm, Em and Dm follow each other, or in the verse of The Move's 'Blackberry Way'. By contrast, a comic song might deliberately mismatch the theme of the lyric with the harmony – imagine a tragic lyric set to a series of major chords and a bouncy beat at a quick tempo, or a happy lyric sung entirely in a minor key at a slow tempo. Madness sometimes did this with their songs, such as 'Embarrassment'.

In most chord progressions, minor chords combine with majors. This causes a subtle alternation of mood and tone that can be aesthetically and emotionally stimulating. Some non-Western types of music do not have chord sequences in this sense; in Indian music, for example, there are long scale sequences that are mono-chordal, without chord or key changes.

The chords of Am, Dm and Em have effective open-string shapes. They are the three 'master-shapes' for the minors.

Much of the work of the songwriter is carried out by selecting major and minor chords for sequences such as verses and choruses. It is perfectly possible to write a song with only major and minor chords. To use an analogy, this is like painting with bold colours. But just as there are many possible shades of any given colour, it is possible to create different 'shades' of a major or minor chord.

Minor chord shapes

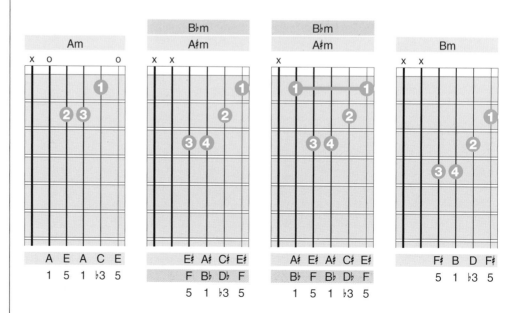

SECTION 2

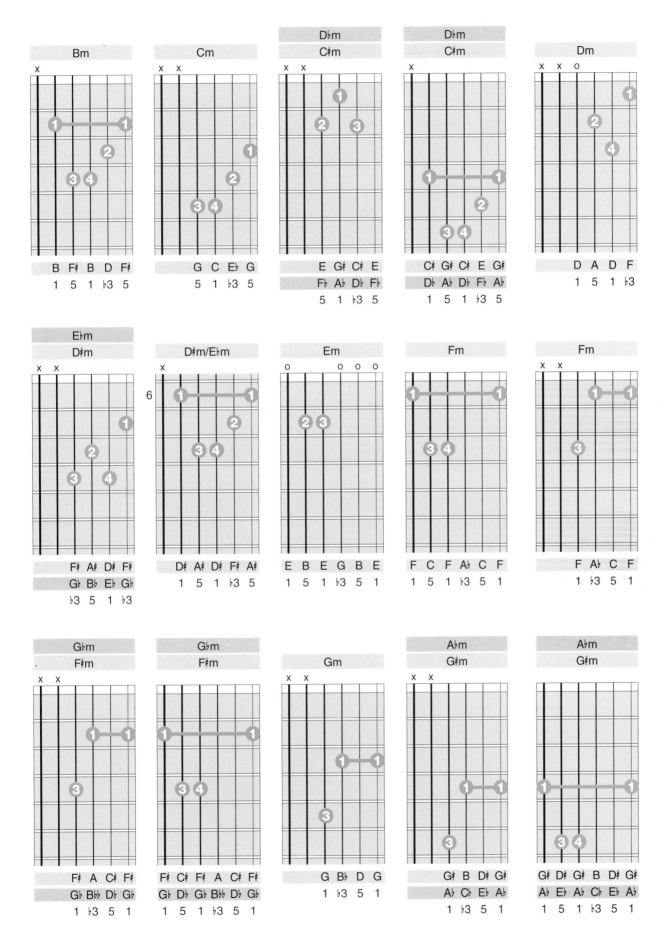

Dominant seventh chords

A different type of chord is created by adding another note to a triad. This note is often identified by a number that indicates its scale degree.

Here is the scale of C major:

1	2	3	4	5	6	7
C	D	E	F	G	A	B

The triad of C major (chord I) is made by combining the notes C, E and G (1-3-5). The dominant seventh chord is formed by adding the note one tone (one full step) below the root note: C major (C E G) becomes C E G B♭. It is called the 'dominant' seventh because in traditional harmony the fifth note of the scale (called the dominant) is the only one on which a dominant seventh chord inevitably results if you build a chord upon it. In the key of C, for example, G is the dominant; G dominant seventh is G B D F. Notice that the fourth note of the chord, F, is one full step below the root, G.

Dominant seventh chords

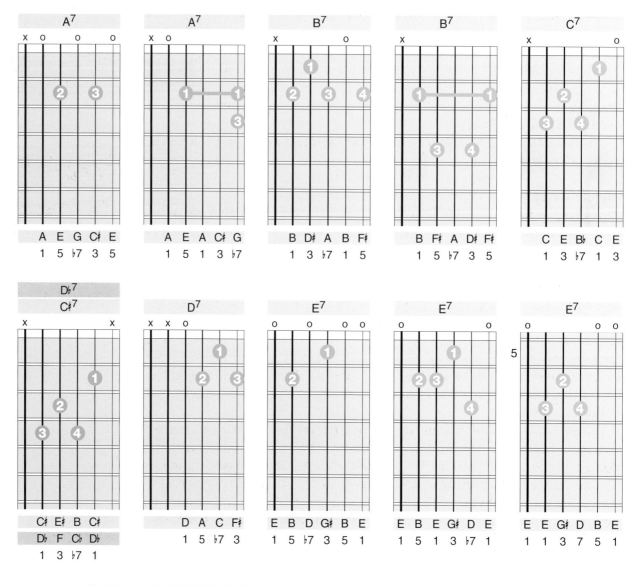

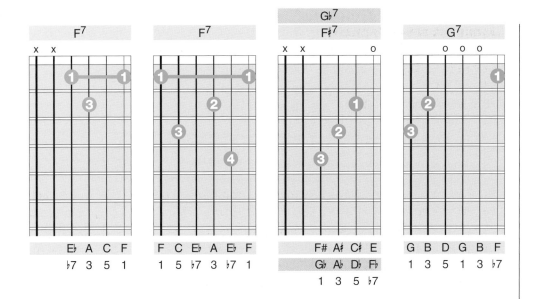

In the blues, however, a dominant seventh chord can occur on chord I or chord IV as well as chord V (the chords built on the first, fourth, and fifth notes of the scale), and in popular music the seventh note of the scale is often flattened. These dominant seventh chords have a hard, bluesy sound. Use a dominant seventh to toughen up a chord sequence, as it does in songs such as The Beatles' 'When I Get Home', 'Baby's In Black' and 'Hard Day's Night', or to emphasise a blues / rhythm & blues influence, as in Amy Winehouse's 'Rehab'. It is also used to establish a new key – there is more about this in Section Ten on key-changing.

The chords of A7, B7, C7, D7, E7 and G7 can be played in first position as open-string shapes.

Major seventh chords

This chord is formed by adding the note one semitone (half-step) below the root. C major (C E G) becomes C E G B. In traditional harmony, it occurs on chords I and IV. Another way of thinking of a major seventh is to think of it as superimposed major and minor triads (C E G = C major; E G B = E minor).

In contrast to the dominant seventh, the major seventh has a soft, romantic quality. For this reason, it is excellent for expressing gentle, intimate emotions, which is why it is often used in ballads, soul, pop, and MOR (the major seventh is central to the style of composers such as Burt Bacharach). It works better at medium-to-slow tempos because at speed the nuance of the chord is easily lost. At quicker tempos it can be heard in Latin-influenced material. In the 60s The Association made frequent use of major sevenths, both in the instruments and in the backing vocals.

There is a string of five major seventh chords in the bridge of Aztec Camera's 'Oblivious'. It is not so common in hard and heavy rock, punk, etc, though Jimmy Page has used them occasionally, as in Led Zeppelin's 'Carouselambra' and 'Ten Years Gone' where all the chords in the A-D-G-C bridge sequence are major sevenths. He also used an Amaj7-Em7 change to devastating effect on the bridge of The Firm's 'Fortune Hunter'. The major seventh is a delightful chord to climax a crescendo, as in 'Tears Of A Clown',

SECTION 2 | 23

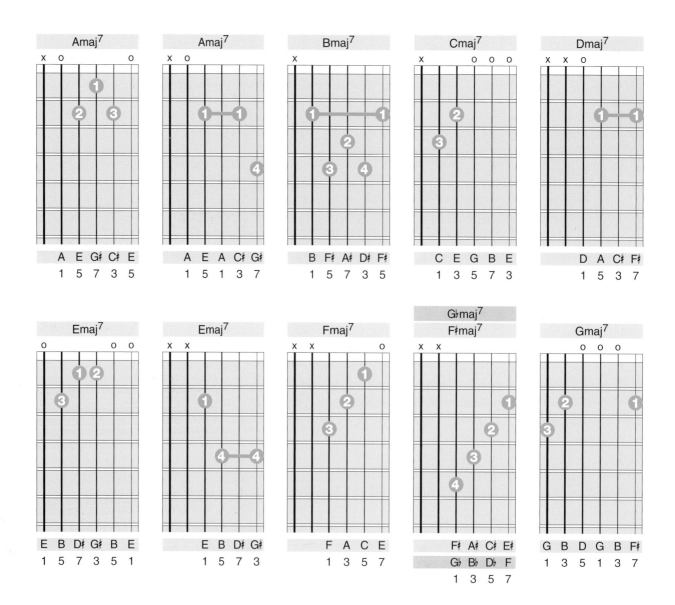

Major seventh chords

where the hook is D-B-Em-Cmaj7. Major seventh chords play a significant role in the songs of Love's album *Forever Changes*, especially the Cmaj7-Fmaj7 change heard in 'Maybe The People' and 'The Good Humour Man'.

Open-string major sevenths can be played for Amaj7, Cmaj7, Dmaj7, Emaj7, Fmaj7 and Gmaj7.

Minor seventh chords

Adding the note that is one tone (full step) below the root of a minor chord produces a minor seventh. C minor (C E♭ G) becomes C E♭ G B♭. In traditional harmony, it occurs on the I, IV and V chords if these are derived from the natural minor scale, and on chords II, III and VI of a major scale. Another way of looking at a minor seventh is to think of it as a major triad superimposed on a minor triad (C E♭ G = C minor; E♭ G B♭ = E♭ major), the opposite of the major seventh.

The minor seventh is a diluted version of the minor chord. It has a sad quality but is not as sad as the straight minor. Songwriters use it instinctively

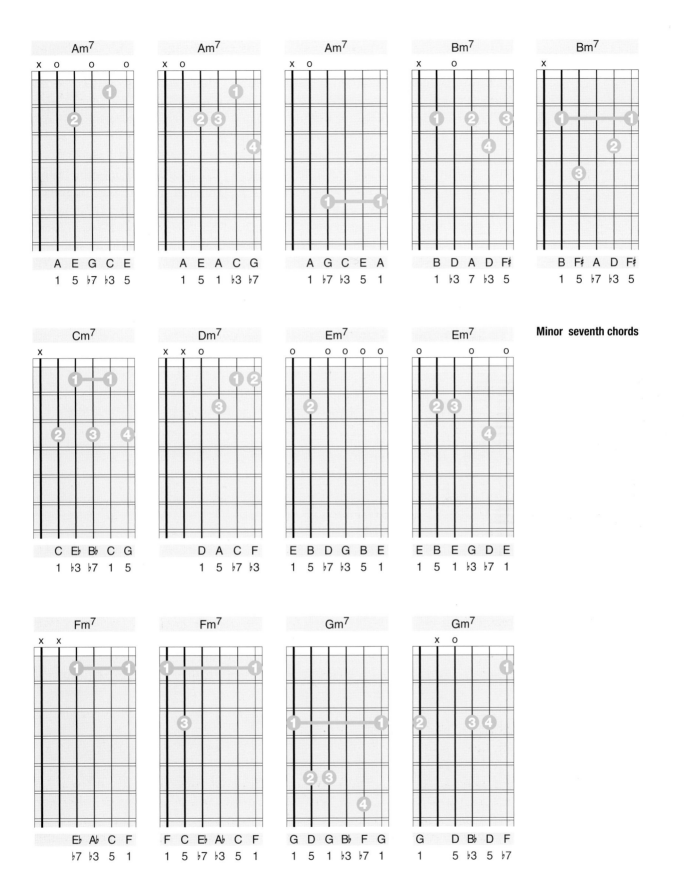

Minor seventh chords

SECTION 2 | 25

where the straight minor would be too depressing, and for combining pleasantly with majors. A song written entirely in minor sevenths would be less depressing than one written only with minors. Minor sevenths combine nicely with major sevenths – a well-known trick in soul music – giving an easy patina of sophistication. Try an ascending I-II-III-IV sequence like C-Dm-Em-F and then play it like this: Cmaj7-Dm7-Em7-Fmaj7.

Minor seventh chords are heard on the early soul / funk influenced songs from the first three Bruce Springsteen albums. The main function of the minor seventh in Springsteen's songs is make a progression mildly jazzy or funky: 'The Fever' has extensive Am7, Bm7, and Em7 chords; 'Kitty's Back' has a slow Am7-Em7 groove in some parts; 'The E Street Shuffle' has a Bbm7-Ebm7 end sequence; and they feature (sometimes pitched high on the neck) in 'Spirit In The Night' (ch), in 'Tenth Avenue Freeze-Out', and throughout 'Blinded By The Light'.

There are open-string minor sevenths for Am7, Bm7, Dm7, Em7, and Gm7.

The Minor/major seventh chord
This chord is formed by adding the note that is one semitone (half-step) below the root of a minor chord. C minor (C Eb G) becomes C Eb G B. This is a tense

Minor/major seventh chord

Am/maj⁷

A E G# C E
1 5 7 b3 5

Am/maj⁷
4

A A C E G#
1 1 b3 5 7

Bm/maj⁷

B F# A# D F#
1 5 7 b3 5

Cm/maj⁷

C Eb G B G
1 b3 5 7 5

Dm/maj⁷

D A C# F
1 5 7 b3

Em/maj⁷

E B D# G B E
1 5 7 b3 5 1

Fm/maj⁷

F Ab C E
1 b3 5 7

Gm/maj⁷

G D Bb D F#
1 5 b3 5 7

chord with a strange sound that is not exactly sad or happy – more like restless or threatening. In pop songs, it is usually found only as a passing chord between the minor and the minor seventh: try Cm-Cm/maj7-Cm7. On the guitar, this is most easily executed starting from open Am, Dm or Em shapes. Minor/major sevenths crop up in soundtrack music for horror and thriller movies. John Barry used them in the soundtracks of the 1960s James Bond films. You will also find one in the coda of The Beatles' 'That Means A Lot' and on the intro of Muse's 'Screenager' (Gm/maj7).

Suspended fourth chords

Having dealt with the four main kinds of seventh chord (there are more, believe it or not!), we move to several chord types that inhabit a strange musical 'neutral zone'. We'll begin with the suspended fourth, which is formed by replacing the third of a chord with the fourth of the relevant scale. C major (C E G) becomes C F G. Since the only difference between C major and C minor is the third (E or E♭), if it is removed you cannot tell whether the chord is major or minor.

Suspended fourth chords

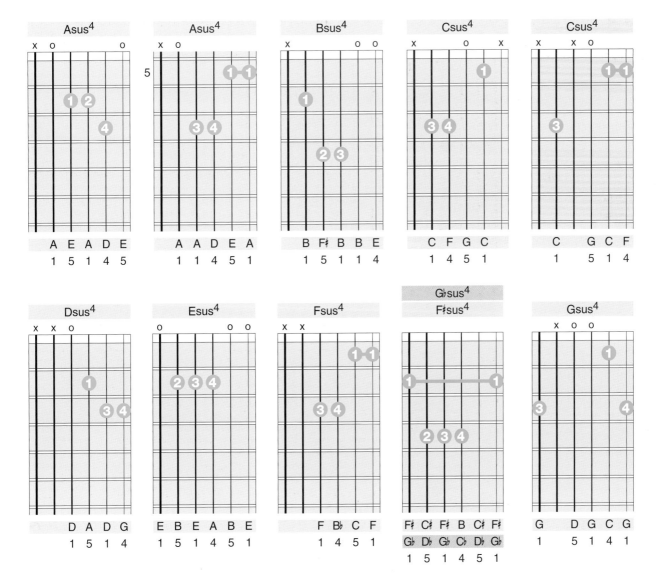

The suspended fourth is therefore neither major nor minor, but neutral, and Csus4 can occur in the keys of C major or C minor.

This is a very tense chord. The fourth wants to resolve by dropping back either a semitone (half-step) to a major chord or a tone (full step) to a minor chord. Songwriters use it to build momentary tension. Pop songs tend to use sus4s at transition points to create excitement – for example, from the end of a verse into a chorus, or at the end of a chorus into a repeat of the chorus. They have a significant role in rock music because of their drama and tension. The Dandy Warhols' 'Bohemian Like You', U2's 'Two Hearts Are Better Than One', Bruce Springsteen's 'She's The One', David Bowie's 'Jean Genie', The Who's 'Pinball Wizard', Argent's 'Hold Your Head Up', and Cat Stevens's 'Can't Keep It In' all feature prominent sus4s.

Effective open-string sus4 are available for Asus4, Dsus4, Esus4 and Gsus4. Some of the other pitches are more awkward to finger.

Suspended second chords
Brother of the sus4, the sus2 is formed by replacing the third with the second of the scale. C major (C E G) becomes C D G. Like the suspended fourth, the

Suspended second chords

suspended second is neither major nor minor. It is not as tense as the sus4, having more ambiguity and space. I sometimes think of the sus4 chord as hot, bright and fiery, whereas the sus2 is cool, dark and watery. It is good for atmospheric songs, especially to convey emptiness, and the sus2 works well with (or as a substitute for) minor chords and the add9 chord.

The sus2 combines nicely with the sus4, as a finger is added, taken off, etc. John Lennon used this on 'Happy Christmas (War Is Over)' and it is also found in The Searchers's 'Needles and Pins', The Who's 'So Sad About Us', The Beatles' 'I Need You', The Byrds' 'I'll Feel A Whole Lot Better', Bryan Adams's 'Summer Of 69' and The Pretenders' 'Brass in Pocket'. Guitarist Alex Lifeson often uses this chord in Rush's more recent material. In The Cure's 'Lullaby' you can a two-chord change in which the note B, the seventh of C♯m7, becomes the second in Asus2.

There are good open-string shapes for Asus2, Csus2, Dsus2, Fsus2 and Gsus2.

Fifth chords

This type of chord is related to the sus2 and sus4 because, once again, the third has been removed. C5 is C G. A C5 chord could be included in a progression in the key of C major or C minor. You can solo over it using a number of different scales and there won't be a clash … (Possibly *The* Clash, but not *a* clash!) This harmonic neutrality makes it suitable for hard rock.

Any book of rock transcriptions features loads of these. They come in two basic forms. There's the 'power chord' fifth (C G), possibly with the root doubled an octave higher (C G C), usually played on the bottom three strings of the guitar with almost any quantity of distortion. This is for aggressive music, be it punk, grunge, hard rock or HM. No matter how different their politics, lyrics, or haircuts, Green Day, Nirvana, Queen, Guns N' Roses and Metallica are united musically in using fifths. For this type of fifth, there are open-string shapes for A5, C5, D5, E5 and G5.

In the other form of this chord, the two notes are doubled or tripled across the strings. Hence the G5 favoured by Noel Gallagher (Oasis), which goes from bottom to top G x D G D G (A-string muted), and Pete Townshend's A5 (A E A E A from the A-string up). With a stark, bold tone, this type of fifth chord

Fifth chords

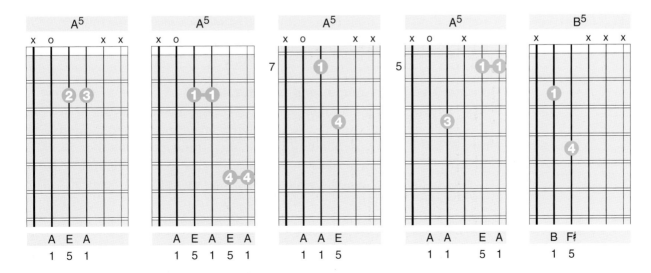

SECTION 2 | 29

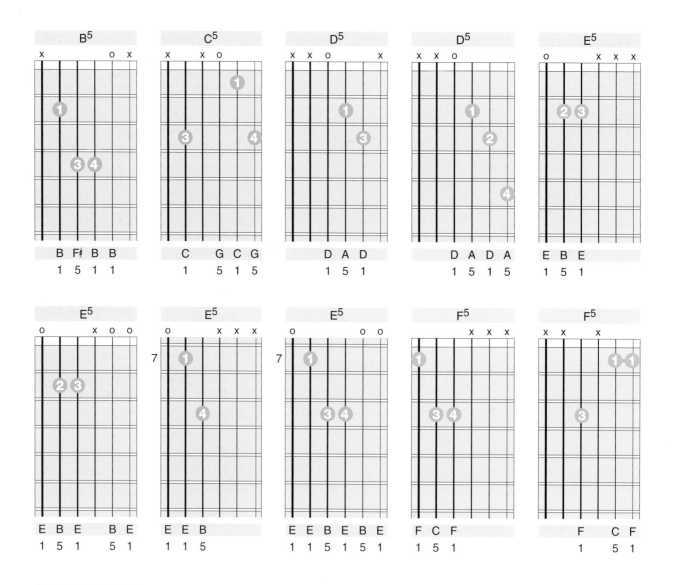

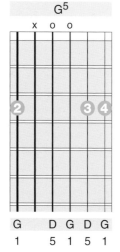

sounds good strummed in moody and aggressive acoustic stuff.

The fifth chord toughens up a progression and arrangement. You can sing a minor or major melody over the same fifth chord – it makes no difference. On a recording with multiple guitar tracks, it combines nicely with full major or minor chords on that same root note. Guitar one plays C, guitar two plays C5; Guitar one plays Em, guitar two plays E5.

Dominant seventh suspended fourth chords

This is quite a popular chord, an amalgam of a dominant seven and a sus4. In C this would be C F G B♭. This chord is neither major nor minor. It can resolve either to C7 or Cm7, depending on whether the F drops to E or E♭. The presence of the seventh makes this chord not as tense as the straight sus4, but it can still be dramatic, as you can hear just a few bars into Led Zeppelin's 'The Song Remains The Same' or on the main riff of Rush's 'A Farewell To Kings'. There are open shapes for A7sus4, D7sus4, E7sus4 and G7sus4.

Fifths (any position)

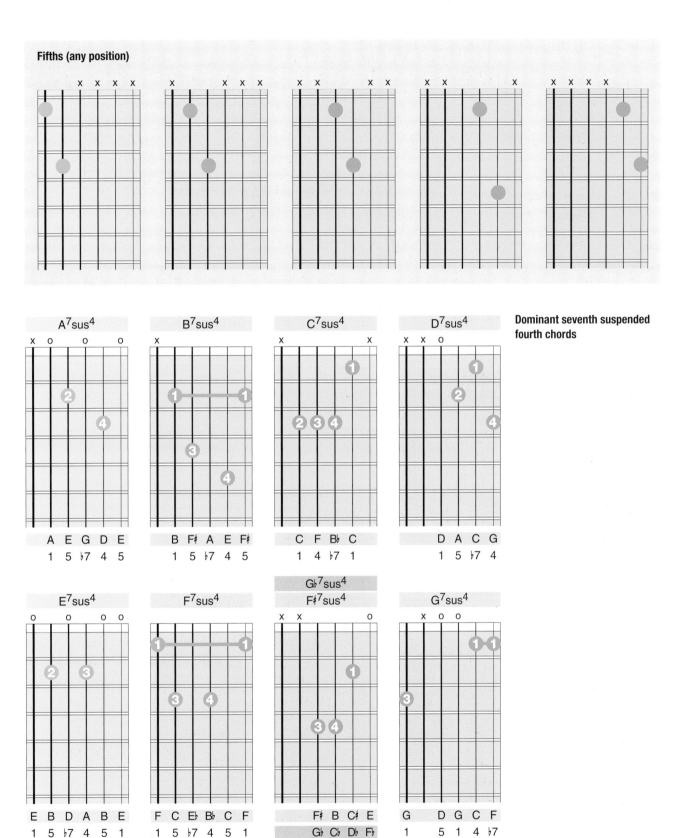

Dominant seventh suspended fourth chords

A⁷sus⁴ — A E G D E — 1 5 ♭7 4 5

B⁷sus⁴ — B F♯ A E F♯ — 1 5 ♭7 4 5

C⁷sus⁴ — C F B♭ C — 1 4 ♭7 1

D⁷sus⁴ — D A C G — 1 5 ♭7 4

E⁷sus⁴ — E B D A B E — 1 5 ♭7 4 5 1

F⁷sus⁴ — F C E♭ B♭ C F — 1 5 ♭7 4 5 1

G♭⁷sus⁴ / F♯⁷sus⁴ — F♯ B C♯ E / G♭ C♭ D♭ F♭ — 1 4 5 ♭7

G⁷sus⁴ — G D G C F — 1 5 1 4 ♭7

SECTION 2 | 31

Major sixth chords

The major sixth is formed by adding the sixth note of the scale to the major chord. C major (C E G) becomes C E G A. It is a slight dilution of the major chord, just as the minor seventh is a dilution of the minor chord. In fact, C E G A are the same notes that make up Am7 (A C E G). Some guitar chordbooks and sheet music give chord boxes shown as major sixths that are really inverted minor chords. It is essential for the major sixth that all four notes be sounded. This is not always easy in standard tuning, hence the compromise of using, for example, Am/C (C E A) as a stand-in for C6 (C E G A).

In most pop contexts a major sixth lends a mildly 'jazzy' sound, and it is often heard in Latin American music. It is associated with The Beatles, who sang a major sixth as the last chord of 'She Loves You', and the verse of 'No Reply' has two major sixths, giving it a slightly Latin quality. Roxy Music's 'Love Is The Drug', Thin Lizzy's 'The Rocker', and Elvis Costello's 'Man Called Uncle' also end on a major sixth. Sixths also lend a distinct flavour to Fleetwood Mac's 'Man Of The World', Catatonia's 'I Am The Mob', and there is one in Arctic Monkeys' 'Riot Van'.

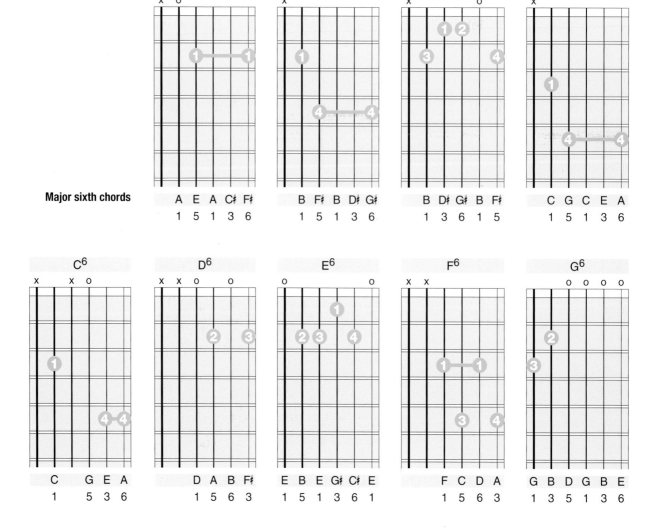

Major sixth chords

Minor sixth chords

The minor sixth chord is formed by adding the sixth of the melodic minor scale (A B C D E F♯ G♯) or the Dorian mode (A B C D E F♯ G) to the minor chord. A minor (A C E) becomes A C E F♯. This chord is close to D7 (D F♯ A C) and makes an interesting substitute for a dominant seventh. A second inversion D7 (A D A C F♯) where the open A string is deliberately strummed will sound similar.

The minor sixth has an angular sound because of the dissonant augmented fourth between C and F♯, as is found in the dominant seventh. It is not a common chord, though around the time of the *White Album* Lennon was fond of it, as is heard in the verse of 'Happiness Is A Warm Gun'. It can be effective to use this chord when a song features a change from the minor form of chord IV to I. In C major, this would be Fm (F A♭ C) to C; try Fm6 (F A♭ C D) instead of Fm. Try playing Am-G-C and then Am6-G-C and notice the change in feeling. Radiohead included a Dm6 in 'There There' and it is the penultimate chord of Teenage Fanclub's 'Sparky's Dream'.

Minor sixth chords

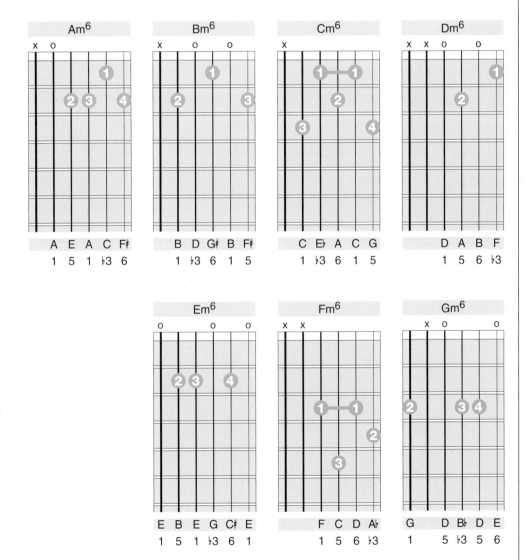

Augmented chords

To complete part one of the Chord Dictionary, we'll look at two chord types that have occasional uses. The augmented chord is a major triad where the top note (the fifth) is sharpened: C E G becomes C E G♯. In traditional harmony, it does not occur on the major scale but is found on the harmonic minor scale as chord III (C E G♯ in A harmonic minor).

This chord is tense sounding and never played for more than a beat or two. It is usually found as a passing chord between a major and a minor, or a major and a major sixth. Try changing D to D+ to Bm, or D to D+ to D6. Chuck Berry famously put the augmented triad at the start of 'No Particular Place To Go' to imitate a car horn. In The Beatles' songs you can catch the augmented strutting its funky stuff in 'All My Loving' (ch: VI-♭VI+-I in E), 'Ask Me Why' (ch: IV-V-I-I+) and 'From Me To You' (end of bridge). There are augmented chords in 'It Won't Be Long', 'Michelle', 'Fixing A Hole', and 'I'm Happy Just To Dance With You'. An E+ kicks off 'Oh Darling', and the chorus of 'Hey Bulldog' has the hypnotic climbing sequence Bm-Bm+-Bm6-Bm7, followed by

Augmented chords

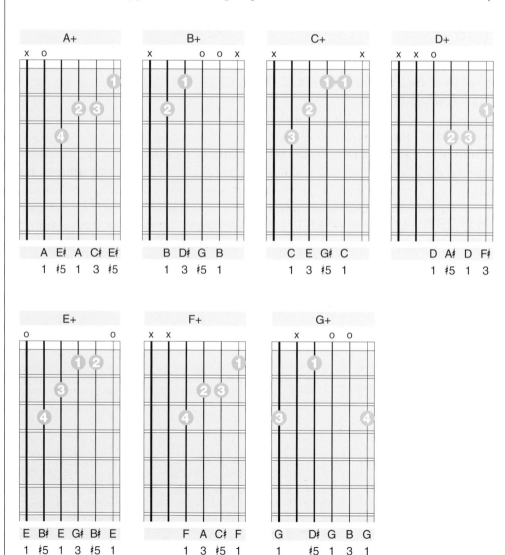

SECTION 2

the same sequence starting from Em. This reveals the lingering influence of jazz standards on The Beatles as they grew up in the 1950s.

It is an essential part of the riff in Led Zeppelin's 'Kashmir' – given a down-market re-fit for the film *Godzilla* and renamed 'Come With Me' by Puff Daddy – and adapted by Kingdom Come for their number 'Get It On'. There is a G+ chord in the chorus of ELO's 'Livin' Thing' and the D-D+ change drives the verse of The Ting Tings' 'Great DJ'. See also Abba's 'Mamma Mia' and John Lennon's 'Just Like Starting Over'. The main riff on U2's early 'An Cat Dubh' has a strong D augmented flavour.

Notice that an augmented chord is made up of two intervals of two tones (full steps) each. If you try to add another one, you come full circle: in C, the note two tones above G♯ is … C. Therefore, the augmented chord cannot be added to by the method which increases the complexity of other chords.

Diminished seventh chords

The diminished triad (C E♭ G♭) is almost never used on its own. Instead, another note one-and-a-half tones above is added to create a diminished seventh: C E♭ G♭ B♭♭ (B double-flat = A in pitch). In sound, this is close to a dominant seventh chord. If we change C E♭ G♭ B♭♭ *enharmonically* (using alternate names for the same notes) to C E♭ F♯ A, the E♭ has to drop only one semitone (half-step) to D to make a D7 chord. That's why this chord has a highly ambiguous quality.

As with the augmented chord, you don't want to stay on a diminished seventh for long. It is the musical equivalent of one of those strange particles found in sub-atomic physics – the sort that are in six different places and/or six different times at once. The diminished seventh is a mutant offspring of the minor chord, whose main employment is as a doorway between different keys.

Each note in a diminished seventh can be regarded as the root, so each shape has multiple names. Bizarre, isn't it? I guess you won't be surprised if I tell you that the number of hit singles with diminished sevenths is pretty small. It sometimes turns up in Meat Loaf numbers, to assist that air of faded

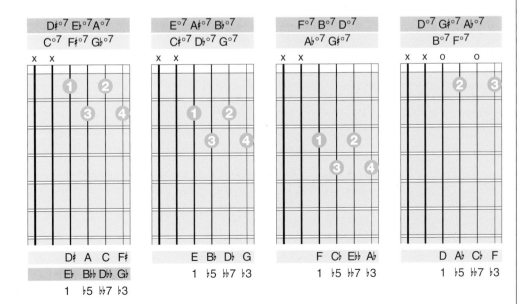

Diminished seventh chords

Diminished seventh chords

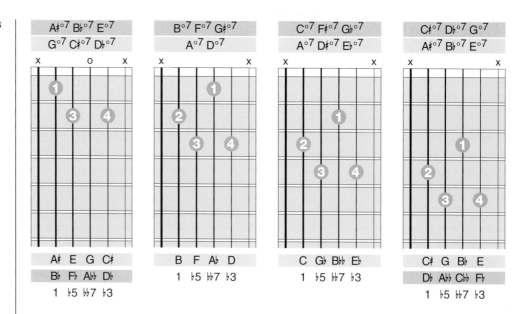

| A♯°7 B♭°7 E°7 |
| G°7 C♯°7 D♭°7 |

| B°7 F°7 G♯°7 |
| A°7 D°7 |

| C°7 F♯°7 G♭°7 |
| A°7 D♯°7 E♭°7 |

| C♯°7 D♭°7 G°7 |
| A♯°7 B♭°7 E°7 |

| A♯ E G C♯ |
| B♭ F♭ A♭♭ D♭ |
| 1 ♭5 ♭♭7 ♭3 |

| B F A♭ D |
| 1 ♭5 ♭♭7 ♭3 |

| C G♭ B♭♭ E♭ |
| 1 ♭5 ♭♭7 ♭3 |

| C♯ G B♭ E |
| D♭ A♭♭ C♭♭ F♭ |
| 1 ♭5 ♭♭7 ♭3 |

grandeur, and there's one in Grandaddy's 'The Crystal Lake'. David Bowie put several in the chorus of 'Quicksand', thus causing a generation of guitar tyros to gnash their teeth because they could not figure out what the hell was going on. But it is popular in jazz. You have been warned….

SECTION 3
CHORD SEQUENCES

Many guitarists write songs without knowing the theory behind the chords they use – they simply rely on their ears: if it sounds good it works. Sometimes during composition a turn of melody or a riff suggests an unusual chord change, and you later discover you have included a chord that is not strictly 'in key'. If it fits in the context of the song, that's fine. The history of music is littered with broken rules, on the other side of which is great music.

Chords in a major key

Here is a simple formula for working out which chords best fit together. Let's demonstrate it in a guitar-friendly key, C major. The notes of the C major scale (below) are: C D E F G A B. They are separated by a set pattern of intervals: tone, tone, semitone, tone, tone, tone, semitone (full step, full step, half-step, full step, full step, full step, half-step). In frets this pattern is 2 2 1 2 2 2 1 (easy

ABBREVIATIONS

Roman numerals **I–VII** indicate chord relationships within a key.

m=minor

maj=major

SONG SECTIONS:

b bridge; **c** coda; **ch** chorus; **f** fade; **hk** hook; **i** intro; **pch** pre-chorus; **r** riff; **s** solo; **v** verse

Most of the chord-sequence examples are standardised for comparison into **C major** or **A minor**. The famous songs are therefore not always in the key of the original recordings.

Scale of C major

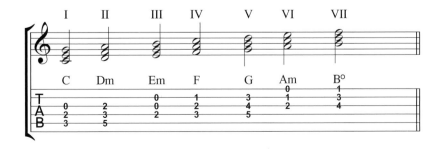

Chords of C major

SECTION 3 | 37

to remember). It governs all major scales, regardless of the starting note. To test this choose any note on any string and go up the string playing notes in the 2 2 1 2 2 2 1 pattern. You will always hear a major scale.

The chords of C major (previous page) are formed from the seven notes of this scale, by stacking in intervals of a third (the numbers here refer to the number of the note in the scale): D F A (2 4 6), E G B (3 5 7), F A C (4 6 1), G B D (5 7 2), A C E (6 1 3) and B D F (7 2 4). The resulting sequence of chords is the same for every major key: major, minor, minor, major, major, minor, diminished. Therefore, the chords that naturally combine in C major are C Dm Em F G and Am. The seventh chord, B diminished, is rarely used. Instead, a musically useful substitute is made by flattening the seventh note and turning it into a major chord. In C major, this would mean flattening B to B♭.

Chords in a minor key

Minor keys are less straightforward because there are different versions of the minor scale. A natural minor (also known as the Aeolian mode) is A B C D E F G A. The pattern of intervals is tone, semitone, tone, tone, semitone, tone, tone (full step, half-step, full step, full step, half-step, full step, full step). In frets this: 2 1 2 2 1 2 2. The chords formed from the seven notes of this scale generate a sequence true for every natural minor key: minor, diminished, major, minor, minor, major, major.

Scale of A natural minor

Chords of A natural minor

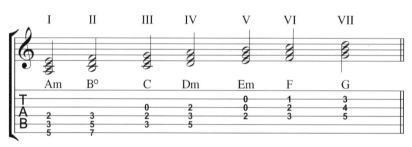

Another possibility is the harmonic minor scale, which has a raised seventh. A harmonic minor is A B C D E F G♯ A. The pattern of intervals is tone, semitone, tone, tone, semitone, tone and a half, semitone (full step, half-step, full step, full step, half-step, step and a half, half-step). In frets: 2 1 2 2 1 3 1. The chords formed from the harmonic minor scale are: minor, diminished, augmented, minor, major, major, diminished.

In songwriting practice, this combination of chords is almost never used. Instead, the major form of chord V (with the G♯ from this scale) is carried over into the natural minor scale chords.

SECTION 3

Scale of A harmonic minor

Chords of A harmonic minor

The Roman numeral system

There is a handy way of notating and thinking about chord progressions without specifying the key. This is possible because the internal chord relationships of all major keys are identical. The same is true of all minor keys as long as they are based on one type of minor scale. The system has been used for hundreds of years in classical music. This is how it works.

There are seven notes (and therefore chords) in a major scale. Each one is given a Roman numeral: I, II, III, IV, V, VI, VII. In C major this means I = C, II = Dm, III = Em, IV = F, V = G, VI = Am, and VII = B diminished. Notice the sequence of chords: major, minor, minor, major, major, minor, diminished, the same for all major keys. Therefore any chord sequence can be notated purely in Roman numerals, as in I-VI-IV-V. Regardless of the major key in which we play this it will always comprise a major chord followed by a minor and then two majors. Their relationship to each other is constant, whatever the key. Compare these examples:

Chord		I	VI	IV	V
Key	C major	C	Am	F	G
	G major	G	Em	C	D
	E♭ major	E♭	Cm	A♭	B♭
	B major	B	G♯m	E	F♯

In *How To Write Songs On Guitar* additional abbreviations attached to Roman numerals give further detail:

i first inversion (in C major, iIV = F with A bass; iVI = Am with C bass)

ii second inversion (in C major, iiIV = F with C bass; iiVI = Am with E bass)

m minor version of what would normally be a major chord. (In C major IVm = Fm instead of F)

^ gives a major version of what would normally be a minor chord, ie, III^

♭ indicates a chord on the flattened note of the scale (♭VII, ♭VI, ♭III)

SECTION 3 |

7 indicates a dominant seventh if the chord is major; minor seventh if it is minor (in C major I7, IV7, V7, ♭VII7 = C7, F7, G7, B♭7; in C major II7, III7, VI7 = Dm7, Em7, Am7; the major seventh chord is indicated with 'maj7', in C major Imaj7, IVmaj7 = Cmaj7, Fmaj7. In C major II^7 is D7 and II^maj7 Dmaj7).

Not only does the Roman numeral system help you to understand keys and progressions, and to see how in different keys they mirror one another, but also to grasp how a single chord can have a different harmonic function according to which key it is in. For example, the chord Am is II in G major, III in F major and VI in C major – same pitch but different roles. There is a practical use, too. If you write out a chord sequence in Roman numerals in the chosen key and discover the melody is too high for you to sing, it's easy to shift it into a lower key without writing out the chords again.

Which chords belong together in which keys?

Many readers have said that the Song Chords table (p42) alone was worth the purchase price of *How To Write Songs On Guitar* for the time it saved them and the ideas it generated. I initially devised this table to assist guitar students to figure out chord sequences from recordings. This can be time consuming and frustrating if you don't use a little knowledge to guide your ears and cut down the seemingly endless possibilities. A vast number of popular songs can be transcribed more easily by first identifying the key and then working with the chords that belong in that key, as set out in the table. For songwriters, creating songs rather than transcribing them, the diagram is a handy guide to which chords sound good together. It is also an aid to identifying which chords certain keys have in common so you can use these to change key. This does not mean that you cannot introduce other chords into sequences than the ones allotted to each key, only that they may sound less natural.

On the left you have the keys. C major is halfway up the table, with no sharps or flats. As you go *down* the table, the keys are increasingly flat; as you go *up*, increasingly sharp. Notice that there are 15 keys but only 12 notes. This anomaly is explained by the fact that three keys are different ways of writing out the same notes (see opposite). Which name for a key in these instances is chosen depends on whether you are working on the flat or sharp side of things.

If you are playing a song in E major (four sharps) and change key to B major (five sharps), it is much easier to continue thinking about sharps than to write the B major chords out as C♭ major (seven flats!).

The Song Chords table in depth

Columns 1–6 show the six most important chords in songwriting for each key. These fit together and sound good in any order. We're not concerned here with whether they are played in extended form as sevenths, sixths, suspensions, ninths, inversions, etc. All we need to think about is the root position major or minor form. As you look *down* the columns, notice that:

I, IV, and V are always major chords
II, III, and VI are always minor chords

Three keys use the same notes but written differently.

SECTION 3 | 41

Song Chords

	I	II	III	IV	V	VI	♭VII	♭VI	♭III	IImaj	IIImaj	IVmin
C# major	C#	D#m	E#m	F#	G#	A#m	B	A	E	D#	E#	F#m
F# major	F#	G#m	A#m	B	C#	D#m	E	D	A	G#	A#	Bm
B major	B	C#m	D#m	E	F#	G#m	A	G	D	C#	D#	Em
E major	E	F#m	G#m	A	B	C#m	D	C	G	F#	G#	Am
A major	A	Bm	C#m	D	E	F#m	G	F	C	B	C#	Dm
D major	D	Em	F#m	G	A	Bm	C	B♭	F	E	F#	Gm
G major	G	Am	Bm	C	D	Em	F	E♭	B♭	A	B	Cm
C major	C	Dm	Em	F	G	Am	B♭	A♭	E♭	D	E	Fm
F major	F	Gm	Am	B♭	C	Dm	E♭	D♭	A♭	G	A	B♭m
B♭ major	B♭	Cm	Dm	E♭	F	Gm	A♭	G♭	D♭	C	D	E♭m
E♭ major	E♭	Fm	Gm	A♭	B♭	Cm	D♭	C♭	G♭	F	G	A♭m
A♭ major	A♭	B♭m	Cm	D♭	E♭	Fm	G♭	F♭	C♭	B♭	C	D♭m
D♭ major	D♭	E♭m	Fm	G♭	A♭	B♭m	C♭	B♭♭	F♭	E♭	F	G♭m
G♭ major	G♭	A♭m	B♭m	C♭	D♭	E♭m	F♭	E♭♭	B♭♭	A♭	B♭	C♭m
C♭ major	C♭	D♭m	E♭m	F♭	G♭	A♭m	B♭♭	A♭♭	E♭♭	D♭	E♭	F♭m

A practical example of a song which uses the primary chords would be Arctic Monkeys' 'Riot Van'. The musical essence of this tale of petty misdemeanours and police-baiting is six bars using chords I to V in A major. The chorus is a two-bar phrase using Dmaj7-C#m7-Bm7 which avoids chord I (A); the verse is a four-bar phrase repeated built on a I-III-II-V turnaround. Likewise, The Eagles' 'Take It Easy' uses chords I, II, IV, V and VI.

The additional columns (7-9, 10-12) offer some extra musical possibilities.

These chords are not truly in key but they are used in songwriting as supplements to the primary six chords.

Columns 7-9: 'flat degree' chords

The chords in columns 7–9 are all major chords built on flattened notes of the scale: the ♭VII, the ♭III and the ♭VI. Chord VII is given in its flattened form as a major, because by strict application of the notes of the scale VII is a diminished chord and therefore not very useful. Let's have a look at them in turn.

The ♭VII chord is very common in popular music because of the influence of blues harmony and the use of the Mixolydian mode (C D E F G A B♭) in many tunes. Both influences have a tendency to lower the seventh note by a semitone. There is an A-G-E change (I-♭VII-V) in 'The View From The Afternoon' and the chorus of 'Dancing Shoes' has I-♭VII-IV-♭III (A♭-G♭-D♭-C♭), both by the Arctic Monkeys. Approaching chord V via ♭VII is heard at the end of the bridge of U2's 'Stuck In A Moment That You Can't Get Out Of'. It is also typical of early 1960s pop numbers, as in the second phrase of the verse of The Beatles' 'Yes It Is'.

The ♭VII can be used to approach chord I instead of V. Compare these two sequences:

I	III	VI	IV	V	I
C	Em	Am	F	G	C

I	III	VI	IV	♭VII	I
C	Em	Am	F	B♭	C

The latter occurs twice in the verse of The Beatles' 'Help' at the close of each vocal phrase.

The ♭III is a significant blues chord. It turns up in many songs on the debut album by Arctic Monkeys, as in the IV-♭III-I (E-D-B) change in 'You Probably Couldn't See For The Lights …' (in B major the expected version of I-III-IV would be B-D♯m-E), and there is IV-♭III-I (E♭-D♭-B♭) in 'Still Take You Home'. There is a ♭III chord in 'Perhaps Vampires Is A Bit Strong But …' in the sequence F♯-A-C♯ (I-♭III-V) and another in the chorus of 'Red Light' . The lowered third note of the scale also provides 'Fake Tales Of San Francisco' with its three-note B-D-E riff (on a B pentatonic minor scale). The Raconteurs' 'Together' uses a straightforward palette of E-G♯m-C♯m-A (I-III-VI-IV) but also includes an accented A-G-E (IV-♭III-I) blues-type sequence which contrasts with the E major harmony in the verse. The I-♭III change dominates 'Rich Woman' by Robert Plant and Alison Krauss. It is also heard in The White Stripes' 'Rag And Bone', Goldfrapp's 'Lovely To See You', and as I-♭III-IV in their 'Ooh La La'.

The ♭VI is also heard in blues and pop-rock. The ♭VI can be found in a non-blues or hard rock context as in the verse of The Beatles' 'Hello Goodbye' or in the chorus of their 1920s' pastiche 'Honey Pie'. There's a ♭VI in the verse of Foo Fighters' 'For All The Cows' in the sequence E-C-B (I-♭VI-V), in the verse of Squeeze's 'Cool For Cats' (leading to a IVm), in Supergrass's 'Pumping On Your Stereo' (♭VI-I: F-A) and one in the verse of Amy Winehouse's 'Rehab' where the

SECTION 3 | 43

chords for the song otherwise are I, III, IV, V, and VI. A common sequence often heard at the end of a phrase is:

♭VI	♭VII	I
A♭	B♭	C

This is an alternative approach to I instead of via V. You can hear it in Oasis' 'She's Electric' (just before the verse), the Kinks' 'Lola', and in the verse of 'Going For The One' by Yes. There is a fine use of the ♭VI at the end of the chorus in Boston's 'More Than A Feeling' – the music pauses on it before sliding by a semitone (half-step) to VI (E♭-Em in G major). The combination of a major-minor change with the half-step is very satisfying.

A hard rock formula

The chords from columns 7–9 are often combined with those in columns 1–6 in songs that have a harder edge. A formula for writing hard rock songs in a generic Rolling Stones/Black Crowes/Bad Company style, or (arranged differently) in the garage rock style of The White Stripes, combines chords I, IV and V with these three flattened chords. You can hear the flat degree chords in The Raconteurs' 'Broken Boy Soldier' which moves around E-G-D-E (I-♭III-♭VII-I) plus C-B-A-G (♭VI-V-IV-♭III).

Here are more examples. (Remember that C major is not necessarily the key of the original recording. All sequences are given in C to facilitate comparison with one another.)

I-♭III-IV: C-E♭-F

The Beatles 'Back In The USSR', 'I Am The Walrus', 'Sgt. Pepper's Lonely Hearts Club Band', Gomez 'Whippin' Piccadilly', Embrace 'One Big Family' (ch), 'Life Is Sweet' (v), and in reversed form as I-IV-♭III in Elastica's 'Connection' (ch) and The Knack's 'My Sharona' (v)

I-♭III-IV-V-♭VII: C-E♭-F-G-B♭

The Beatles 'Baby You're A Rich Man', Eddie Floyd 'Knock On Wood' (i), Wilson Pickett 'In The Midnight Hour' (i)

I-♭III-IV-♭VI-♭VII: C-E♭-F-A♭-B♭

Jimi Hendrix 'Hey Joe', Led Zeppelin 'Trampled Underfoot'

I-♭III-IV-V-♭VI-♭VII: C-E♭-F-G-A♭-B♭

Rolling Stones 'Brown Sugar'

I-IV-♭VII: C-B♭-F

The Beatles 'Another Girl' (v), 'Get Back'

I-IV-V-♭VII: C-F-G-B♭

The Beatles 'A Hard Day's Night', David Bowie 'Jean Genie', The Sex Pistols 'Pretty Vacant' (v), Cream 'Sunshine Of Your Love'

I-V-♭VII: C-G-B♭

The Beatles 'I'm a Loser' (v), reversed to I-♭VII-V in Led Zeppelin 'Misty Mountain Hop'

The three flat degree chords play a significant part in the music of The White Stripes. 'Dead Leaves' uses I, ♭III, IV, V, ♭VI and ♭VII in A; 'Hotel Yorba' has I, IV, V and ♭VII in G; 'I'm Finding It Harder To Be A Gentleman' has I, ♭III and ♭VII in its verse, and ♭III in its hook; 'Fell In Love With A Girl' has a I-♭VII-♭III-IV sequence, and V, ♭VII, ♭III and IV, in B; and 'The Same Boy You've Always Known' uses I, ♭III, IV, and ♭VII in A. 'You Don't Know What Love Is' features a heavily accented ♭III-♭VII-I change

The chorus of The Hold Steady's 'Same Kooks' uses I-♭VII-V-IV-♭III (A-G-E-D-C). The flat degree chords can be used to toughen one section and make it contrast with another. So the verse of Robert Plant and Alison Krauss's 'Gone Gone Gone' has a verse with chords I, IV, V, and VI, but a link that uses IV-♭III-I.

The Mixolydian song

Foo Fighters' 'Times Like These' and 'Overdrive' are two examples of what I call Mixolydian songs. The scale known as the Mixolydian mode is equivalent to a major scale with the seventh note lowered by a semitone. That scale produces a ♭VII chord and a minor chord V. The term 'Mixolydian' serves as shorthand to describe a song that brings in the ♭VII, or turns chord V into a minor (a harmonic consequence of the lowered seventh). In D major we would then find Am instead of A. This happens in 'Times Like These' which has both C and Am present, and 'Overdrive' which has a prominent Am. Plant and Krauss's 'Polly Comes Home' is in D major with Vm (Am) and ♭VII (C) chords. Madness's 'Embarrassment' has a I-III-Vm-II sequence for some of its verses.

Reverse polarity

Columns 10–12 of the Song Chords table offer another group of possible additional chords to the primary I-VI. These are adjusted versions ('reverse polarity') of chords II, III and IV, where what was a minor chord turns into a major and vice versa. These are often used as substitutes in a primary chord (I-VI) progression. Play these popular sequences to hear the effect:

I	II	IV	V	I	III	IV	V	I	VI	IV	V
C	Dm	F	G	C	Em	F	G	C	Am	F	G

Now try the 'reverse polarity' trick:

I	II^	IV	V	I	III^	IV	V	I	VI^	IV	V
C	D	F	G	C	E	F	G	C	A	F	G

The major version of II (II^) creates a momentary expectation of a key change to G minor or G, but the move to F cancels this out. This expectation would be heightened if you played D7 instead of D. The chorus of The Beatles' 'All You Need Is Love' has I-II^-V. Roxy Music's 'Virginia Plain' uses I, IV and V but adds II^. U2's 'Walk On' links a I-V-IV-II with a I-V-IV-II^, where the switch to the reverse polarity version of II (D-A-G-E instead of Em) makes for an unexpected twist.

The major version of III (III^) creates the momentary expectation of a key change to A minor or A (as heard in chorus of The Beatles' 'Golden Slumbers'). Once again, the move to F cancels this out, and you can heighten the expectation by turning the major III into a dominant seventh (E7). A dramatic example occurs in the verse of Queen's 'Innuendo' (E to G♯).

Major versions of II and III are heard in the verse of Foo Fighters' 'Alone And Easy'. The chorus of Abba's 'Dancing Queen' depends on II^ and III^ and the expectation they arouse for its power. The progression in A is:

V	III^	VI	II^	IV	II	I
E	C♯	F♯m	B	D	Bm	A

Notice the delay of chord I to the very end, the fleeting modulation to F♯m and the sudden sadness that goes with that chord, the unexpected change from B to D, the second sad change with D to Bm and the final resolution of these emotions on the key chord.

In some of Arctic Monkeys' songs reverse polarity chords are combined with the flat degree chords. 'Still Take You Home' has a sequence that goes I-IVm-♭VI-V (B♭-E♭m-G♭-F). In 'When The Sun Goes Down' B-D♯-Emaj7-D♯m are the first four chords, which offers two forms of chord III, the normal and the reverse polarity. The same III / III^ combination is heard in the verse of 'Mardy Bum'. 'From The Ritz To The Rubble' has the unusual B-D-Em chord sequence (I-♭III-IVm). Caution should be exercised when using flat degree and reverse polarity chords in the same song section because they may damage the sense of the home key.

The minor version of chord IV (column 12) is an MOR favourite because it lends itself to romantic emotion. It is found either as the chord change I-IVm or coming after IV in its normal major form and then resolving to I or V. Play this popular sequence:

I	I	IV	I	V	IV	I
C	Dm	F	C	G	F	C

Now try:

I	II	IV	I	V	IV	IVm	I
C	Dm	Fm	C	G	F	Fm	C

The Beatles use the IVm in the verses of 'Do You Want To Know A Secret?', 'In My Life', 'I'll Follow The Sun', 'That Means A Lot', 'Hold Me Tight', 'All I've Got To Do', 'I Call Your Name', 'She Loves You' (ch), and in 'Bungalow Bill' (ch and v). 'Nowhere Man' has a bridge of Dm-Fm-C (II-IVm-I). It can finish a minor-key song with an unexpected lift, as in 'And I Love Her', which ends Gm-D. Paul McCartney put one in the intro of Wings' 'Band On The Run' (on the word "mama").

See also R. Kelly's 'I Believe I Can Fly', Grandaddy's 'The Crystal Lake',

Elvis Costello's 'Riot Act', Space's 'Female Of The Species', Peter and Gordon's 'World Without Love' (br), and Echo And The Bunnymen's 'The Killing Moon' (ch). The Hollies' 'The Air That I Breathe' has I-III-IVm-I and I-III^-IV-IVm. Bob Dylan used a IVm for a dramatic first chord in the verses of 'Idiot Wind'. The IVm can be heard in a I-VI-♭VI-IVm sequence in the verse of ELO's 'Livin' Thing'. There's a I-IVm-V sequence in 'Since I Don't Have You', and I-IVm-♭VII in Robert Plant's 'Heaven Knows'. Goldfrapp's 'Satin Chic' has I-♭VI-Ivm for the verse and Dido's 'All You Want' has it in the verse and the chorus.

Try a Imaj7-IVm7 for a more sophisticated version of this change, or approach from VI to intensify the IVm. A song with the VI-IVm change in its verse is The Beatles' 'The Night Before'. Its deeply tragic potential is heard in Stephen Stills's 'To A Flame'. Rock bands have generally not been keen on this change, judging it too 'soft', which perhaps makes it more affecting when they do make it the lynch-pin of a song, as Led Zeppelin did in 'Ten Years Gone' and Fleetwood Mac in 'Man Of The World'. Radiohead have incorporated this chord change into their brand of contemporary rock in songs such as 'Airbag', 'Creep' 'Subterranean Homesick Alien', and 'No Surprises'. Muse are also fond of this change, as 'Hate This' reveals (it ends Gm-D).

Here are some unusual chord alterations and possibilities not on the Song Chords table.

V as a minor

Along with chord I, chord V determines the feeling of being in a particular key. Therefore if chord V is turned into a minor it darkens the minor key at the price of a little ambiguity. Nevertheless, this can be heard in Suede's 'Trash' (ch: C-Gm-F-A♭), Dido's 'Honestly OK', 'Who Makes You Free', and 'Don't Think of Me' (with V as major also), Lightning Seeds' 'Sense' (ch: Dm-C-G when the key is G), Eric Clapton's 'She's Waiting' (v: I-IV-Vm-IV: G-C-Dm-C), Goldfrapp's 'Fly Me Away' (I-Vm-♭VII: B-F♯m-A) and The Who's 'Behind Blue Eyes' (br: I-Vm-IV-I: E-Bm-A-E).

The chorus of Blur's 'Park Life' features the even rarer ♭V chord (E B♭ B). This is sometimes used as a chromatic approach to chord V – but usually coming from chord IV, not chord I. For its use with the ♭VII chord see the paragraph above on the Mixolydian song. Supergrass's 'Richard III' has this striking I-♭V change as A-E♭.

VI as a major

The major version of chord VI creates the expectation of a key change up a tone. It is much used for quick key changes, as in the verse of The Beatles' 'Good Day Sunshine' and Blur's 'Charmless Man'. You'll also find it in the intro to 'Goldfinger' (E-C). The John Barry/Bond association was exploited by Sneaker Pimps' 'Underground', which adds a Bond sample to the chord change just to emphasise the point. Listen to the first two chords of 'Seen The Light' by Supergrass (I-VI^).

Using the Song Chords table for minor keys

If writing a song in a minor key, you can still use the Song Chords table. The trick is to approach the table from a different angle. Here's how:

- Locate the minor key in which you're composing in column 6.
- Your main chords in that minor key will be found in columns 1–7 plus columns 10 and 11.
- All that changes is the numbers relative to the chords.

Let's say you want to write a song in A minor. If you look down column 6, you find that Am occurs there in the key of C major:

1	2	3	4	5	6	7	8	9	10	11	12
C	Dm	Em	F	G	Am	B♭	E♭	A♭	D	E	Fm

So for A minor, we take chords 1–7 plus 11 and re-number them, starting with the Am:

1	2	3	4	5	6	7	[10]	[11]
Am	B♭	C	Dm	Em	F	G	D	E

Whether you use the major or minor form of chords IV and V in a minor key depends on the harmony you want and the melody of the song. For a tune in A natural minor (Aeolian mode: A B C D E F G), you need chords 1, 3–7. For a tune in A Dorian (A B C D E F♯ G), you need chords 1, 3–7, with 4 as D major rather than D minor. Tunes using the harmonic (A B C D E F G♯) minor scale will need the major version of the V chord. It is perfectly allowable to combine different minor harmonies in a single song *as long as the chord and the melody note match*. You can have D and Dm in a song in A minor, but if so the note F in the melody must be sung over Dm (D F A); a D major chord (D F♯ A) requires F♯ in the melody.

A good example is The Zombies' 60s hit 'She's Not There'. Both the verse and the chorus repeatedly change from Am to D (I-IV^, which has an F♯ in it) and then Am to F in adjacent bars (I-VI). Chord V appears in the chorus both as Em and E (V^). Goldfrapp's 'You Never Know' has the unusual and haunting progression G♯m-D♯-F♯-D♯m (I-V^-VII-V).

Both Franz Ferdinand and Muse often write songs in minor keys. Em, Dm, and Gm are favourites of Muse, whose chord sequences often imply the harmonic minor by having the major version of chord V. 'Feeling Good', for example, is Gm Gm/F Eb Dsus4 D (I-VI-V^).

Song Chords and key-changing (modulation)

If there is a change of key in a song you are transcribing, or if you want your song to change key, find or choose the new key on the Song Chords table in column 1 and work with the chords that belong to it.

Now we're ready to look at how songwriters combine chords into songs.

The two-chord song

There are one-chord songs, but they're pretty rare. 'Exodus' by Bob Marley stays on one chord much of the time, as do Pink Floyd's 'Careful With That Axe, Eugene', The Beatles' 'Within You Without You' and 'Tomorrow Never Knows', and Roy Harper's 'Frozen Moment'. There is a tradition in the blues of one-chord songs such as Muddy Waters' 'I'm A Man', Howlin' Wolf's 'Smokestack Lightning' and Sonny Boy Williamson's 'Bring It On Home'. More commonly a single chord might carry a verse, as with Morcheeba's 'Shoulder Holster', The Beatles' 'The Ballad Of John And Yoko' and Marvin Gaye and Kim Weston's 'It Takes Two', where IV and V come in with the hook.

A list of two-chord songs might include K. C. & The Sunshine Band's 'That's The Way (I Like It)' (Cm-Fm), The Spice Girls' 'Spice Up Your Life', Underworld's 'Born Slippy', Stereo MCs' 'Step It Up', James Brown's 'Sex Machine', and 'Say It Loud – I'm Black And I'm Proud'. The challenge of writing a two-chord song is to avoid monotony. Composing an arresting song with only two chords is not easy, which is why most songwriters prefer to include (at least) a third chord.

Two-chord changes

Before tackling progressions with three or more chords, it is useful to explore basic chord changes, so that you get a feel for their varied qualities. Let's start from a C major chord and look at all the possible changes. These could form a two-chord song, but the point here is simply to sense the moods these changes evoke so you can incorporate them into songs with any number of chords. Note that *on the guitar* the effect of any change is modified by the key in which it is played. For example, I-II in C (C-Dm) using standard open shapes has a rising quality, whereas I-II in D (D-Em) plunges downward.

I-II: C-Dm

This is a short movement where all the notes change, typical of reggae and ska. This change features in The Zutons' 'Valerie' (ch), Bob Marley's 'Wait In Vain' (ch), Thunderclap Newman's 'Something In The Air' (v), The Beatles' 'Don't Let Me Down' (v + ch), Supergrass's 'Alright' (v), Madonna's 'Like A Virgin' (ch), Wham!'s 'Wake Me Up Before You Go-Go' (ch), Phats & Small's 'ATB 9pm (Till I Come)', Fleetwood Mac's 'Over My Head', The Faces' 'Debris' and 'Glad And Sorry', Nick Drake's 'Hazey Jane I' and 'Northern Sky', Genesis's 'The Carpet Crawlers', and Santana's 'Samba Pa Ti' (cd). I-II is a signature chord change of Smokey Robinson, who used it in 'Ooh Baby Baby' (ch), 'If You Can Want', 'Baby, Baby Don't Cry', and 'More Love', which is why Amy Winehouse's 'He Can Only Hold Her' is reminiscent of him. Four Razorlight tracks – 'Up All Night', 'Which Way Is Out', 'Rip It Up', and 'Get It And Go' – make some use of a I-II chord change, and it features in The Strokes' songs 'Someday' and 'Last Nite'.

I-III: C-Em

This is an expressive major-to-minor change with two notes in common (C = CEG, Em = EGB). Its potential is brought out in Tori Amos's 'A Northern Lad' (ch), Blur's 'The Universal' (I +v), and Elvis Costello's 'Party Girl' (v).

I-IV: C-F

This has a lighter, more relaxed feel than I-V. Bruce Springsteen's 'Born In The USA' (B-E), and 'Stolen Car' (G-C), The Temptations' 'My Girl' (v) The Beatles' 'Paperback Writer' (v G-C), and 'It's All Too Much' (C-F), R.E.M.'s 'Electrolyte' (v G-C), U2's 'Angel Of Harlem' and 'All I Want Is You', Kate Bush's 'Kite', Joni Mitchell's 'Both Sides Now' (v), The Dave Clark Five's 'Glad All Over', Lou Reed's 'Walk On The Wild Side', Rod Stewart's 'Tonight's The Night' (v), The Four Tops' 'Baby I Need Your Loving' (v), Marvin Gaye's 'How Sweet It Is To Be Loved By You', Lone Justice's 'Ways To Be Wicked' (v), Gerry and the Pacemakers' 'Don't Let The Sun Catch You Crying' (v), Aretha Franklin's 'Respect', Lightning Seeds' 'Life Of Riley', Levellers' 'Hope Street', Goldfrapp's 'Number 1', Supergrass's 'Going Out', and The Verve's 'Numbness'. It is dreamy when played as Imaj7-IVmaj7; harder-edged as I7-IV7.

I-V: C-G

This has a strong sense of major tonality that holds the key firm. Excellent for writing light, novelty, comic or children's songs or where the words and melody are paramount. The Scaffold's 'Lily The Pink', Chuck Berry's 'Memphis Tennessee', The Equals' 'Baby Come Back', Dire Straits' 'So Far Away' (v), Aretha Franklin's 'Respect' (ch), Plastic Ono Band's 'Give Peace A Chance', The Beatles' 'Yellow Submarine' (ch), The Honeycombs' 'Have I The Right'.

I-VI: C-Am

This is significant as one of the strongest changes from major to minor. Only one note alters between these chords (C = C E G, Am = A C E) yet the mood change is great. Elvis Presley's 'His Latest Flame', The Smiths' 'Rusholme Ruffians', Lulu's 'Shout', The Searchers' 'Needles And Pins', The Small Faces' 'Itchycoo Park' (ch), Marvin Gaye's 'What's Going On' (ch), Boomtown Rats' 'Rat Trap' (i), Smokey Robinson And The Miracles' 'You Really Got A Hold On Me' (i), Tears For Fears' 'Head Over Heels' (v), Razorlight's 'In The Morning' (v + ch) and 'Who Needs Love?', Bruce Springsteen's 'Twelfth Avenue Freeze-Out' and 'Living In The Future'.

I-♭VII: C-B♭

This is often implied in riff-based songs. Led Zeppelin's 'Whole Lotta Love', The Who's 'My Generation', The Kinks' 'You Really Got Me', Stevie Wonder's 'We Can Work It Out' (v), Thin Lizzy's 'The Rocker' (v), Bryan Adams's 'Somebody' (v), Siouxsie And The Banshees' 'Hong Kong Garden'.

The above are the changes from chord I to another chord based on columns 1-7 of the Song Chord table. Here are some other, more exotic variations. Some are examples of 'reverse polarity' (where a chord that should be minor becomes major and *vice versa*) :

I-Im: C-Cm

This is an arresting chord change that unsettles the sense of key. The first change of the verse of 10cc's 'I'm Not In Love' is from a major to a minor on the same root. It is also in Mary Hopkin's 'Those Were The Days' (Am-A-Dm), Super Furry Animals' 'I Don't Want You To Destroy Me' (A-F♯m-E-Em), The Carpenters' 'Close To You' (C-Bsus4-B-Bm). The Kinks' 'Autumn Almanac' has several at the end of one section and start of the next. The verse of Louis Armstrong's 'We Have All The Time In The World' has E- Em in the key of A major.

I-♭II^: C-C# or D♭

This is highly unusual – listen to the verse of Led Zeppelin's 'Dancing Days'. Voiced as power chords (such as E5-B♭5), it's important for the 1980s heavy metal of bands like Metallica. It is implied in the riff of 'Conquest' by The White Stripes.

I-II^: C-D

This is ambiguous because it sets up the expectation of a key change to the dominant key, ie, here G.

I-♭III: C-E♭

This is a classic hard-edged blues change found in T. Rex's 'Children Of The Revolution' (v) and 'Venus Loon', and Suzi Quatro's 'Can The Can' (ch). It can also be exotic, as in the verse of Tears For Fears' 'Head Over Heels'. 'Late In The Day' by Supergrass has this change given an unusual colour with both I and ♭III as major sevenths (Dmaj7-Fmaj7).

I-IIImaj: C-E

This is ambiguous because it sets up the expectation of a change to the key whose root note is the sixth note of the scale, ie, here A or A minor. Compare the stark C-E♭m (actual pitch A-Cm) change in the 'hymn' section of 'Paranoid Android'.

Try strumming F-A, B♭-G, A-C, or F-D: all occur in songs on Nirvana's *Nevermind*. Notice that all these pairs of chords are either a major third (2 tones) or a minor third (1½ tones) apart. The sound of major chords a third apart is possibly the most distinctive harmony effect in Nirvana's music.

I-IVm: C-Fm

This is a staple chord change of ballads and MOR. It's expressive to the point of sentimentality.

I-Vm: C-Gm

This is ambiguous, because it sets up the expectation of a key change to, or being in, F (or whichever key's root note is on the fourth degree of the scale). This can be heard on the disconcerting intro of Paul Young's version of 'Don't Dream It's Over' and at the start of The Beatles' 'She's Leaving Home'.

I-♭VI: C-A♭

This is slightly strange-sounding, though the note C is common to both chords. Sometimes deployed by film composer John Barry: see 'Goldfinger'. It occurs in Go West's 'We Close Our Eyes'.

I-VI^: C-A

This is ambiguous because it sets up the expectation of a change to whichever key is represented by a root note at the second note of the scale, ie, here D or D minor. See Otis Redding's '(Sittin' On) The Dock Of The Bay' (ch), and Talking Heads' 'Road To Nowhere' (v).

I-♭VIIm: C-B♭m

This is a very unusual change that implies a IV-V change in the minor key whose root note is the fourth of the home key's scale, ie, here F minor. It occurs in the bridge of ELO's 'Livin' Thing'.

Minor key two-chord changes

What happens if instead of starting with a major chord, we start from a minor? These changes work differently in minor keys where, depending on which minor scale or mode is operating, the most common would be:

I-III: Am-C

This is heard in Edwin Starr's 'War'. Compare Radiohead's 'Morning Bell' Am to C♯m, where the minor chords are two tones apart.

I-IV: Am-Dm

This is a very common minor-key change, heard in Johnny Kidd and the Pirates' 'Shakin' All Over', The Rolling Stones' 'Fool To Cry' and 'Miss You', Siouxsie And The Banshees' 'Fireworks', Beats International's 'Dub Be Good To Me', and The Verve's 'Sit And Wonder'.

I-IV^: Am-D

This is heard in Pink Floyd's 'Another Brick In The Wall' (v), Santana's 'Oye Como Va', U2's 'Miss Sarajevo' (v), Sly And The Family Stone's 'It's A Family Affair', Dexys Midnight Runners' 'Jackie Wilson Said', R.E.M.'s 'Drive' (v), Carole King's 'It's Too Late' (v), and Happy Mondays' 'Kinky Afro'. It is a powerful change, especially in the major key where it occurs from II to V. Sometimes it isn't easy to assess whether the change is I-IV^ in a minor key or II-V in the major key a tone below.

I-V: Am-E

This is a very common minor-key change, heard in The Spice Girls' 'Spice Up Your Life'. The White Stripes give the angular Em-B♭ (I-♭V) change a new twist in 'The Union Forever'.

I-Vm: Am-Em

This is a gloomier version of the I-V change, heard in the verse of R.E.M.'s 'Losing My Religion' and Kraftwerk's 'The Model'.

I-VI: Am-F

This is a very common change, heard throughout The Beatles' 'Eleanor Rigby', Goldfrapp's 'Let It Take You', Fleetwood Mac's 'Dreams' and 'Rhiannon', Oasis' 'Live Forever' (cd), Franz Ferdinand's 'The Fallen' (hk to v) and Dido's 'Life For Rent'.

How you voice this change makes a big difference to the effect. I-VImaj7 (Am-Fmaj7) and I-VI7 (Am-F7) have a very different quality; the latter is in the verses of The Beatles' 'From Me To You' and 'Glass Onion'.

I-♭II: Am-B♭

Bob & Earl's soul classic 'Harlem Shuffle' makes astonishing use of this otherwise awkward change – and, to avoid monotony, subjects it to a semitone (half-step) key change, from A minor to B♭ minor.

I-VII: Am-G

This is a common change featured in R.E.M.'s 'Maps And Legends' (ch) and 'The One I Love' (v), America's 'Horse With No Name' (with G as an inverted G/B), and Cat Stevens's 'Matthew and Son' (v).

I-#VII: Am-G#

This gives a haunting change in the minor key. This oddly-named chord ♯VII arises because as I have conceptualised the minor key the natural minor scale is taken as normative and the seventh note of that scale is a tone away from the final note. What would have been called a ♭VII in the major key (G in A major) is here in the normative minor key labelled plain VII (G in A minor). This creates the possibility of a major chord on a raised seventh note of the minor scale – hence G♯ (♯VII) in A minor. This unusual change can be heard in Neil Finn's 'Try Whistling This' and Beck's 'O Maria'.

Techniques for writing a two-chord song

To get the most from the restricted harmony of a two-chord song, try these techniques:

- Put the emphasis on the melody and lyric, as in a narrative song.
- Vary the tempo or time signature.
- Change the order of the chords from section to section.
- Use first and second inversions of the two chords.
- Change key and play the same change in the new key. Wings' 'Mull Of Kintyre' starts as a two-chord song in A and changes key to D.
- Change the bass note to imply a change of chord. An E under a G chord implies Em (chord III in C) even if you're still strumming a G.
- Use the 'bar-stretching' technique: if the rate of change is one chord to a bar in the chorus, make it two bars to a chord in the verse or vice versa.

The 'three-chord trick'

The 'three-chord trick' is the commonest songwriting device with chords. It means a song with just chords I, IV, and V of any major or minor key. Since these are the three chords that are used in 12-bar blues, a vast number of 1950s rock'n'roll songs by Elvis Presley, Chuck Berry, Carl Perkins, Jerry Lee Lewis, Little Richard, Bill Haley, Buddy Holly, Eddie Cochran, etc, as well as ones by later rock acts who played 12-bar boogie, such as Canned Heat and Status Quo, are three-chord tricks. This is also the formula for many pop songs such as The Beatles' 'Twist and Shout', The Clash's 'I Fought The Law' and 'Should I Stay Or Should I Go?', Babybird's 'You're Gorgeous' (ch), and Ritchie Valens's 'La Bamba'. With care it can be expressive, as in the verse of Elton John's 'Don't Let The Sun Go Down On Me', which uses just I, IV, and V (the first minor chord is not featured until the chorus). The track 'Killing The Blues' by Robert

Plant and Alison Krauss shows the three-chord trick in a slow country style. The three chords can occur in any order. Sting's 'Consider Me Gone' has two chords to carry the verse and one for the chorus. The Stone Roses' 'She Bangs The Drums' carries the verse with IV and V before hitting I on the chorus.

The three chords can go in any order. Compare Roxy Music's 'Over You' or Mink de Ville's 'Spanish Stroll' (I-IV-V, C-F-G) with the I-V-IV, C-G-F of Corner Shop's 'Brimful Of Asha', George Harrison's 'If Not For You', Neil Young's 'Helpless', The Rolling Stones' 'Sway', The Who's 'Baba O'Riley'. Jimi Hendrix's 'The Wind Cries Mary' (v), Rod Stewart's 'Maggie May' (v), Dido's 'Life For Rent' (ch) and U2's 'Elevation' (ch) use the displaced form V-IV-I.

Variations on the 'three-chord trick'
If we widen the definition to allow any three chords in a key, not only I, IV, and V, there are many other combinations for a song. These include putting a minor chord, a flat degree chord or a reverse polarity chord in with I and V:

I-II-V: C-Dm-G
Thin Lizzy 'Boys Are Back In Town' (ch), Bryan Adams and Mel C 'When You're Gone' (II-V-I), Richard Hawley 'Seasons' and 'Dark Road' (v II-V-I), R.E.M. 'Wendell Gee' (v), '(Don't Go Back To) Rockville' (ch).

I-V-II: C-G-Dm
R.E.M. 'Near Wild Heaven' (ch), Pretenders 'Back On The Chain Gang' (v), Mazzy Star 'Fade Into You', Bob Dylan 'Knockin' On Heaven's Door' (I-V-II, I-V-IV), Shakespeare's Sister 'Stay' (ch).

I-III-V: C-Em-G

I-V-III: C-G-Em

I-III-VI: C-Em-Am
Plastic Ono Band 'Instant Karma' (ch), Aimee Mann 'Choice In The Matter' (v in B, ch in E).

I-VI-IV: C-Am-F
The Hold Steady 'You Can Make Him Like You' (displaced as VI-IV-I), Dido 'See You When You're Forty'.

I-VI-V: C-Am-G
Four Tops 'Still Waters Run Deep'.

I-V-VI: C-G-Am
Thin Lizzy 'Jailbreak' (v, voiced as fifths).

V can be replaced with chord IV for a softer, less definite effect:

I-II-IV: C-Dm-F
Radiohead 'High And Dry' (displaced as II-IV-I).

CHORD SEQUENCES

I-II^-IV: C-D-F

Oasis 'Cigarettes And Alcohol' (v E-F♯-A).

I-IV-II: C-F-Dm

Jimmy Ruffin 'Gonna Give Her All The Love I've Got' (ch).

I-III-IV: C-Em-F

Van Morrison 'Queen Of The Slipstream'.

I-VI-IV: C-Am-F

Bruce Springsteen 'If I Should Fall Behind'.

The Mixolydian 'three-chord trick'

You can also create a three-chord song by bringing in a 'blues' chord from columns 7–9 of the Song Chords table and combining it with I and IV, or I and V.

I-♭III-IV: C-E♭-F

Beatles 'Magical Mystery Tour', U2 'Pride (In The Name Of Love)' (br), Edwin Starr 'Twenty Five Miles'.

I-♭III-♭VII: C-E♭-B♭

Thin Lizzy 'The Rocker' (ch), Ike and Tina Turner 'Nutbush City Limits' (v).

I-♭VII-IV: C-B♭-F

U2 'Desire', The Who 'Won't Get Fooled Again' (v, and many other Who songs), R.E.M. 'Crush With Eyeliner' (v), Robert Palmer 'Addicted To Love', The Rolling Stones '(This Could Be) The Last Time', Cast 'Alright' (v), Patti Smith 'Rock and Roll Nigger', Bachman Turner Overdrive 'You Ain't Seen Nothing Yet' (v, I-♭VII-IV with a three-chord trick ch I-V-IV), Fatboy Slim 'Praise Him', Alanis Morrisette 'Hand In My Pocket' (hk), Bad Company 'Can't Get Enough' (v), Fleetwood Mac 'Don't Stop' (v), Oasis 'Cigarettes And Alcohol' (ch), Joe Cocker 'With A Little Help From My Friends', Them 'Gloria', Sunhouse 'Chasing The Dream' (as ♭VII-IV-I), The Verve 'Valium Skies' (ch, as ♭VII-IV-I), Robert Plant and Alison Krauss 'Please Read The Letter', R.E.M. 'Until The Day Is Done' (♭VII-IV-I), Franz Ferdinand 'Do You Want To' (v, I-IV-♭VII).

♭VI-♭VII-I: A♭-B♭-C

Seal 'Kiss From A Rose', The Boo Radleys – the end of 'Wake Up Boo!', The Beatles 'Lady Madonna' (v).

Note that the presence of the ♭VII chord sometimes leads to uncertainty as to which key the music is in. The Mixolydian three-chord trick in C (C-B♭-F) happens to be the same chords as a I-IV-V in F (F-B♭-C). Green Day exploit this in 'Longview'. Its verse has an E♭-D♭ change (I-♭VII) with E♭ sounding as though it is the key chord. The chorus goes B♭-A♭-E♭ with B♭ sounding like the key chord (a progression of I ♭VII IV in B♭). So we're not sure what key it is in. 'Walking Contradiction' has a verse of I-IV-♭VII-I in A♭ but a chorus of D♭-G♭-A♭

(I-IV-V in D♭) which exploits the ambiguity of G♭ being chord ♭VII in A♭ but IV in D♭.

The three-chord turnaround

In blues guitar, the term 'turnaround' means a distinctive phrase played in the last two bars of a 12-bar. In songwriting, it is a short sequence of chords repeated either as an intro, a verse, part of a verse, a chorus, or in a bridge. The turnaround circles its chords, creating an awareness in the listener that it makes a unit within itself. A song can feature one or more turnarounds. In combinations of the three-chord trick with the turnaround device, it must be said that three-bar three-chord turnarounds are rare. Songwriters prefer the symmetry of a four-bar phrase (especially in 4/4 time). However, a 12-bar verse could divide into four three-bar phrases:

G-C-D	G-C-D	G-C-D	G-C-D

This creates an interesting tension because of the way the three pulls against the expectation of four. Each phrase will sound as though a bar is missing, because we are so accustomed to four-bar phrases.

Three-chord four-bar turnarounds in a major key

It's more common to make a four-bar turnaround out of three chords with a return to the first (or one of the other chords) in bar four. Here are some examples with I, IV and V:

I-IV-V-IV

The Troggs 'Wild Thing', China Crisis 'Wishful Thinking', Aswad 'Don't Turn Around' (v).

I-IV-V-I

Eric Clapton 'Lay Down Sally' (ch).

I-IV-I-V

Buddy Holly 'Peggy Sue' (i), Crosby Stills Nash & Young 'Teach Your Children' (v), Van Morrison 'Brown-Eyed Girl' (v).

I-V-IV-I

Sleeper 'What Do I Do Now' (ch).

I-V-IV-V

George Harrison 'What Is Life?', Led Zeppelin 'Tangerine', Roxy Music 'Avalon' (v), The La's 'There She Goes' (v), Cat Stevens 'The First Cut Is The Deepest', Neil Young 'Like A Hurricane' (ch), Shakespeare's Sister 'Stay' (v), Melanie 'Ruby Tuesday'.

Here are examples with other combinations of three chords:

I-II-III-II: C-Dm-Em-Dm
The Beatles 'Ask Me Why' (v), 'I'm Only Sleeping' (ch), Bob Dylan 'I Shall Be Released', Genesis 'Follow Me, Follow You' (ch), Smokey Robinson 'Ooh Baby Baby' (v).

I-II-IV-I: C-Dm-F-C
The Bee Gees 'Massachusetts' (v), Bobby McFerrin 'Don't Worry, Be Happy'.

I-II-♭VI-I: C-Dm-A♭-C
David Bowie 'Boys Keep Swinging' (v).

I-II^-IV-I: C-D-F-C
The Beatles 'Eight Days A Week'.

I-♭III-II-I: C-E♭-Dm-C
Beck 'Nobody's Fault But My Own' (v).

I-♭III-IV-♭III: C-E♭-F-E♭
The Jesus and Mary Chain 'Far Gone And Out' (ch).

I-♭III-♭VII-♭III: C-E♭-B♭-E♭
Hole 'Doll Parts' (v).

I-III-IV-III: C-Em-F-Em
The Isley Brothers 'I Guess I'll Always Love You' (ch)

I-IV-II-I: C-F-Dm-C
The Lightning Seeds 'Sense', Jackie Wilson 'Higher And Higher'.

I-IV-♭VII-I: C-F-B♭-C
Big Star 'Feel'.

I-IV-♭VII-IV: C-F-B♭-F
The Wonderstuff 'The Size Of A Cow', Green Day 'Warning'.

I-V-II-V: C-G-Dm-G

I-V-IVm-I: C-G-Fm-C
Fleetwood Mac 'Man Of The World'.

I-V-VI-V: C-G-Am-G
The Proclaimers 'Letter From America' (i).

I-V-♭VII-V: C-G-B♭-G
The Association 'Cherish' (v).

I-Vm-IVm-I: C-Gm-Fm-C
Nancy Sinatra 'You Only Live Twice', Robbie Williams 'Millennium'.

I-VI-I-V: C-Am-C-G
Marvin Gaye 'Wherever I Lay My Hat' (v).

I-VI-II-I: C-Am-Dm-C
The Supremes 'Stoned Love'.

I-VI-IV-I: C-Am-F-C
U2 'One', David Bowie 'Soul Love' (v).

I-VI^-VI-I: C-A-Am-C
Blondie 'Heart Of Glass'.

I-♭VII-IV-I: C-B♭-F-C
The Who 'I Can't Explain', The Beatles 'Hey Jude' (cd), Wishbone Ash 'Blowin' Free' (v), The Charlatans 'Just When You're Thinking Things Over' (ch). Goldfrapp 'Ride A White Horse' (v).

I-♭VII-IV-♭VII: C-B♭-F-B♭
Simple Minds 'Don't You Forget About Me' (v), The J.Geils Band 'Centerfold'.

Three-chord songs in a minor key
Analysing minor-key sequences in popular music is problematic because the six primary chords for songwriting in the natural minor key (I, III-VII) are the same pitches as the relative major but in a different order. In classical music, minor keys tend to be more clearly signalled by the harmonic or melodic minor forms of the scale, where the seventh note of the scale is only a semitone (half-step) away from the key note, rather than the natural minor. Keep this in mind when looking at the following examples. It is not always easy to judge whether a progression is in the natural minor key or its relative major (A minor or C major, for example).

The 'default' for the minor key is assumed to be the natural minor scale and its chords: Am Bdim C Dm Em F G. F is called VI and G VII, not ♭VI and ♭VII, because on the natural minor scale the seventh note has not been flattened in the way that it can be on the major scale. So in A minor I think of Am-G-F as I-VII-VI, not I-♭VII-♭VI, in contrast to A-G-F as I-♭VII-♭VI in A major.

Minor-chord sequences in pop and rock are dominated by I, VII, and VI moving in either direction. In A minor this is Am G F; in E minor it is Em D C (two easy guitar sequences). You will have to check whether in a particular instance this really is in a minor key or is in the relative major, because Am-G-F could be VI-V-IV in C and Em-D-C could be VI-V-IV in G. (Look up the chords on the Song Chord table to get a clearer sense of this.)

The same chord sequence can have a different harmonic meaning depending on the key. Fleetwood Mac's 'You Make Loving Fun' has a verse that features Gm-F-E♭ as a turnaround. This could lead us to think that the song is in G minor, in which case this would be a I-VII-VI in that key. However, the chorus starts on a strong B♭ and we realise that actually the song is in B♭ major and the Gm-F-E♭ progression was actually VI-V-IV in B♭. A similar ambiguity arises in Texas's 'White On Blonde'.

In U2's 'Sometimes You Can't Make It On Your Own' the chorus is VI-V-IV in A major (F♯m-E-D).

I, VII, and VI in the minor key

Songs that use I, VII, and VI in the minor key include: Phil Collins's 'In The Air Tonight', Dire Straits' 'Sultans Of Swing', Derek And The Dominoes' (Eric Clapton) 'Layla', Led Zeppelin's 'Stairway To Heaven' (behind guitar solo) and 'Achilles Last Stand', Lionel Ritchie's 'Hello', Blue Oyster Cult's 'Don't Fear The Reaper', Fleetwood Mac's 'Dreams', Kate Bush's 'Breathing', Oasis's 'Slide Away' (v), Patti Smith's 'Because The Night', The Waterboys' 'The Glastonbury Song', Free's 'Wishing Well', and Thin Lizzy's 'Don't Believe A Word' (cd.).

It is used ascending in The Police's 'Bring On The Night', The Verve's 'This Time', Elvis Costello's 'The Beat' (v), Kate Bush's 'Running Up That Hill', S Express's 'Theme From S-Express', Skunk Anansie's 'Weak', and All About Eve's 'Wild Hearted Woman'. In some of these examples, VII may not as strong as in others – sometimes it is felt only as a passing chord (Am-Am7 or Am/G-F).

Played as power chords in A or E (A5-G5-F5 or E5-D5-C5), I-VII-VI is a favourite of 1970s metal bands (Iron Maiden seemed to base much of their career on it). You can hear it in Black Sabbath's 'Paranoid' between the verses.

Top 1980s UK singles act Madness evolved a distinctive style that, despite a madcap image and quick tempos, was often reliant on minor chords. Slade's 'Coz I Luv You' is a minor key song with three chords – I, IV and ♭II. Remembering that these examples are not necessarily originally in A minor, other minor-chord combinations include:

I-III-VII: Am-C-G

R.E.M. 'Orange Crush' (v).

I-IV-V: Am-Dm-Em

Curtis Mayfield 'Move On Up', Stevie Ray Vaughan 'Dirty Pool', Sufjan Stevens 'The Seer's Tower' (v).

I-IV-V^: Am-Dm-E

The Turtles 'Elenore' (v) Madness 'One Step Beyond', Dido 'Isobel' (v).

I-IV^-V: Am-D-Em

Tasmin Archer 'Sleeping Satellite' (ch).

I-IV^-VI: Am-D-F

'Ritz' Steve Harley and Cockney Rebel, Dido 'Don't Think Of Me' (ch).

I-IV-VII: Am-Dm-G

U2 'Party Girl'.

I-V-IV^: Am-Em-D

I-VI-IV: Am-F-Dm

The Cure 'Why Can't I Be You'.

SECTION 3 | 59

I-VI-V: Am-F-Em
The Cure 'Fascination Street'.

I-VI-V^: Am-F-E
Eurythmics 'Sweet Dreams Are Made Of This'.

I-VII-III: Am-G-C
Van Halen 'Ain't Talkin' 'Bout Love'.

I-VII-IV: Am-G-Dm
Neil Young 'Cortez The Killer'.

I-VII-IV^: Am-G-D
Dodgy 'In A Room', Crosby Stills Nash & Young 'Almost Cut My Hair'.

I-VII-V: Am-G-Em
The Police 'Spirits In The Material World'.

Three-chord four-bar turnarounds in a minor key
I-IV-V-IV: Am-Em-Dm-Em
Madonna 'Into The Groove' (v) Ace 'How Long' (ch).

I-IV^-I-VII: Am-D-Am-G
The Stranglers 'No More Heroes' (hk).

I-V-I-IV: Am-Em-Am-Dm

I-VI-VII-I: Am-F-G-Am
10cc 'Wall Street Shuffle'.

I-VI-VII-VI: Am-F-G-F
The Verve 'Appalachian Spring'.

I-VI-I-V: Am-F-Am-Em

I-VI-IV-VI: Am-F-Dm-F
Dire Straits 'Where Do You Think You're Going', Dido 'Hunter'.

I-VII-I-III: Am-G-Am-C
Air 'Sexy Boy' (ch).

When you use a four-bar three-chord turnaround, be conscious of the fact that it may begin and end on the same chord. If so, you will need to take this into account in terms of lyric and melody at the start of each phrase. This question does not arise with the four-chord turnaround because the last chord is usually different (see below).

The four-chord song

After the three-chord trick, we can advance to using four chords. If we have only used I, IV, and V, the three major chords of a key, we can now bring in one of the minors (II, III, or VI), or even keep it all major with a flat degree ♭III, ♭VI or ♭VII. In a song that is economical with chords, the fourth chord could be reserved for the chorus or bridge.

Consider the songs of Green Day. 'Maria' is a classic three-chord I-IV-V song in A. Sometimes another chord is added to these. 'Pop Rock And Coke' has F♯5, instead of the usual VI in A, F♯m. 'Geek Stink Breath' has an I-♭VII-IV intro in F♯; 'Jaded' has this progression in A♭ at the start of the verse; 'J.A.R.' starts as a three-chord trick but brings in the ♭VII (B in this key of C♯) for the bridge. 'Redundant' is based on a I-IV-V and ♭VII verse in A. 'Basket Case' has a ♭VII chord (D) in its chorus.

The four-chord turnaround

While many songs have only four chords, some put them in a fixed four-bar or eight-bar phrase that then repeats, either for the verse, chorus or bridge, or some combination, or even goes all the way through the song. The four-chord turnaround is one of the strongest musical hooks going. There is a significant symbiotic relationship between it and pop's favourite time signature, 4/4, which in itself has a tendency to cause melodic and verse/chorus lengths to fall into fours or multiples of four. This is both a blessing and a curse. The turnaround lends itself to lazy songwriting, and this is one reason why the last few decades have generated fewer classic songs that artists want to cover.

The 'tyranny of four'

When the various parts of a song are all measurable by four, there is a risk of producing something literally 'four-square' and too predictable (although possibly a hit). Here is an instance in songwriting where artistic and commercial considerations do not see eye to eye. In a nightmare scenario of the 'tyranny of four', we get a song that has a four-bar intro, leading to a 16-bar verse made up of four four-bar four-chord turnarounds, a chorus of eight bars (twice round a different four-bar turnaround), and an eight-bar middle eight – all in 4/4! In 1990s chart pop and dance hits, it was not uncommon to hear songs constructed from a single four-bar four-chord turnaround. Verses and choruses were distinguished only by small changes in the arrangement.

Symmetry is pleasing, but too much of it is boring. By analogy, think about architecture. What is more engaging, more mysterious, more human: the unpredictable passages and lanes of a small fishing village where the eye is continually surprised by irregularity and curve, or the wide concrete spaces of a plaza where everything is straight lines, squares, 90-degree angles and can be seen all at once?

Sometimes 'less is more'. But sometimes less really is *less*. Simplicity is not automatically a virtue in music, nor a cast-iron defence against monotony. The resources of music are very rich, so why limit yourself; especially when seen in the context of a symphony, such decisions in popular song are decisions about tiny increments of simplicity.

The liberation of asymmetry

One of the most important points of craft a songwriter can develop is a sensitivity to the emotional and artistic possibilities of *asymmetry*, which in its simplest form means working with odd numbers. This is evident in Radiohead songs like '2+2=5' and 'There There'. Asymmetry is the deliberate cultivation of irregularity in a song. It often involves the use of odd numbers – either for a section length, or the number of repeats. Asymmetry covers anything that takes the song away from the dull predictability of everything going in units of four. Effectively and sparingly used, asymmetry can be beautiful and expressive. You can introduce asymmetry into a turnaround by adding a fifth chord within the four bars, or by making the turnaround last five bars, or with an extra bar every second or fourth time through. You can also have asymmetrical sections by length. Try writing a verse, bridge or chorus that is built on the odd numbers 3, 5, 7, 9, 11 etc:

Popular four-chord turnarounds

Turnarounds are so significant in popular songwriting that there are many variations. For convenience, I've sorted them into groups. Remember that the songs mentioned as examples may use the turnaround only for a section, not for the whole song. These sequences not only sound good in themselves but may be incorporated into larger structures. For instance, you might take two turnarounds and join them to make an eight-bar phrase that could then be repeated to make a 16-bar verse.

Group 1

The most popular turnarounds start on chord I and end on chord V, assuring that the sense of key is strong. They are also satisfying because of their positive upward energy. Some of the song illustrations mention 'displaced' and 'stretched' turnarounds – see Section 4 for an explanation of these terms.

The first three examples are satisfying because they move onto a minor but then draw back from the sadness it represents to the reassuring major.

I-II-IV-V: C-Dm-F-G

The Troggs 'Love Is All Around' (ch), R.E.M 'Fall On Me' (ch), Maria McKee 'Show Me Heaven', Nena '99 Red Balloons', The Bee Gees 'I've Just Got To Get A Message To You' (ch), Johnny Tillotson 'Poetry In Motion', Tori Amos 'A Northern Lad' (v), Bryan Adams 'Somebody', The Who 'They Are All In Love' (v), Don McLean 'Vincent' (v), The Jam 'Away From The Numbers', 'Eton Rifles' (v, in 'stretched' form: I-II [x4]-IV-V), Jefferson Airplane 'Somebody To Love' (ch displaced as IV-I-II-V), Sheryl Crow 'If It Makes You Happy' (ch displaced as II-IV-V-I).

I-III-IV-V: C-Em-F-G

The Jam 'Down In The Tube Station At Midnight' and 'Going Underground', Thin Lizzy 'Waiting For An Alibi' (ch), Marvin Gaye 'Let's Get It On', Van Morrison 'Have I Told You Lately' and 'Bright Side Of The Road' (v, notice the difference if you make F here F7), Morrissey 'The More You Ignore Me, The Closer I Get' (v).

I-VI-IV-V: C-Am-F-G

This is the Big Daddy of all pop turnarounds. During the doo-wop era of 1958–63, many hits were written with this sequence. It took The Beatles to break its stranglehold on the charts, though even they used a displaced version for 'I Wanna Hold Your Hand' (ch IV- V-I-VI). Later Lennon evoked its 1950s associations ironically in 'Happiness Is A Warm Gun', and its innocence was appropriate for 'Octopus's Garden'. Alice Cooper put a ghoulish twist on it for his 'I Love The Dead'. It has been used in countless songs – here are a *very* few!

The Who 'I Can't Explain' (br), Unit 2+4 'Concrete And Clay' (ch), The Jam 'Strange Town' (v), T. Rex 'Teenage Dream' (v), Dion 'Runaround Sue' (v), Marty Wilde 'A Teenager In Love' (v), Ben E. King 'Stand By Me', The Police 'Every Breath You Take' (v), Everly Brothers 'All I Have To Do Is Dream' (ch), The Marvelettes 'Please Mr Postman' and 'When You're Young And In Love', Roxy Music 'Dance Away', Gene Chandler 'Duke Of Earl', Elton John 'Crocodile Rock', Chubby Checker 'Let's Twist Again', Led Zeppelin 'D'yer Mak'er', Mud 'Lonely This Christmas', Madonna 'True Blue' (ch), The Righteous Brothers 'Unchained Melody' (v), Betty Everett 'It's In His Kiss' (hk), Whitney Houston 'I Will Always Love You', The Pretenders 'Brass In Pocket' (v), Jimmy Cliff 'Wonderful World' (v), Ash 'Angel Interceptor' (i), Destiny's Child 'Say My Name', The Isley Brothers 'I Guess I'll Always Love You' (v), Martha Wainwright 'Factory'.

This turnaround is now difficult to use in a 'straight' way because it sounds corny and over-familiar. It probably works better in the displaced form IV-V-I-VI, as heard in Honeybus's 'I Can't Let Maggie Go' (ch), The Jam's 'Eton Rifles' (ch), Scarlet's 'Independent Love Song', Bruce Springsteen's 'Sad Eyes' (ch), Crowded House's 'Don't Dream It's Over' (ch), and Meat Loaf's 'Dead Ringer For Love' (ch). Neil Young's 'Heart Of Gold' (v) displaces it to VI-IV-V-I. David Bowie's 'Ashes To Ashes' has it on the verse and displaced on the chorus. Marc Bolan of T. Rex was fond of combining a 12-bar progression in one part of a song with I-VI-IV-V in another (see 'Beltane Walk' and 'Rabbit Fighter').

I-VI-V-IV: C-Am-G-F

Embrace 'Come Back To What You Know' (ch), The Spin Doctors 'Two Princes', Prince 'Purple Rain' (v), Thin Lizzy 'Dancing In The Moonlight' (v).

This switches the last two chords of the previous sequence in order to make a descending progression. The sequence is displaced to VI-V-IV-I in Big Country's 'Chance' (v), Lone Justice's 'Ways To Be Wicked' (ch), Arthur Conley's 'Sweet Soul Music' (hk), Chairmen of the Board's 'Give Me Just A Little More Time' (ch), Stephen Stills's 'Love The One You're With' (ch), and Oasis's 'Cast No Shadow' (prech).

I-IV-VI-V: C-F-Am-G

Boston 'More Than A Feeling' (ch), Tracy Chapman 'Talking About A Revolution', Take That 'Never Forget', Foo Fighters 'Dig Me', Kate Bush 'Room For The Life', The Libertines 'Can't Stand You Now'.

Here are some related sequences in which the middle chords have changed place:

I-II-VI-V: C-Dm-Am-G

I-II-V-VI: C-Dm-G-Am
Keane 'Nothing In My Way' (twice for v).

I-IV-V-VI: C-F-G-Am
The Hold Steady 'Hot Soft Light' (v).

I-VI-II-V: C-Am-Dm-G
The Beatles 'Tell Me Why' (v), 'All My Loving' (displaced as II-V-I-VI), 'This Boy' (v), 'I Will' (v), 'You're Gonna Lose That Girl' (ch), Paul Anka 'Diana' (v), Gerry & The Pacemakers 'How Do You Do It' (ch), Connie Francis's 'Lipstick On Your Collar', T. Rex 'Metal Guru' (v in stretched form), Bruce Springsteen 'Hungry Heart', Dusty Springfield 'You Don't Have To Say You Love Me', Elvis Presley 'Return To Sender', 'The Wonder Of You' (v), Harry Nilsson 'Without You' (ch), The Everly Brothers 'All I Have To Do Is Dream', Aztec Camera 'Oblivious' (ch). Richard Hawley 'Tonight The Streets Are Ours'. This turnaround is closely related to I-VI-IV-V and can substitute for it.

I-III-VI-V: C-Em-Am-G
Tiffany 'I Think We're Alone Now', Thin Lizzy 'Waiting For An Alibi' (v, displaced as VI-I-III-V).

II-III-IV-V: Dm-Em-F-G
Martha Reeves & The Vandellas 'Come And Get These Memories' (v), The Isley Brothers 'This Old Heart Of Mine' (v), Thin Lizzy 'Do Anything You Want To' (v). This creates a sense of suspension because I is delayed until another part of the song. The classic use of this progression is as a prechorus, as in Martha Reeves and the Vandellas' 'Heatwave', Wham!'s 'Wake Me Up Before You Go-Go', and Tears For Fears' 'Everybody Wants To Rule The World'. It is the main hook of Gene's 'Olympian' and a link in Razorlight's 'Hold On'.

Group 2
This is a variation on group 1: change IV to its relative minor (II) or switch their positions.

I-III-II-V: C-Em-Dm-G
Peter Starsted 'Where Do You Go To My Lovely?', The Beatles 'Goodnight' (v), Sixpence None The Richer 'Kiss Me' (as displaced II-V-I-III), Gerry and the Pacemakers 'Ferry Cross The Mersey' (ch), Arctic Monkeys 'Riot Van' (v).

I-IV-II-V: C-F-Dm-G
Razorlight 'America' (displaced as II-V-I-IV, ch), R.E.M. 'The Sidewinder Sleeps Tonight' (ch) (displaced), The Four Tops 'Loco In Acapulco' (ch), Roxy Music 'More Than This' (v), Aswad 'Don't Turn Around' (ch).

I-IV-II-♭VII: C-F-Dm-B♭
Echobelly 'Great Things' (ch), R.E.M. 'What's The Frequency, Kenneth?' (v).

I-IV-III-V: C-F-Em-G
The Monkees 'A Little Bit Me, A Little Bit You' (the gut-wrenching drop from F to Em is 'saved' by the reassuring climb back to V).

I-VI-III-V: C-Am-Em-G
The Beatles 'She Loves You' (v), Aimee Mann 'That's Just What You Are' (v).

I-VI-V-III: C-Am-G-Em
The Four Tops 'Baby I Need Your Loving' (ch). This sequence is easily confused with IV-II-I-VI in G major.

Group 3
A variation on Group 1. When V goes to the second place and IV is last, it has a softer, less assertive effect.

I-V-II-IV: C-G-Dm-F
Travis 'Driftwood', Texas 'Halo' (ch). The popularity of this progression is indicated by the number of variations on it, as with R.E.M.'s 'Try Not To Breathe' (v, displaced to V-II-IV-I), Bryan Adams's 'On A Day Like Today' (ch, displaced to II-IV-I-V), and The Police's 'Walking On The Moon' (ch, displaced as IV-I-V-II).

I-V-III-IV: C-G-Em-F

I-V-IV-II: C-G-F-Dm
Ocean Colour Scene 'The Day We Caught The Train' (ch), Big Star 'September Girl' (v).

I-V-IV-III: C-G-F-Em
Adam and the Ants 'Stand And Deliver' (ch).

I-V-VI-II: C-G-Am-Dm
R.E.M. 'Half A World Away'.

I-V-VI-IV: C-G-Am-F
Rainbow 'Since You've Been Gone' (ch), Natalie Imbruglio 'Torn' (ch), U2 'With Or Without You' and 'Miracle Drug', The Police 'So Lonely', Bob Marley 'No Woman No Cry', The Rolling Stones 'Beast Of Burden' (v), Bryan Adams 'Inside Out', Elvis Costello 'Possession' (ch), Idlewild 'Actually It's Darkness', The Hold Steady 'First Night' (ch, displaced as VI-IV-I-V).

The most popular of these sequences, it makes for a punchy chorus. Chord V can be played as a first inversion so the bassline moves down in steps (in C major, C G/B Am), as in Jimi Hendrix's 'Bold As Love' (v), Men At Work's 'Down Under' (ch), Macy Gray's 'Still', Kantner, Slick & Balin's 'Sketches Of China', Manic Street Preachers' 'Motorcycle Emptiness', and The Cure 'Just Like Heaven'.

Group 4
Another variation on Group 1: change V into its relative minor, III.

I-II-IV-III: C-Dm-F-Em

I-VI-IV-III: C-Am-F-Em
Spandau Ballet 'True' (i).

I-VI-III-IV: C-Am-Em-F
Mercury Rev 'Holes'.

Group 5
I-IV-III-II: C-F-Em-Dm
Blind Faith 'Presence Of The Lord' (i = IV-III-II-I), The Beatles 'Long Long Long' (v), Badfinger 'Day After Day' (hk), Minnie Riperton 'Lovin' You', Nick Lowe 'So It Goes', R.E.M. 'Hollow Man' (ch). This has a mournful quality because of the descending minors. You get a different effect by changing these into all majors or fifth chords, as in Sex Pistols' 'Holidays In The Sun' (i), 'God Save The Queen' (cd.). A variation is IV-III-II-V, as in The Isley Brothers' 'This Old Heart Of Mine'.

I-II-III-IV: C-Dm-Em-F
A powerful ascending sequence, heard in The Beatles' 'Here, There And Everywhere' (v).

Group 6
I-II-VI-III: C-Dm-Am-Em
R.E.M. 'Daysleeper' (ch).

I-III-IV-II: C-Em-F-Dm
Catatonia 'I Am The Mob', R.E.M. 'At My Most Beautiful'.

I-III-VI-IV: C-Em-Am-F
The Beatles 'A Day In The Life' (v), Verve 'Sonnet' (ch), The Raconteurs 'Together'.

I-III-VI-V: C-Em-Am-G
David Gray 'Please Forgive Me' (v).

I-III-VI-II: C-Em-Am-Dm
Santana 'Samba Pa Ti' (v).

I-VI-II-IV: C-Am-Dm-F
Bruce Springsteen 'New York City Serenade'.

I-VI-IV-II: C-Am-F-Dm
Costello & Bacharach 'Toledo'.

Group 7

This group takes the sequences of Group 1 but turns the minor chords into majors (reverse polarity). These turnarounds arouse an expectation – perhaps of a key change – that does not happen.

I-II^-IV-V: C-D-F-G

Tom Petty and the Heartbreakers 'American Girl', The Rolling Stones 'As Time Goes By', Hawkwind 'Silver Machine' (v). This can evoke 1960s pop.

I-IV-II^-V: C-F-D-G

Smokey Robinson 'Shop Around' (i + v), Elton John 'Goodbye Yellow Brick Road' (opening of v displaced to II-V-I-IV), The Beatles 'Hold Me Tight' (all voiced as dominant sevenths.) This progression sounds as though you have changed the key to G. To nullify this effect, make the G a G7.

I-II^-III-IV: C-D-Em-F

David Bowie 'Modern Love' (ch).

I-III^-II-V: C-E-Dm-G

The Beatles 'You're Gonna Lose That Girl' (v).

I-III^-IV-II^: C-E-F-D

Otis Redding '(Sittin' On) The Dock Of The Bay' (v). With two reverse polarity chords there is plenty of surprise in this sequence.

I-III^-IV-IVm: C-E-F-Fm

Radiohead 'Creep'.

I-III^-IV-V: C-E-F-G

Thin Lizzy 'Waiting For An Alibi' (ch), John Lennon 'Imagine' (br, displaced as IV-V-I-III^).

I-III^-VI-IV: C-E-Am-F

Oasis 'She's Electric' (v).

I-IV-III^-V: C-F-E-G

This has an unpredictable sound.

I-IV-III^-VI: C-F-E-Am

Supergrass 'Caught By The Fuzz' (v) Gives the impression of a key change to A minor.

I-IV-VI^-V: C-F-A-G

A disorientating progression.

I-IV-VI-II^: C-F-Am-D

R.E.M. 'Green Grow The Rushes'.

I-VI^-IV-V: C-A-F-G

I-VI-IV-III^: C-Am-F-E
Crowded House 'Don't Dream It's Over' (v).

I-VI-II^-IV: C-A-D-F

Group 8
These turnarounds are mostly major.

I-♭III-IV-V: C-E♭-F-G
A tougher-sounding ascending sequence than I-III-IV-V. It occurs in rapid form after the first phrase of The Beatles' 'Please Please Me'.

I-♭III-♭VII-IV: C-E♭-B♭-F
Cilla Black 'Step Inside Love' (ch). Displaced as ♭III-♭VII-IV-I in Eels' 'Daisies Of The Galaxy' along with ♭III-♭VII-II-I.

I-♭III-V-♭VII: C-E♭-G-B♭
Played only once with strong accents in Yes's 'Going For The One' as a link to the last verse. As a turnaround it has a powerful ascending energy.

I-IV-V-♭III: C-F-G-E♭
Desmond Dekker 'Israelites'.

I-IV-♭VI-♭VII: C-F-A♭-B♭
Living Colour 'Desperate People' (v).

I-IV-♭VII-V: C-F-B♭-G
Roxy Music 'Street Life', R.E.M. 'Can't Get There From Here' (ch) displaced as IV-♭VII-V-I, Elvis Costello 'Alison' (cd).

I-V-♭VI-♭VII: C-G-A♭-B♭
Garbage 'Only Happy When It Rains' (ch).

I-V-♭VII-IV: C-G-B♭-F
The Vapors 'Turning Japanese' (ch), Chairmen Of The Board 'Give Me Just A Little More Time' (v), Aretha Franklin 'You Make Me Feel Like A Natural Woman' (v), Wizzard 'Ball Park Incident' (v), Air 'Sexy Boy (v), The Raconteurs 'Steady, As She Goes' (v).

I-♭VI-♭VII-IV: C-A♭-B♭-F
Hole 'Violet' (ch).

I-♭VII-♭III-IV: C-B♭-E♭-F
The Who 'Pinball Wizard' (ch), R.E.M. 'Crush With Eyeliner' (ch), Foo Fighters 'I'll Stick Around', U2 'Vertigo' (ch).

I-♭VII-♭III-V: C-B♭-E♭-G
Green Day 'Welcome To Paradise' (v).

I-♭VII-IV-V: C-B♭-F-G
Oasis 'Champagne Supernova' (ch, with IV as iIV). As I-♭VII-V-IV (C-B♭-G-F) in Hole's 'Asking For It' (v), The Association's 'Windy' (v). This is a popular sequence with a strong circularity.

I-♭VII-IV-VI: C-B♭-F-Am
Sunhouse 'Crazy On The Weekend'.

I-♭VII-IV-♭III: C-B♭-F-E♭
The Pretenders 'Middle Of The Road', R.E.M. 'The Wake-Up Bomb' (v).

I-♭VII-VI-V: C-B♭-Am-G
Embrace 'My Weakness Is None Of Your Business' (v) with a variation in which ♭VII becomes ♭VIIm (C-B♭m-Am-G).

Group 9
Here are some typical minor-key turnarounds. Remember that the default minor harmony is one based on the natural minor scale. In A minor this means I = Am, III = C, IV = Dm, V = Em, VI = F, VII = G.

I-III-IV-V: Am-C-Dm-Em

I-III-IV-V^: Am-C-Dm-E

I-III-IV-VI: Am-C-Dm-F
Love 'A House Is Not A Motel' (v).

I-III-VI-V^: Am-C-F-E
Elvis Costello 'I Want You'.

I-III-VII-IV: Am-C-G-D
Oasis 'Wonderwall' (v), Bryan Adams 'Run To You' (ch).

I-III-IV-VII: Am-C-Dm-G
R.E.M. 'Swan Swan H' (v).

I-III-VI-IV: Am-C-F-Dm
The Band 'The Night They Drove Old Dixie Down' (v, where III is actually C/G).

I-III-VI-VII: Am-C-F-G
R.E.M. 'Harbour Coat' (v), Kate Bush's 'Breathing' (ch). A strong rising progression.

I-III-VII-VI: Am-C-G-F
The Verve 'Love Is Noise' (v + ch).

I-IV-♭VII-V^: Am-Dm-G-E
The Pretenders 'Talk Of The Town' (v), David Bowie 'Fame' (ch).

I-V^-IV^-VI: Am-E-D-F
Sleeper 'Sale Of The Century' (v).

I-V^-VII-IV^: Am-E-G-D
The Undertones 'You've Got My Number', Deep Purple 'Fireball' (ch) displaced as VII-IV^-I-V^ (G-D-Am-E).

I-VI-III-VII: Am-F-C-G
Iggy Pop 'The Passenger', alternates with I-VI-III-V^ (Am-F-C-E), Bruce Springsteen 'Radio Nowhere' (v).

I-VI-IV-VII: Am-F-Dm-G
Dire Straits 'Expresso Love' (v).

I-VI-IV^-VII: Am-F-D-G

I-VI-VII-IV: Am-F-G-Dm
The Police 'Message In A Bottle' (v), Kate Bush 'December Will Be Magic Again' (i).

I-VI-VII-V^: Am-F-G-E
Siouxsie and the Banshees 'Overground', Franz Ferdinand ''The Fallen' (v).

I-#VI-III-VII: Am-F#m-C-G
Siouxsie and the Banshees 'Israel' (v).

I-VII-VI-IV: Am-G-F-Dm
Paul Weller, 'You Do Something To Me' (v) displaced VII-IV-V-I.

I-VII-VI-IV: Am-G-F-Dm
Suede 'Animal Nitrate' (v), All About Eve 'Paradise' (v).

I-VII-VI-V: Am-G-F-Em
Neil Young 'Like A Hurricane', Alan Stivell 'Trimartolod', The Cure 'Lovesong'.

I-VII-VI-V^: Am-G-F-E
Dire Straits 'Sultans Of Swing' (v), Zager & Evans 'In The Year 2525', The Beach Boys 'Good Vibrations', Del Shannon 'Runaway' (v), The Four Tops 'Standing In The Shadows Of Love' (ch), The Supremes 'Love Child' (ch), Portishead 'Roads' (v).

A popular variant of the previous.

Group 10

Here are some exotic turnarounds which you will not come across very often. Add one of these to spice up a song!

I-III-♭VII-II: C-Em-B♭-Dm

Bob Dylan 'Lay Lady Lay', Alice Cooper 'No More Mr. Nice Guy' (v).

I-IV-II-♭VII: C-F-Dm-B♭

R.E.M. 'What's The Frequency, Kenneth?' (v).

I-IV-♭III-♭VI: C-F-E♭-A♭

An ambiguous, harmonically dislocated sequence associated with Nirvana's 'Smells Like Teen Spirit'. It could also be described as V-I in F followed by V-I in A♭ – a turnaround half in one key and half in another. Compare this with the sequence C F D G, which is also in two keys but more symmetrical. It is the asymmetrical nature of Cobain's riff (the original started on F) that makes it memorable.

I-IV-IVm-V: C-F-Fm-G

A combination of romantic and unpredictable.

I-IV-♭VI-Vm: C-F-A♭-Gm

Dubstar 'Not So Manic Now' (i).

I-♭VI-V-III^: C-A♭-G-E

Kate Bush 'Wuthering Heights' (v).

I-♭VII-VI-V: C-B♭-Am-G

The Jam 'The Bitterest Pill' (v).

I-♭VII-♭VI-Vm: C-B♭-A♭-Gm

Kate Bush's 'The Sensual World' (v).

This is not an exhaustive list of turnarounds – and there are always new combinations to be created. But all the popular sequences are here and we have already covered a huge amount of potential song material. Draw on the above ten groups in any number of ways. For example, by using one turnaround in a chorus and then having a non-turnaround verse and bridge, or by linking them with each other. You can mix any of the sequences in these ten groups with any earlier in the section. It all comes down to what sounds pleasing to your ears and which chords you can pitch a good melody over. A turnaround might be deployed in each section of a song – one for the verse, one for the chorus, and one for the bridge – but I would advise against this because the energy and feel of these sections will seem too alike.

SECTION 4
DEVELOPING SEQUENCES

As your ears get familiar with their sound you will be astonished at how common turnarounds are in recent popular music. This is partly because the element of repetition and the fact that they are short makes them easy to remember. But don't get trapped by the 'tyranny of four'. Turnarounds are seductive; they can make you a lazy and predictable songwriter. To inject more interest into their use there are various techniques for developing turnarounds. These are the subject of this next section.

It's important to try and do more with them – different turnarounds could be used for different parts of a song, verse, chorus, bridge, etc.

I-VI-IV-V (v) + I-VI-II-V (ch)
The Marvelettes 'Beechwood 4-5789'

Two different turnarounds can be linked together to make a longer phrase. Two four-bar turnarounds linked would make an eight-bar phrase; repeated, that would be a 16-bar verse, but each of the turnarounds would have been played only twice.

I-IV-II-V + I-IV♭VII-V
The Beatles 'Yes It Is' (v)

I-II-IV-V + I-II-VI-V (v)
The Verve 'Valium Skies'

The important factors that determine the effect of a turnaround are:

- direction – is it going harmonically up or down?
- tonality – the mix of major, minor and flattened chords
- expectation – the inclusion of a chord that suggests a key-change that doesn't actually happen, or is momentary

- where it starts and finishes (especially the position of I or V)
- displacement
- stretching
- use of inversions
- frequency of chord change
- repetition
- the type of chord, ie, whether II in a sequence is a minor seventh, a sixth, ninth, etc

Displacement

The classic turnaround starts on I and often ends on V. This strongly emphasises the key. A *displaced* turnaround is one in which chord I has been re-positioned so it no longer leads the sequence. Displacement can change the balance and energy of a turnaround, making it more interesting and less predictable. Consider the way the chorus of Abba's 'Knowing Me Knowing You' starts on V and no sooner lands on I ("do") than it moves off to IV and then back to V. Wings' 'My Love' comes in on IV, uses a VI^ and doesn't land on chord I until bar eight, at a slow tempo. Displacement is stronger if chord I moves into the middle of the sequence. Kate Bush's 'Wuthering Heights' has a chorus with an excellent example of displacement: IV-II-V-I-IV-V-I-IV. In this instance Bush made chord I feel like a place where you cannot rest. The music keeps moving off it and on to IV. A similar thing happens in the chorus of Bruce Springsteen's 'You'll Be Coming Down'. The verse of The Verve's 'Rather Be' takes the unusual minor turnaround of of I-II^ ♭III-II (D-E-F-Em) and displaces it to F-Em-D-E.

The ultimate displacement is to omit chord I altogether. The Marvelettes' 'When You're Young And In Love' has a chorus of VI-II-IV-V. The Eurythmics' 'There Must Be An Angel (Playing With My Heart)' creates anticipation by delaying chord I to the end of each phrase: II-V-VI-IV-IV-V-♭III-I. Notice also the unusual resolution from bIII to I, instead of the more predictable IV-I or V-I.

Substitution

To create a more interesting musical effect, it is possible to substitute turnarounds for each other in such a way that minor chords turn into their relative majors (and vice versa) but retain the same position in the sequence. For example:

Main turnaround
I-VI-IV-V: C-Am-F-G

Substitutes
I-VI-II-V: C-Am-Dm-G

I-VI-IV-III: C-Am-F-Em

This kind of substitution can powerfully illustrate something in the lyric. Imagine a love song with the turnaround C-Am-F-G.

DEVELOPING SEQUENCES

Verse:

```
C                 Am      F    G
The world is suddenly strange, I feel a fear
```

```
C              Am                F       G
My steps falter, can't find my way, the path is unclear
```

```
C              Am      F          G
I stumble in the dark in the middle of the day
```

```
C      Am            Dm      G
Right is wrong since you've gone far away
```

The switch from F to Dm in the last line puts extra weight on the word "gone" – which is, after all, the reason the speaker is complaining. Instead of merely repeating a single turnaround, a touch of harmonic variety is introduced.

Another type of substitution is to retain the root-note sequence but use techniques such as 'reverse polarity' (major to minor, minor to major).

I	VI	IVm	V
C	Am	Fm	G

I	VI^	IV	V
C	A	F	G

The stretched turnaround

There are two basic methods for 'stretching' a turnaround. First, simply stay on a chord for several more beats or an extra bar. Second, repeat a change within the turnaround several times before you proceed to the next one.

Smokey Robinson & The Miracles' 'Tracks Of My Tears' exquisitely stretches its three chords like this, with two beats on each chord:

I	IV	IV	V
C	F	F	G

Graham Parker & The Rumour's 'Heat Treatment' is based on I-VI-IV-V but repeats the I-VI change before IV and V:

I	VI	I	VI	I	VI	IV	V
C	Am	C	Am	C	Am	F	G

Razorlight's 'Who Needs Love?' has a I-VI-IV-V sequence where the I-VI change is repeated before the IV appears. The Marvelettes' 'When You're Young And In Love' plays about with the later chords:

I	VI	IV	V	IV	V
C	Am	F	G	F	G

You can displace *and* stretch in a progression at the same time – and the turnaround no longer sounds as 'four-square'. Take George Harrison's 'My Sweet Lord', where a I-VI-II-V has metamorphosed into this:

II	V (x4)	I	VI	I	VI
Dm	G	C	Am	C	Am

If we assume Hurricane #1's 'Step Into My World' to be in F♯ minor, we get a I-VII-VI-IV stretched to this:

I	VII	I	VII	VI	IV	VI	IV
F♯m	E	F♯m	E	D	Bm	D	Bm

Slade's 'Cum On Feel The Noize' takes I-VI-II-V and uses the same repeat approach:

I	VI	I	VI	II	V	II	V
G	Em	G	Em	Am	D	Am	D

Stretching by harmonic variation

You can also stretch by harmonic variation. This means lengthening a sequence by changing a chord from simple major or minor to seventh, sixth, etc, on the same root note. The commonest harmonic variation is probably when a major chord moves through its major and dominant seventh chord types: I-Imaj7-I7. This is satisfying to the ear because the root note can be heard falling (on a C chord) from C to B to B♭. After that, it can either return to C or fall to A and be harmonised by an F, A, Am or Dm chord (or something more exotic). This happens in The Beatles' 'Something' (v), Derek and the Dominoes' (Eric Clapton) 'Bell Bottom Blues' (ch), Roxy Music's 'Pyjamarama', and Harry Nilsson's 'Everybody's Talkin''. In The Casuals' 'Jesamine' and The Supremes' 'Up The Ladder To The Roof', the intro progression is I-I7-IV-IVm-I; in The Supremes' 'I'm Living In Shame' I-Imaj7-I7-IV-IVm.

The equivalent on a minor chord, which is Em-Em/maj7-Em7, can be heard in The Beatles' 'Cry Baby Cry' (where it continues to Em6 and then C), 'Got To Get You Into My Life', and 'Michelle'. Augmented chords can facilitate similar effects: D D+ D6 D7 (where the ear hears a rising pitch from A to A♯ to B to C).

Stretching by division

Another way of putting turnarounds to different use is to split them in half and assign the first two chords to a verse and the last two to a chorus. R.E.M. did this in 'Everybody Hurts', where the verse is a repeated I-IV change and the chorus is II-V. In such a song the turnaround has disappeared, but you might have started with one before deciding to do this.

Disguising turnarounds

Turnarounds are less obvious if they are slow, displaced (not centred on chord I) or arranged in a less conventional manner. If no instrument plays the whole chord but several instruments contribute to its overall sound, then it will seem less 'solid' and the turnaround not so obvious. Two great examples are the harpsichord parts on Tori Amos's 'Caught A Lite Sneeze' and the strings on Kate Bush's 'Cloudbusting'.

This effect is also often heard in U2's music, typified by a track such as 'With Or Without You'. It's a simple four-chord sequence (I-V-VI-IV: D-A-Bm-G). Most bands would have had the guitar chugging out those chords. U2's arrangement has the bass *imply* those changes whilst The Edge gets on with other ideas around the chord of D.

To apply this arranging technique to a turnaround, let the bass play the root notes but don't follow the chord sequence with full guitar chords.

The five-chord turnaround

It is possible to have a turnaround of five or even more chords. Consider the chord sequence of Jimi Hendrix's 'Hey Joe': ♭VI-♭III-♭VII-IV-I (C-G-D-A-E). This also occurs in the middle eight of The Beatles' 'A Day In The Life' (after the word "dream"). These chords cover only four bars, which then repeat throughout the song. Another example would be 'Hard Day's Night', which is I-IV-I-♭VII-I – only three different chords but used in a fixed pattern of five.

A turnaround stops being a turnaround once the the rate of chord change is no longer fast enough for the ear to hear it as a single unit of music repeated. 'Hey Joe' crams five chords into four bars, so we are aware of the fact that it is a single unit. If those chords were spread out across eight bars at the same tempo, it is less likely we would hear it as a turnaround. The effect of the turnaround depends partly on tempo and number of bars. Quicker tempos emphasise it.

Here are other examples of five-chord patterns (not necessarily using five different chords):

I-II-V-♭III-II: C-Dm-G-E♭-Dm
'A Design For Life'
I-II-III-V-I: C-Dm-Em-G-C
'I Shall Be Released'

I-♭III-IV-♭VI-♭III: C-E♭-F-A♭-E♭
'Stardust' (v)

I-III-IV-I-V: C-Em-F-C-G
'Hymn To Her' (ch)
I-III-IV-II-V: C-Em-F-Dm-G
'Trash'
I-III-VI-IV-V: C-Em-Am-F-G
'Till Death Us Do Part' (ch)

I-IV-♭III-♭VII-♭VI: C-F-E♭-B♭-A♭
'Free Man In Paris'
I-IV-III-IV-V-I: C-F-Em-F-G-C
'The Drugs Don't Work'
I-IV-V-II-III-II: C-F-G-Dm-Em-Dm
'Je T'Aime'
I-IV-♭VII-IV-I: C-F-B♭-F-C
'Fine Time'

I-V-II-IV-III^: C-G-Dm-F-E
'Country House'
I-V-II-IV-V: C-G-Dm-F-G
'Live Forever' (v) (with VI-V-II-IV-V as a variation), 'I Try'
I-V-II-V-IV: C-G-Dm-G-F:
'Where Did Our Love Go?'
I-V-VI-V-IV: C-G-Am-G-F
'Might Be Stars'

I-VI-III-II-V: C-Am-Em-Dm-G
'Across The Universe'
I-VI-III-IV-V: C-Am-Em-F-G
'Going For The One'
I-VI-IV-I-V: C-Am-F-C-G
'Some Might Say' (v)
I-VI-IV-V-I: C-Am-F-G-C
'He's On The Phone' (v)

I-♭VII-IV-♭III-V: C-B♭-F-E♭-G
'Living Well Is The Best Revenge'

Five-chord turnarounds can be stretched in the same way as the four-chord types. The Vapors' 'Turning Japanese' has a verse where a I-VI-I-VI-II-IV-V sequence is extended by a repetition of the first chord change. The chorus of Bryan Adams's 'Can't Stop This Thing We Started' (IV-V-VI-IV-I) and The Beatles' 'It's Only Love' (VI-V-III-IV-I) both use displacement.

Beyond turnarounds

As popular as turnarounds are, songwriters (fortunately) often construct longer chord progressions, sometimes non-repeating, such as a 16-bar verse in which there is only a single chord progression. A turnaround might then be used for the chorus and sound more effective by contrast. Let's have a look at one of these longer structures.

Sequences usually combine major and minor chords, but there are songs that stay on minor chords for lengthy periods for dramatic effect. The Move's 'Blackberry Way' is extraordinary for the stream of minor chords in its verse: Em-F♯-Am, then Em-Bm-B♭m-Am-Cm-Em. Kate Bush's 'December Will Be Magic Again' has Cm-Gm-Dm-Am-Em-Bm in its first verse and the second time adds Fm-Cm at the end of this progression!

SECTION 4 |

Sticking to major chords without reference to key is an effect associated with 60s psychedelia in music. The Beatles' 'I Am The Walrus' has no minor chords, and songs such as Hawkwind's 'Silver Machine' and Pink Floyd's 'Arnold Layne' and 'Astronomy Domine' are dominated by major chords. The psychedelic effect is heightened if the music spends a long time on a dominant seventh chord, or employs chromatic half-step shifts, as in Hendrix's '1983' and Pink Floyd's 'Interstellar Overdrive'.

You can, of course, construct verses, choruses, and bridges without reference to a turnaround at all. Consider Bob Dylan's 'Like A Rolling Stone', where the verse is I-II-III-IV-V (x2) + IV-V (x2) + IV-III-II-I (x2) + II-IV-V, or Eddie and the Hot Rods' 'Do Anything You Wanna Do', where the verse is V-I-IV + V-I + II-III-IV-V-IV-III-II-I.

Peter & Gordon's hit 'World Without Love' (written by Lennon and McCartney) shows what can be done with two reverse polarity chords and a flat chord:

I	III^	VI	I	IVm	I	II	V	I
E♭	G	Cm	E♭	A♭m	E♭	Fm	B♭	E♭

Notice how this progression pulls off chord I on to different chords and then returns, in a sense giving different views of it. After the vocal line finishes, there is a ♭VI-V (C♭-B♭) link. Dubstar's 'Just A Girl She Said' is worth studying for its progressions, including this one heard on the intro:

I	II	IV	V	III	VI	IV	V
A	Bm	D	E	C♯m	F♯m	D	E

The expectation of a turnaround generated by the first four chords is quickly dispelled by chord III.

Rate of harmonic change

When composing a song, be attentive to the duration of chords and when they change. It is easy to fall into the trap of having every chord occupy a bar and every change happen on the first beat of a bar. Inject variation so the chords change at differing rates.

Change halfway through a bar or after one-and-a-half bars, or write a sequence where the changes are every two beats, or include a bar where there is a different chord on each beat.

Including several turnarounds in an uptempo song risks creating a feeling of bewilderment. You will need to have a small stretch where the chords do not change so frequently to allow the listener to grasp what's going on. Think of the I-V changes in The The Beatles' 'I Should Have Known Better' and the chord-change rate of one every two beats in the chorus of Oasis's 'Some Might Say'. The Kinks' 'Days' has rapid chord movement in its chorus. 'Violet Hill' by Coldplay features a chorus with unexpectedly frequent, accented chord changes. In a song with rapid changes, there may be a need to cool out for a bit and hang on a single chord, as in The Monkees hits 'I'm A Believer' and 'A Little Bit Me, A Little Bit You'. Give the listener a breather!

Unusual chord changes

In the January 1995 issue of *Mojo*, Noel Gallagher was quoted as saying, "There's 12 notes in a scale and there's 36 chords and that's the end of it. All the configurations have been done before." The context for this remark was a certain defensiveness because Oasis had been criticised for being derivative. It isn't literally true, of course. First, there aren't just 36 chords, and Noel Gallagher's number was merely rhetorical. Second, compared to the harmonic range of 20th-century 'classical' music, the harmony of popular song is like a piece of A4 paper compared to a football pitch. Third, Gallagher's view does not encourage innovation. If you think all the "configurations" have been done before, you aren't likely to go looking for new ones.

Perhaps that's one of the reasons Oasis have not yet come up with a song like Radiohead's 'Just', which has several innovative touches. The intro is I-♭III-II^-IV (all majors, C-E♭-D-F), and the verse is Am-A♭-E♭-F, Am-A♭-E♭-B♭, Am-A♭-G-F♯-F. The chord changes are unusual, and the melodic phrases fall into three bars each. The chorus adds a C-F♯-F to the C-E♭-D-F change from the intro. 'Just' was probably the first song on a commercially successful album to have these particular unusual chord movements.

One of the challenges for a songwriter is to find less common chord changes but make them work. Common chord changes are popular because they sound pleasant and are self-reinforcing – that is to say, familiar. They have been heard so often that they feel comfortable and seem to express familiar emotions. In an emotional sense they are recognised faster (an important point for commercial songwriting) on first listen. Unusual chord changes are by their nature disconcerting because they have not been heard very often. They are not immediately recognised and make the emotion of the song seem less familiar, too. They do, however, offer the songwriter a tantalising hope. I call this Rodgers & Hammerstein's Law, which states:

> *If you can make an unusual chord change accessible in a song, you have immediately distinguished your song from thousands of others, past and present, that use common changes.*

There have been thousands of hit records based on I-IV-V. But there is only one I know that bases its verse on the haunting change of two minor chords three semitones (half-steps) apart. That is 'Light My Fire' by The Doors, in which the verse moves from Am to F♯m and back again. This change is so rare that it conjures up only that one song. Anyone else trying to use it has the immediate problem of wresting it away from that association, whereas anybody can write a I-IV-V song and not have it confused with any other specific I-IV-V song.

Consider also what I call the 'Songwriter's General Theory of Relativity': *the weirdness of the change is relative to the strength of the sense of key.* Too many weird chords erase the sense of the original key, or the listener will decide you've changed key anyway – in which case their ear will orient the chords around a new key centre and the original 'oddness' you aimed at disappears.

What qualifies as an unusual chord change?

In simple terms, we're talking about chords that don't belong together in the same key. The technical name for this is 'non-diatonic' or 'chromatic'. In C major, this could mean changing from the chord of C to:

♭IImaj/min	C♯/D♭ major or minor
♭IIImin	D♯/E♭ minor
♭Vmaj/min	F♯/G♭ major or minor
♭VImin	G♯/A♭ minor
VImaj	A major
♭VIImin	A♯/B♭ minor
VIImaj/min	B major or minor

The verse of 'Light My Fire' is haunting precisely because of its harmonic ambiguity. We think at first the key must be A minor, but the F♯m confuses the ear. Because F♯m is not in A minor, we decide F♯ minor is the 'true' key. The return to Am is equally confusing because you can't have Am in F♯ minor either. The ear gives up trying to fix the key and accepts this strange movement. The same change occurs in Eric Clapton's 'Edge Of Darkness' (Em-Gm) without going back to Em, and behind the guitar solo in Queen's 'Tenement Funster' (G♯m-Bm); with a similar effect there's a Gm-Bm change in Queen's 'Stone Cold Crazy'. No clear sense of key emerges from the main turnaround in Coldplay's 'Lost' (A7-C-Bm-D).

Contexts for unusual chord changes

Some lyric subjects encourage strange chord changes. Songs about madness often use peculiar progressions to evoke the mental displacement of the subject. David Bowie's 'The Bewlay Brothers' has a coda that juxtaposes Bm with F. This is another change that cannot be reconciled with either chord being the key chord. (In F you would have B♭; in Bm you would have F♯.) Bowie used unrelated chords for a similar reason on the coda of 'Ashes To Ashes'. In 'I Want You', Elvis Costello communicates the deranged jealousy of the speaker not only through the lyric but through a D♯m chord which periodically interrupts the Em-G-C-B turnaround; D♯m is unrelated to E minor. The coda of The Beatles' 'I Want You (She's So Heavy)' is worth examining not only for the unusual changes (a five-chord turnaround), and 6/8 time, but also for its asymmetry.

Strange chord changes sometimes suit comic songs. UK outfit Madness scored a string of hits in the 1980s with a wacky mix of ska, new-wave, and pop. The bittersweet humour of their songs partly arises from the music's frequent use of minor chords and keys, and unusual changes. 'Night Boat To Cairo' features a C-B♭m change and a sequence that moves from Fm-G♯m-Fm-D♭ (twice) before Eb and C. The chorus of 'Baggy Trousers' uses repeated changes from a major chord to a minor on the same note (IV-IVm-I-Im). Few bands have created such a distinctive musical world through such specific harmonic means.

Non-diatonic chords

Other ways of using odd chords include putting a chromatic chord between two diatonic ones: C-F♯-Am; G-C♯-D. In the verse of The Beatles' 'Do You Want To Know A Secret?', we find III-♭IIIm-II. If you extend this as IIIm7-♭IIIm7-IIm7-

V7-I, you have a popular sequence from the 1920s. In Elvis Costello's 'Pump It Up', the chords are B-B♭-A for the main bit of the verse; the B♭ is a passing chord. In Amy Winehouse's 'Me and Mr Jones' a ♭II chord is inserted between I and II in its chorus (F♯m-F-E).

The movement of major chords a semitone (half-step) apart is a rock'n'roll trick that goes back to 1950s rockers like Eddie Cochran and was revived in both glam and punk rock. The delinquent quality which chromatic changes can have at medium to fast tempos is heard on The Damned's 'New Rose' and Blondie's 'One Way Or Another'. Semitone shifts also occur in The Beatles' 'I'm So Tired' and 'Sexy Sadie', where Lennon moves from I to VII^7 before landing on IV or III. In G this would be G-F♯7-C or G-F♯7-Bm.

Bruce Springsteen used chromatic chords that move in semitones to heighten the build-up, in some of his longer songs, during a transition from one section to another. 'Kitty's Back' has a chromatic chord passage at 3:10-34 with an anarchic jazz feel; 'Rosalita' has its chromatic passage at 3:18-42 where the music edges up a semitone at a time from C to E, building to the sax bridge.

Songs by UK rock group Muse feature an above average number of chromatic chord changes like Gm-F♯, or the sequence Gm-F♯-Fm-E-Fm-E-Em from 'Fillip', and changes from major to minor (or vice versa) on the same root note; consider also the chorus of 'Plug In Baby', which goes G-Bm-F♯m-G-Bm-F♯.

Many of the songs on Love's *Forever Changes* feature unexpected combinations of chords. 'Alone Again Or' starts with its poignant F♯m to Em6/9, its verse kicking off with a flamenco-influenced F♯-G (III^-IV) change. Unexpected semitone shifts also happen in 'The Red Telephone' (C-Am-G-F♯-F-F♯) and 'Live And Let Live (A-B♭). 'Old Man' has no less than 12 chords and semitone shifts from Bm-B♭, Bm-Cm, and F-Em.

Altered harmony

The correct sequence of sevenths for a major key is Imaj7-IIm7-IIIm7-IVmaj7-V7 and VIm7. Using different types of sevenths changes the effect. Take, for example, a I-♭III-IV sequence. If this were in G major, it would be G-B♭-C, and given the presence of the ♭III might suggest a G7-B♭7-C7 blues harmony. In the George Harrison song 'I'd Have You Anytime' the effect of these chords is considerably altered by the harmony, which is Gmaj7-B♭maj7-Cm7, an unorthodox but beautiful progression for a verse. The first three chords of the verse of David Bowie's 'Absolute Beginners' are D-Bm-Amaj7. In the key of D major chord V would be A7, so the Amaj7 is startling.

Similarly 'Protection' (Massive Attack with Tracy Thorn) uses a three-chord change where the first chord is initially Bmaj7 but then turns into Bm7.

If a song has some unsettling changes, it makes good artistic sense to juxtapose them with conventional ones. 'The Ballad Of Tom Jones' by Space starts in fine John Barry-esque style with Em-G-Fm-B♭, a sequence that cannot sit in any one key. It is followed by a Dm-G change, repeated four times, that turns out to be II-V in C and then a chorus of Cmaj7-Fm-G (I-IVm-V) – exotic but not weird. As for Barry himself, the verse of 'Thunderball' is based on I-IV-V^ in B♭ minor, but in bar ten a wonderfully unexpected Dm chord appears as Barry neatly works in part of the 007 theme. The middle eight has a key change to E♭m that leads to some colourful changes.

Linking unrelated chords

Odd chord juxtapositions can be made less so if the chords have a note in common. This can be seen in a number of songs by Snow Patrol. During the first sequence of 'How To Be Dead' (the chords F-F/A-Bb-G or Gm) a high guitar plays an Fsus2 arpeggio (the notes F G C). Over the F and F/A chords these notes are heard as the 1, 2, and 5 of the scale. But over the Bb chord the harmonic identity of the notes changes to 5, 6, and 9, and over the G chord to b7, 1, and 4. During the verse of 'Wow' the chord changes go G#-A-E and the note E is played across all three. The note E sits happily in chords A and E (as 5 and 1 respectively) but forms a tense 6 against the G#. In the opening sequence of 'Run' the note C is constant to Am, F, and Gsus4 (as 3, 5, and 4). In 'Spitting Games' there is a descending sequence of D-C-Bm (or B)-G. The note F# is heard against all four chords, functioning in turn as a 3, #4, 5, and 7. The 3 and 5 blend, the #4 is very tense, the 7 is mildly tense but expressive. 'Somewhere A Clock Is Ticking' has the chord sequence Cm-Bb-F with a four-note keyboard phrase over the top made of the notes Bb A Eb F. Over those chords this motif changes from 7 6 3 4, to 1 7 4 5, and then 4 3 b7 1. Same notes, different qualities.

In Radiohead's 'There There' the note B is present in all four chords of the final sequence: B is the 1st of Bm, the 9th of Am add9, the 6th of Dm6, and the 5th of Em. So it sounds through the entire 11-bar sequence. This is a technique which can apply to a host of musical situations. Keane's 'Atlantic' has a B-E-A#-F# turnaround whose chords are linked by a persistent G# in the piano. R.E.M's 'Man Sized Wreath' has an initial verse change of G-C#7 (I-#IV, with the note B in common).

Another example lies with Roxy Music's hit 'Avalon': the verse is a stately I-V-IV-V in F (F-C-Bb-C). The hook (where Bryan Ferry sings the title) goes to a chilly bVII-VI-V (Eb-Dm-C). These three chords would normally have no note in common to all three (Eb and C both have the note G). If the progression is voiced as Ebadd9-Dm-Csus4-C the addition of the note F in the Ebadd9 and Csus4 smooths the transition:

Notes in the chord	F	F	F	E
	Bb	A	G	G
	G	F	F	E
	Eb	D	C	C
Chord name	Ebadd9	Dm	Csus4	C

Notes in the triad	Bb	A	G	
	G	F	E	
	Eb	D	C	
Chord name	Eb	Dm	C	

Notice how whilst its pitch remains constant, the harmonic function of the note F alters. In the first chord (Eb) F is a 9th; in the second (Dm) it is a 3rd; and in C it is the suspended 4th which finally resolves to E.

Having looked at harmony and chords, it is time to think about song structure and how these ideas can slot into place in verses and choruses.

SECTION 5
SONG STRUCTURES

The classic popular song structure has three primary sections: a verse, a chorus and a bridge/middle eight. These are sometimes referred to by the letters A, B and C – which is where Genesis got the title for 'ABACAB'. Secondary sections include an intro, a pre-chorus, an outro (or coda, literally meaning 'tail') and any instrumental solos, links, or riffs that join one primary section to another. Let's look at these one at a time, starting with the intro. It may not seem to be as interesting as the main parts of a song, but professional songwriters and producers take trouble with their intros, because this is the very first thing a listener will hear.

The Intro

The intro establishes tempo, key, style, and mood. It is strongly affected by the question of who your audience is. If the song is intended to be a single, the intro has to be shaped to commercial considerations. It must be brief – perhaps only a few seconds – and it must grab the listener's attention. If the song is not intended as a single, then you can take more time – but this is one area where commercial considerations and aesthetic values need not conflict. An intro can be very short (Manic Street Preachers' 'A Design For Life' takes five seconds to get to its verse) or extended.

The intro of Oasis's 'Some Might Say' is 36 seconds, owing to an initial guitar solo, and their 'Do You Know What I Mean' takes as long to get to its first chorus as many 1960s rock singles required to get to their codas! The Stone Roses' 'Ten Storey Love Song' has a 50-second atmospheric intro and there are several ambient fade-in intros on The Verve's 2008 album *Forth*. David Bowie's 'Andy Warhol' has about 45 seconds of Bowie talking to producer Tony Visconti over various synth noises. Many of the tracks on The Raconteurs' debut album have messy beginnings or endings: 'Hands' comes in with 12 seconds of a false intro, as if an earlier idea had only partly been erased, and isn't sure whether it is in A, D, or E; 'Yellow Sun' has several false beginnings.

Radiohead's 'There There' begins with about 28 bars of static harmony on Bm7, before the chords start changing after the opening lyrics. Many amateur

ABBREVIATIONS

Roman numerals **I–VII** indicate chord relationships within a key.

m=minor

maj=major

SONG SECTIONS:

b bridge; **c** coda; **ch** chorus; **f** fade; **hk** hook; **i** intro; **pch** pre-chorus; **r** riff; **s** solo; **v** verse

Most of the chord-sequence examples are standardised for comparison into **C major** or **A minor**. The famous songs are therefore not always in the key of the original recordings.

songs are spoiled because there has not been ruthless enough cutting of the length of various sections. Guitarists in particular need to be aware of this. A riff may be fun to play but do you really need to do it 36 times before the verse starts? (Leave that for live performance.)

It is perfectly legitimate to have no intro at all. You could start straightaway with a few words in a pickup bar followed by the instruments entering on the first beat of the first whole bar, as on Elvis Costello's 'Accidents Will Happen'. This might be a verse or a chorus. Think about the dynamics of your intro. Ballads can start quietly to set a mood. A dance song needs to be loud. Sudden beginnings like Bruce Springsteen's 'The Ties That Bind' and 'Night', or Simple Minds' 'Waterfront', or The Who's 'Won't Get Fooled Again', make people sit up and pay attention. Some songs, such as The Pretenders' '2000 Miles', The Stone Roses' 'I Wanna Be Adored', or The Beatles' 'Eight Days A Week', fade in – but this is not as effective on the radio as when listening at home.

One common device is to take part of section A, B, or C as the intro and simply not have a vocal on it. It could be an instrumental version of the chorus or a section of the verse. You might have some kind of instrumental theme or motif, possibly part of the chorus melody. This means that the listener will have heard the chorus tune already when the first chorus is reached. Intros require drama, involvement, expectation. Try starting a song with a crescendo, as in Bowie's 'Let's Dance', or with an ascending or descending figure. That gets our attention immediately because we know it's moving *towards* something, and we are curious to hear what it will be.

Guitar intros

Since the guitar has been a central instrument in popular music, there are many different types of guitar intros. The instrumental motif could be a rhythm guitar riff, as on Led Zeppelin's 'Whole Lotta Love', Sheryl Crow's 'If It Makes You Happy', Dodgy's 'In A Room', The Jam's 'In The City', or The Faces' 'Stay With Me' and 'Miss Judy's Farm'. It could be a burst of lead guitar, like Chuck Berry's signature phrase on 'Johnny B. Goode', mimicked on The Beatles' 'Revolution'. It could be an arpeggio, like Slash's on Guns N' Roses' 'Sweet Child O' Mine', or the opening of Led Zeppelin's 'Achilles' Last Stand', or the low-string melody that starts Golden Earring's 'Radar Love' in such a threatening way (and at a different tempo to the main song). It could be a single chord, as with The Who's 'The Kids Are Alright' (*Bbrraaanggg!* "I don't mind …"), The Beatles' 'Hard Day's Night' (try G7sus4 on a 12-string for an approximation), Keef's chopped open-G tuning chord for The Rolling Stones' 'Brown Sugar' and 'Start Me Up', or the crunching E chord on T. Rex's 'Twentieth Century Boy'.

Dissonance will sure as hell get people's attention. Think of Hendrix's grinding flattened fifth to kick-start 'Purple Haze' or the Aleister Crowley-meets-the Arabian-Nights snakebite of Jimmy Page's bent augmented fourth (C♯ against G) for Led Zeppelin's 'Dancing Days'. There's a flattened fifth in the riff of R.E.M.'s 'Feeling Gravity's Pull' where it is not as expected as it might be in a heavy rock number such as Metallica's 'Enter Sandman'. A song like Robert Plant's 'Big Log' starts with an instrumental guitar passage because the song itself is half guitar instrumental anyway.

Other instruments

The intro instrument could be a horn, as on The Beach Boys' 'God Only Knows', or a keyboard, as on Stevie Wonder's 'Superstition'. A trumpet has the intro to many a Bacharach tune like Louis Armstrong's 'We've Got All The Time In The World'. It's a saxophone on Gerry Rafferty's 'Baker Street', and there's what critic Dave Marsh aptly called the "rattlesnake" tambourine on the intro of Marvin Gaye's 'I Heard It Through The Grapevine'. It might be the lush orchestral intro of Siouxsie & The Banshees' 'Dazzle' or the solo bassline of The Temptations' 'My Girl', Madonna's 'Erotica', or R.E.M.'s 'Cuyahoga'. Think of the repeated bass motif that starts Queen's 'Under Pressure'. What about having an unusual instrument play the intro, like the Coral electric sitar heard on The Supremes' 'No Matter What Sign You Are' and Stevie Wonder's 'Signed, Sealed, Delivered' – guaranteed to make people ask "What the hell is that?"

People who are recognised stars on their instruments get to start songs with short solos, like the guitar break that opens Dire Straits' 'Brothers In Arms'. Some songs start with other people's tunes. Dire Straits put an extract of 'The Carousel Waltz' at the beginning of 'Tunnel Of Love' because it conjured up a fairground. The copyright will cost you, of course.

Drum intros have strong impact, especially in music for dancing. John Bonham's drum intros for Led Zeppelin's 'Rock And Roll', 'When The Levee Breaks' (sampled on, among others, Bjork's 'Army Of Me') and 'The Crunge' are exemplary. Other notable drum intros include those on Elvis Costello's 'Lipstick Vogue', Kate Bush's 'Sat In Your Lap', T. Rex's 'Jeepster', and Jimi Hendrix's 'I Don't Live Today'. On hits such as 'Can The Can', Suzi Quatro turned the drum intro into a trademark.

Vocal intros

Think of the way Elvis's 'Hound Dog' comes straight in with unaccompanied vocal, or Martha Wainwright's 'Far Away'. You could whistle, or use a spoken phrase like "Is she really going out with him?", as on The Shangri-Las' 'Leader Of The Pack', which The Damned appropriated for 'New Rose'. There's Ian Hunter's cheery "Allo!" on 'Once Bitten Twice Shy', or even a laugh, as Kate Bush put on the single of 'The Man With The Child In His Eyes'. Motown was fond of spoken intros, such as the ones Smokey Robinson put on 'Shop Around' and 'Baby, Baby Don't Cry', and the party chatter that starts Marvin Gaye's 'What's Going On' and The Temptations 'I Can't Get Next To You'. But these might be considered kitsch now, unless they're funny – like the heavily echoed "Hey! don't watch dat, watch dis!" of Madness's 'One Step Beyond'. How about Little Richard's immortal rock'n'roll war-cry, "Awopbopaloobop-alopbamboom", at the start of 'Tutti Frutti', Lennon's scorching first phrase on 'Mr Moonlight', or the Beatlesque dominant seventh crescendo that begins Bowie's 'Let's Dance'? Intros require drama, involvement, expectation. A crescendo or an ascending or descending figure gets our attention immediately because we know it's moving towards something, and we are curious to hear what it will be. Anticipation can be aroused by suggesting that you are about to land on chord I but delaying it to the verse (or later). 'Can't Ignore The Train' by 10,000 Maniacs does this.

Sampling voices from films can produce excellent results (though again with copyright implications) – witness Kate Bush's use of a fevered male voice exclaiming, "It's in the trees! It's coming!" ('Hounds Of Love', from the film *Night of the Demon*), or Siouxsie & The Banshees' "Did you know that more murders are committed at 92 degrees Fahrenheit than any other temperature? I read an article once ... at lower temperatures people are easy going, over 92 it's too hot to move, but [at] just 92 people get irritable!" ('92 Degrees', dialogue from a Ray Bradbury film, *It Came From Outer Space*). Joan Osborne's 'One Of Us' has a field recording of on-the-porch singing before the song proper starts. Robert Plant's 'Tie Dye On The Highway' sets the hippie scene with a sample from the film *Woodstock*.

You might use a sound effect of some sort. This could illustrate the theme of the song, as with The Kinks' 'Apeman' and Madness's 'Driving In My Car' (car horns), or R.E.M.'s 'Exhuming McCarthy' (a typewriter). It could be trains (The Who's '5.15', The Jam's 'Down In The Tube Station At Midnight'), rain and storm (The Doors' 'Riders On The Storm', and all over The Who's *Quadrophenia*), the waterfront (Oasis's 'Champagne Supernova') or seagulls (The Temptations' 'I Wish It Would Rain'). Pink Floyd started 'Money', appropriately, with cash-tills ringing. Kate Bush used whale song to open 'Moving' and birdsong on *Aerial*. How about a sax imitating a ship's foghorn (Madness's 'Night Boat To Cairo')? You could also use pure sound effects generated on a synth, as the acoustic guitar fed through synth that spits out the intro to The Who's 'Relay'. Samplers have been used to put the sound of crackling vinyl at the start of songs, for that extra touch of analogue warmth, as on Madonna's 'Erotica' and Robert Plant's 'Your Ma Said You Cried In Your Sleep Last Night'.

The 'false intro'

We assume that an intro leads to what follows. But an interesting effect can be created by having an intro that does not dovetail with the rest of the song – a 'false intro'. False intros work by arousing a sense of what we think the song will be and then giving us a mild shock. They manipulate tempo, harmony, or both. You could start in one style and then proceed in another, although that's a fairly way-out trick. R.E.M. put a few seconds of goofing around pretending to be James Brown before the country rock of '(Don't Go Back To) Rockville'.

Tempo variations often work well. Elvis Costello's 'Man Out Of Time' starts in double-time with a manic punk thrash that suddenly subsides into a stately piano-driven song. Intros can be in free time, such as in The Beatles' 'Here, There And Everywhere' and Don McLean's 'American Pie', where the time is controlled by the singer's phrasing. Wings' 'My Love' has a clever false intro in which a horn plays the note A. We are tempted to register A as the key note – but the first chord that fades in is a B♭ (B♭ D F), so the A note makes a B♭maj7 chord (B♭ D F A). In reality the song is in F major.

The Libertines' 'Last Post On The Bugle' starts with four bars of drums. The second musical event occurs on the right channel. A high guitar part, which we'll call Guitar I, enters playing notes (B♭ A G over D) which imply a Gm chord, but no full chord is sounded. When a second guitar enters (Guitar II) with a chord, the chord isn't Gm, as we might have expected, it's Cm. Guitar II comes in on the left at 0:11 with what will be the chord sequence of the chorus. Using the chorus progression as an instrumental intro is effective because when the first chorus is sung the underlying sequence will be half-familiar to the listener.

Red Hot Chili Peppers' 'Under The Bridge' has a 'false intro' in the D-F♯ change heard at the beginning. This musical idea doesn't re-occur in the song. The first verse of 'Under The Bridge' increases the tempo and changes key into E major. Keane's 'Atlantic' opens with an arpeggio using the notes G♯-A♯-D♯. If the listener thinks the G♯ (the lowest note) is the root then this implies a G♯sus2 chord. But twenty seconds in the bass guitar comes in with a B under this arpeggio which transforms it into a B6 and we have to adjust the way we hear it.

You might also start on an unrelated chord. Bebop Deluxe's 'Maid In Heaven' starts with the chords F-D5-A5. We initially assume that F is the key chord and that therefore the D5 is a version of chord VI (Dm) and A5 a version of chord III (Am). But on the third time the F leads to a G. Is this chord II^ in F? No, because it cadences onto a D major chord and we have arrived in the song's proper key by a ♭III-IV-I progression.

Some intros are almost long enough to be termed 'pre-verses'. This is where you realise that the boundaries between sections of a song are not always rigid and easily identified. Take The Beatles' 'If I Fell': it opens with a descending chord sequence in C♯ major or D♯ minor, which changes key to D major for the first chorus. An intro could be in a different tempo and a different key from the song proper. Led Zeppelin's 'Tea For One' starts medium-tempo in F before subsiding into a 12/8 slow blues in C minor. R.E.M.'s 'I Believe' commences with a banjo in G, but the band enter in F at a faster tempo, almost as if they have cut across the banjo.

Intros offer an opportunity to play around with the listener's sense of key. Smokey Robinson did this on 'More Love', and The Isley Brothers' 'Put Yourself In My Place' starts with a bewildering progression of E-A-C-Bb-G/B before settling in C major at the commencement of the verse.

The Verse

The verse is lyrically where you describe a situation and establish the song's style. Verses are anything from about eight bars up to 24 or more in length, often in a figure divisible by four. Verses of any length can have their own internal structure. Two lines of lyric could be set to a four-bar four-chord turnaround repeated, or four lines to four times round (each chord name here represents a bar of music):

C	Am	G	F	(x4)

It would be more interesting to use the turnaround only three times and then change to something else:

C	Am	G	F	(x3)	G	F	G	F

This type of 3 + 1 formula is very common, as is the making of a verse by constructing an eight-bar sequence and repeating it:

| C | G | F | G | F | Em | Am | G | (x2) |

Notice how this stays off the key chord, C, until the start of the next eight bars. 'Hotel California' is a famous eight-bar progression:

I	V^	VII	IV^	VI	III	IV	V^
Bm	F♯	A	E	G	D	Em	F♯

Sam Cooke's 'Cupid' does this with just four chords:

I	VI	I	IV	I	V	I	V
C	Am	C	F	C	G	C	G

Notice how it never loses touch with chord I. The changes are like short steps away from the key centre, not a long journey. Compare it with 'Hotel California' where once the music has left the key chord of B minor it does not reach it again until the start of the next phrase. Manfred Mann's 'Fox On The Run' has a lovely chord progression:

I	V	II	IV	II	V	IV	I
C	G	Dm	F	Dm	G	F	C

Notice how the second Dm is poignant because unexpected and the approach to the last C via F is softer than it would have been with G.

A common trick is to repeat an eight-bar phrase with a change of the last chord second time around. Big Star's 'The Ballad Of El Goodo' does this:

I	IV	II	V	III	VI	IV	♭VI
G	C	Am	D	Bm	Em	C	E♭

The second time through E♭ is replaced by F.

The final verse of The Libertines' 'Last Post On The Bugle' employs a classic arrangement strategy when it strips back to drums, handclaps, and minimal vocal (thus alluding to the intro). Many songs thin out the instrumentation before the final chorus, which has the effect of making the return of the chorus more dramatic.

Verse asymmetry
Asymmetrical verse extensions can be great, because they break the 'tyranny of four'. A verse could have an odd number of bars tacked on the end, sometimes to allow a few extra words to be added. The chorus might appear a couple of bars early or late, either of which can be exciting. Another handy technique is to take out a bar to make a second phrase arrive a bar earlier than expected. The Beatles' 'It Won't Be Long' cuts a bar from its verse after the first phrase so the second has more impact. (Try singing the song with the 'cut' bar restored and notice how much less interesting it is.) In Dionne Warwick's 'Do You Know

The Way To San Jose', there is a good example of asymmetry: the chord sequence I-IV-I-V is five bars long, with chord V covering two bars. Try counting the bars to each phrase in The Herd's 60s classic 'From The Underworld' – more complex than its I-IV-V progression suggests.

The through-composed verse

A verse can also be 'through-composed'. I use this term for a verse that has no repeated chord-change unit, such as a turnaround, but is a single structure without internal repeats that is maybe 12 or 16 bars (or even longer). This type of song is less common because it is more demanding to write. It is also less favoured in a commercial context because the listener has to wait until the end of the verse to grasp the whole. The lack of chord repetition can be offset by repeating lyric phrases or having melodic motifs in the instruments that can be repeated regardless of the changing harmony. Although unusual, the through-composed verse does offer marvellous opportunities for developing the melodic line. Gilbert O'Sullivan's 'Alone Again (Naturally)' and The Carpenters' 'For All We Know' would be examples.

If a verse is very short, the distinction between verse and chorus can be blurred. There is one song structure that has two sections, A and B, where A is a verse that climaxes with a hook – in other words a 'mini-chorus' is incorporated into it. In Edison Lighthouse's 'Love Grows (Where My Rosemary Goes)', there are only two lyric lines sung in four bars before the song arrives at the hook. The whole section completes in about eight bars. Badfinger's 'No Matter What' is another example with an eight-bar A section. Both songs have a bridge that modulates away from the home key. The Beatles' early albums contain many examples of this AB structure.

Verses can be constructed by using 8-, 12- and 16-bar blues-derived forms.

8-bar three-chord verse

I-IV-I-V-I-IV-V-I
The Beatles 'Act Naturally'.

I-I-IV-I-I-V-IV-I
The Beach Boys 'Barbara Ann'.

IV-I-IV-I-IV-I-V-I
The Everly Brothers 'Bye Bye Love'.

I-I-IV-♭Vdim-I-VI-II-V-I-IV-I-V
Fleetwood Mac 'Need Your Love So Bad'.

Typical 12-bar

I-I (or IV)-I-I-IV-IV-I-I-V-IV-I-V

12-bar in Dm

I-I-V-V-I-I-IV-IV-I-V-I-I
Fleetwood Mac 'Black Magic Woman'.

Songs can have verses with different sequences and structures, all leading to the same chorus.

The Pre-Chorus

One further refinement of the verse is the 'pre-chorus', a section that sounds a step beyond the first part of the verse. It may be a musical or a lyrical phrase that gives this feeling of moving forward. For example, if the verse has used only the key chord, a pre-chorus would bring in IV or V or both. A classic pre-chorus chord change is to move from IV to V repeatedly, creating the musical expectation that you will land on chord I at the start of the chorus, as in Culture Club's 'Karma Chameleon'. It might even feature a sequence like II-III-IV-V, which progresses strongly toward the chorus.

The rate of chord change in a pre-chorus can increase on what it was in the verse, as in The Beatles' 'Got To Get You Into My Life'. The pre-chorus definitely has its eyes and ears fixed on the upcoming chorus. It can also be a way of introducing another hook into the song. The pre-chorus usually retains the same lyrics from one verse to another, even if the verse changes. In a song that goes verse, chorus, verse, chorus, middle eight, a pre-chorus can provide the transition to the last set of choruses if it is felt that putting in a third verse would delay things too much.

The Chorus

A great chorus to a popular song is pure magic. The chorus is the passionate, joyous, declamatory, tearful, wistful, angry, assertive heart of the popular song. It has you walking two feet off the carpet. Put another nickel in that machine! Musically, it's where we find the hook, the notes that lodge in your mind (and millions of other minds – you're in good company, you know); the notes that make you want to hear the song again; the notes that drive you to your local music shop or online music provider. A hook is a catchy melodic and harmonic phrase, possibly reinforced by backing vocal, instrumental counter-melodies, a riff, or rhythm. This is where we reach the centre of the lyric's meaning. It could be a resolution ('I'm Gonna Make You Love Me', 'I'll Pick A Rose For My Rose'), a revelation ('She Loves You', 'You're All I Need To Get By'), a realisation ('It Must Be Love'), a question ('Do You Wanna Dance?'), a metaphor ('Blinded By The Light') or a statement ('I Want To Know What Love Is'). Lyrically, the chorus sums up the central issue and/or expresses the over-riding emotion.

Choruses often involve repetition of words and/or the accompanying harmony. The music intensifies and focuses, and this can be achieved in a variety of ways. You could delay chord I until the chorus, or quicken the rate of harmonic change (chords changing twice a bar instead of once a bar). Listen to the way the chorus in Aretha Franklin's 'I Say A Little Prayer' gains urgency as the chords change every two beats. The same trick happens in Madonna's 'Cherish', where the chords change on the beat.

You can lift the melody to higher notes, bring in other instruments, change the key, quicken the tempo, alter the predominant rhythm, or strengthen the beat. Great choruses really need an inspiration – this is where you pray to the Muse when composing.

The Link

After the chorus, you have to find a way to return to the verse. You can have no link and go straight to the verse. Whether this works depends on what the melody does at the end of a chorus. Is there enough time between the end of that phrase and the start of the verse lyric? Does it sound rushed and breathless? Does the listener need a break? Does the singer need a bar for taking breath?

The faster the tempo, the more likely it is you will need a link. A couple of bars will probably do the trick. In a hard-rock song, the guitar riff often returns at this point for an outbreak of headbanging. You could reprise the intro, perhaps in a shortened form. It is often good to have a change of dynamics and texture at this point.

The Middle Eight/Bridge

The middle eight usually comes after the second chorus, though it might be inserted after the second verse as a way of delaying the next chorus. If it is short enough, it can even be inserted more than once.

The term 'middle eight' reminds us that the commonest length for a third song section is eight bars, though the term is used regardless of its length to refer to what songwriters technically call 'the middle bit'. The term 'bridge' reminds us of its function, which is to link different parts of the song. After the second chorus, songs often need to go somewhere else for a bit. New lyrical and musical material is introduced. The easiest thing to do is introduce a solo of some sort – a rock song would have a guitar solo, an MOR ballad might opt for soft, breathy sax. (That way you don't have to write more lyrics.) This tactic is not as common as it once was.

Harmonically, a middle eight might have a key change, or work towards one. The traditional key change is to the dominant key – the key whose root note is the fifth of the scale (eg, from C to G), whence it is easy to return to the home key. Consider this bridge sequence for a song in C major:

F	G	Am	F	C	F	D7	G

This middle eight modulates to the dominant key, G major. But since G major is also chord V of C, you can easily go to a C chord at the start of the next verse and be back in C major. Buddy Holly's 'That'll be The Day' does this. A couple of beats of G7 will make the change back obvious.

A simpler technique than changing key is demonstrated by The Beatles' 'I Saw Her Standing There' and Madonna's 'Into The Groove', where a repeated IV-V change – two major chords a tone (full step) apart – comprises the bridge. This idea was previously encountered as a prechorus technique.

Harmonically, the middle eight may contain chords not played elsewhere in the song. The Beatles had a wonderful trick of combining 12-bar verses that were all tough dominant seventh chords (I7, IV7, V7: C7, F7, G7) with bridges that sweetened the emotion with minor chords II, III or VI (Dm, Em or Am). For this, listen to 'Can't Buy Me Love', 'I Feel Fine', and 'Hard Day's Night'. 'You Can't Do That', which is in G major, has a brilliant bridge in which the sharp-talking bluesy swagger of the verse lapses momentarily into vulnerability:

III^	VI	II	III	I7	III^	VI	II	III	V7
B7	Em	Am	Bm	G7	B7	Em	Am	Bm	D7

The fleeting modulation to a wounded E minor in bar two is cancelled out by the surly G7 (key-wise E minor needs an F♯ but G7 has an F in it).

Lyrically, the middle eight might give a new or different slant on the theme of the song – perhaps leading to a realisation that will be settled in the last verse. A middle eight might be full of questions that are answered in the song's conclusion.

Cream's 'Badge' was named after one of the writers misread the word 'bridge' on the piece of paper that had notes for the song scribbled on it. And now you know why Robert Plant was looking for that 'confounded' bridge at the close of Led Zeppelin's 'The Crunge'.

Last Chorus

Since the chorus is the beating heart of the pop song, songs often end with several choruses back to back. Assuming that there is a coda and not just a fade-out on the chorus itself, last choruses often have an extra something to spice them up. This can be achieved through the arrangement itself, adding more instruments, maybe changing a word or two in the lyric, adding more voices, etc. The corniest device is to increase the excitement by changing key up a semi-tone (half-step) or tone (full step). This is discussed in Section 10.

Reharmonising is a delightful way of adding interest to a final chorus. This means the melody stays the same (or nearly the same) but the underlying chords are changed. This can be very expressive. In Crowded House's 'Don't Dream It's Over', the first two choruses use a IV-V-I-VI sequence (F-G-C-Am, a displaced version of I-VI-IV-V), but the third chorus is II-III-I-VI (Dm-Em-C-Am). The first two major chords, F and G, have turned into their relative minors. This adds a sudden, tragic colouration that heightens the emotional effect. (Wisely, they do it only once.)

In the consciously Beatlesque 'This Year's Model', Elvis Costello harmonises the hook-line with the chords IV-V-I (G-A-D). In the last choruses, it is reharmonised IV-V-I-VI (G-A-D-Bm), IV-V-III-VI (G-A-F♯m-Bm) and finally IV-V-I. The appearance of the minor chords adds an emotional flourish that suggests the speaker has more sympathy with the beleaguered model than the satire of the lyric has let on.

The Outro or Coda

All good things, even great singles, have an ending. Sad but true.

After the last chorus, you have to find a way for your song to finish. The time-honoured pop tradition is to fade out on repetitions of the chorus. This is effective, especially to leave an impression of the music going on forever (a profound metaphysical idea; perhaps the chorus of 'God Only Knows' eternally echoes in the mind of God, along with everything else, of course!). Using a fade does mean, however, that if you perform the song live you'll have to think of an ending later.

Occasionally songs fade out only to return. Roxy Music's 'In Every Dream Home A Heartache' fades out on a solo and then, after a few seconds of silence, returns in a blizzard of phasing. The fade-out-fade-back approach was obviously not designed for radio, as it is liable to catch the DJ in the middle of the next announcement. One of my favourite endings is the 'tape-cut'. Love's 'A House Is Not A Motel' from the classic *Forever Changes* album has a coda consisting of two duelling electric guitars playing solos that are unrelated to each other. The song abruptly ceases as if the tape had vanished. (Whoever faded this out on the remastered CD deserves to be shot.)

Some codas merely reprise the chorus instrumentally, with vocal ad libs or another solo, or have another refrain over the music for the chorus, or use the intro sequence. Many songs have a refrain so you can join in. Extended instrumental codas can create an engaging mood of their own, as with Roxy Music's 'More Than This', Hurricane #1's 'Step Into My World', The Eagles' 'Hotel California', Lynyrd Skynyrd's 'Freebird', Dire Straits' 'Tunnel Of Love', and Bruce Springsteen's 'Thunder Road'.

The Smiths' 'Panic' reaches its coda at a mere 1:42, with a satirical use of kids' voices – satirical because children are so often used on certain types of ghastly pop records; in 'Panic' the kids get their revenge with the gleeful refrain inviting everyone to "hang the DJ". A few hit records have codas longer than the main part of the song. In The Beatles' 'Hey Jude', the "na-na-na" coda goes on for several minutes. Another Number One single with a long coda was T. Rex's 'Hot Love', where the verse provided the music for the "la la" coda. The full-length version of Eric Clapton's 'Layla' has a long instrumental coda that introduces new melodic ideas; it was edited out from the single.

If a coda does not fade, the last chord is usually the key chord: major for a happy ending, minor for a sad one. The precise form of the last chord I will contribute to the effect – the dominant seventh is hard, the major seventh soft, the sus2 empty, the sus4 tense, the major sixth slightly jazzy. The dominant chord is a viable alternative that gives a pleasing feeling of suspension, of stopping somewhere new but not unrelated. Bryan Adams and Mel C's 'When You're Gone' is in C but ends on an F, chord IV, leaving you with the feeling that it has changed key.

Approaching chord I via the minor form of IV is fine for slushy, romantic finishes. You can hear this in the weeping melodrama at the end of 'The Kick Inside', where Kate Bush implies the singer's suicide by ending with IV to IVm. It is also at the end of 'I Got The Blues' by The Rolling Stones. Intensify this cadence by using IVm7-Imaj7 (Fm7-Cmaj7), for more slush than a New York winter.

There is a centuries-old tradition of ending a minor-key song on the tonic major for a redemptive gesture, technically known as a *tierce de picardie*. The opposite – ending a major song on a minor chord – is disconcerting. The Beatles' 'From Me To You' is in C but ends on Am, which provokes the response, does that last minor chord fit the lyric? Something dissonant can also make an ending ear-catching. The penultimate chord of R.E.M.'s 'The One I Love' (its notes are E B♭ D♯ G B E, which can be called Em/maj7/add♭5) is certainly notable before the final Em.

In 1990s UK chart music, it became fashionable to end a song with a solo vocal. Manic Street Preachers' 'A Design For Life' had the unusual ending of drums only.

STRUCTURES

Having looked at the individual bits of songs, let's consider different ways of piecing them together.

The groove song

Dance music has given us the groove song. It does not even have a chord sequence, because for long stretches it stays on one chord. James Brown tracks such as 'Sex Machine' are a good example, as are some of John Lee Hooker's blues tunes. This approach can also be used just for the verse, as in Madonna's 'Erotica'.

The loop

The simplest song structures are no more than four- or eight-bar loops that simply repeat. Boredom is regulated to barely tolerable (ie, pre-psychotic hi-fi/radio smashing) levels by the manipulation of the arrangement to make it sound as though the sections are different. 'I Will Survive' is an eight-bar sequence of eight chords (minor key: I-IV-VII-IIImaj7-VImaj7-IIm7♭5-Vsus4-V^) that spins round memorably until Gloria Gaynor disappears down the hole in the middle.

U2's 'With Or Without You' is a I-V-VI-IV turnaround that gradually gathers in intensity, thanks to a highly dynamic arrangement. Madonna's 'Justify My Love' is essentially a four-bar loop with breaks created by pulling out everything except voice and drums.

Rarely, a lyric will justify this type of structure by its theme. Stevie Wonder's 'I Was Made To Love Her' is a four-bar five-chord turnaround, with only a brief four-bar break to interrupt the flow. But the simplicity of structure expresses the theme of unchanging truth. He's loved this girl from childhood and nothing will change their love. Any risk of tedium is avoided through the sheer quality of the musicianship – whether it be Stevie Wonder's exhilarated vocal, the lovely guitar fills, or James Jamerson's astonishing bassline.

Standard song structures

1 verse verse verse verse

'Strophic' form, common in old ballads, blues, and folk music. The hook may be a short refrain tacked on at the end of each verse. The intro might be no more than a few bars on the key chord.

2 intro verse verse bridge verse bridge verse

This form was favoured by The Beatles in the early years of their career. Again, the hook is part of the verse itself. One of the bridges or verse three could be instrumental rather than vocal. The last verse is likely to have the hook repeated. There is an old formula for a 32-bar song that goes: verse one, eight bars; verse two, eight bars; bridge, eight bars; verse three, eight bars.

3 intro verse chorus verse chorus verse chorus coda or fade

This structure dispenses with a bridge. It can be appropriate in a song where the emphasis is on a lyric story.

4 intro verse chorus verse chorus bridge chorus coda or fade
This is probably the most common structure in popular songs since the early 1960s. It ensures a rapid return of the chorus toward the end.

5 intro verse chorus verse chorus bridge verse chorus coda or fade
In contrast to example four, this form puts an additional verse after the bridge.

6 intro verse chorus bridge verse chorus coda or fade
This is the structure of the single version of Boston's 'More Than A Feeling'. This edited version is much snappier than the album track, offering a good example of how radio edits are often aesthetically right, too.

7 intro chorus verse chorus bridge verse chorus coda or fade
This is a radio-friendly format because it starts with the chorus.

8 intro verse verse verse solo/bridge verse extended coda
The extended coda of this structure provides an opportunity to take the song somewhere else in its closing minutes. The challenge is to make sure the listener is intrigued enough to stay with it that long.

9 intro riff chorus verse verse chorus coda on intro riff
Used by The Byrds for their highly compressed adaptation of Dylan's 'Mr. Tambourine Man' (Dylan's original has many more verses).

10 intro verse 1 verse 2 verse 3 verse 4 solo verse 2 verse 3 verse 4
This is the structure of Smokey Robinson's 'The Hunter Gets Captured By The Game'. What's interesting is that it never returns to verse one (in D major); the rest of the song is in B minor. Each verse is short, and in The Marvelettes' version the whole thing comes in under three minutes.

Remember that it is perfectly possible either to cut a first chorus in half, or to cut a second or third verse in half, in order to tighten up a song's form.

Other types of structure

When thinking about structure, keep sight of the overall 'shape' of a song. A song may have a dynamic curve that overrides its verse/chorus sections, as in the case of 'With Or Without You', 'You'll Never Walk Alone', and 'It's Over', songs that build to a climax and then ebb away or stop. It's important to realise that songs can be made to seem almost seamless – Madonna's 'This Used To Be My Playground' is a good example. In too much recent songwriting, the 'joins' between sections are too obvious.

Some of Springsteen's longer early songs, such as 'Rosalita' and 'Jungleland', have complex structures with many dynamic moments of crescendo and ebb. These were written with live performance in mind and partly influenced by the 'soul revue' approach (for detailed discussion see my book *Songwriting Secrets: Bruce Springsteen*). I coined the term 'multiverse' to describe a more complex verse than is normal in rock. It's a verse which has more than one section, causing a delay of the chorus. 'Incident on 57th Street' is a fine example of a song with a 'multiverse'. It lasts 7:44 with subtle dynamics and the cinematic quality typical of Springsteen's second album. It has the extended song structure Springsteen often deployed at this time. Meat Loaf is a performer who, against the odds, has made a career out of batty (pun intended) long numbers that resemble mini-operas. In rock, examples of unconventionally structured songs would include Radiohead's 'Paranoid Android', Queen's 'Bohemian Rhapsody' (and its lesser-known precursor, 'March Of The Black Queen'), The Beatles' 'Happiness Is A Warm Gun', Led Zeppelin's 'Stairway To Heaven', Wings' 'Band On The Run', and whole stretches of the back-catalogues of bands like Jethro Tull, Genesis, Rush, and Yes. Be warned, however – that way, the rock opera and concept album lie!

If you have never written a song, it can seem daunting to listen to a piece of music three or four minutes long and think, how am I going to invent all that? But this is a false anxiety because the 'all that' doesn't add up to much. It gets much less daunting when you reflect on how short each section is. Let's say we need an intro, a verse, a chorus and a bridge: 4 + 8 (twice) + 4 (twice or four times) + 8. That's a total of only 24 bars of music for the whole song. Cut down to size like this, songwriting need not seem so difficult.

SECTION 6
RHYTHM

Rhythm is a vital aspect of popular music. In fact, it is one of the things that makes popular music popular. Rhythm is fundamental to human consciousness. In the womb, we grow to the beat of our mother's heart. Everyday activities have rhythm – walking, or tapping our fingers on a table. Rhythm can be intoxicating, and it can carry people out of themselves. Armies march to the sound of beats, and some religious rituals have used drums to assist with the inducing of trance and altered states of consciousness. The overtly rhythmic nature of rock music itself was characterised by some critics in the 1950s as primitive, a reversion to the jungle. Rhythm fills the dance halls of every decade.

By contrast, in classical music the beat is implicit. A conductor signals the beats with waves of a baton, but rarely do classical pieces have a percussion instrument marking every beat for prolonged periods. Percussion is deployed at specific moments to accent a theme, a chord or a dynamic change. By employing the drum kit (and, more recently, the drum machine and sampled loops), popular music has always made the beat explicit. This is part of its long-established connection with dance. In any music intended for dancing, which much popular music always has been, overt rhythm is obviously important. But a catchy rhythm can do more than just set your feet tapping; it can be an important part of what makes a song memorable.

Songs driven by rhythm

In Section 1 we looked at this formula:

> **A song = lyric + melody + harmony + rhythm**

Often, we hear a hit song where the rhythm seems more important than anything else. This might be because of an unusual drum pattern or percussion instrument, or because of a stark arrangement that exposes the drums. Much dance music – from 1960s rhythm & blues, Stax, James Brown, Motown and funk to 1970s Philly and disco to 1990s dance tracks – centres on rhythm. The drum track is usually loud in the mix, and the harmonic and melodic elements are secondary. The impulse to reduce the melodic and harmonic elements of popular music as much as possible led to genres such as drum'n'bass.

The Chemical Brothers' 'Loops Of Fury' offers a good example of this reductionism. The instrumental lasts 4:38 and its harmonic content is a riff with a couple of variations based on a I-♭VII change in B. The various sections are largely differentiated by the presence or absence of the drum track. A breakdown of the structure looks like this:

- **A**: Intro: riff 1, one bar, no drums (x4)
- **A**: riff 1, drums in (x8)
- **B**: riff 2, one bar (x16)
- **C**: synth figure (x16)
- **D**: drum break, four bars
- **C**: (x8)
- **E**: drum break, vocal sample (x2)
- **C**: (x8)
- **F**: [E] drum break (x8)
- **C**: (x8)
- **E**: (x2)
- **C**: (x8)
- **G**: synth figure 2 (x7) + one bar drums
- **F**: (x4)
- **C**: with EQ effects (x16)
- **B**: riff 2 (x16)

The rigidity of structure is typical of 1990s dance music. Notice how the 'tyranny of four' is in full operation here, with section lengths based on multiples of four, with the added reductive factor of individual sections usually consisting of a single bar repeated. The tempo is unvarying and the drums simply enter and exit at the mixing stage, without any warning fills.

Fat Boy Slim's 'Praise Him' is similar. It consists of two riffs: the first is ♭VII-IV-I in G over two bars; the second is I-IV-♭VII in D for one bar. The first riff is repeated about 40 times and the second about 30 times. Almost all the sections repeat four times, occasionally eight. Only the abrupt addition or subtraction of percussion, or bass, or a guitar phrase, varies the arrangement. The musical content of the song amounts to little more than three bars. Dreadzone's 'Little Britain' takes a two-bar chord phrase and repeats it over 70 times. This does beg an interesting question: why would anyone want to listen to anything so repetitive?

The singles charts have from time to time featured records that push percussion to the front of the mix, including The Pretenders' 'Message Of Love', Simple Minds' 'Waterfront', Kate Bush's 'Sat In Your Lap', and the claps and foot-stomping of The Supremes' 'Baby Love', and Simon & Garfunkel's 'Cecilia'. There have been chants like Hotlegs' 'Neanderthal Man' (1970), recorded by future members of 10cc. In 1971, 'Burundi Black' brought the sound of African drumming to the UK chart, later used on Joni Mitchell's *The*

Hissing Of Summer Lawns and Adam Ant's *Kings Of The Wild Frontier*. That same year also saw two hit singles by the South African John Kongos, 'Tokoloshe Man' and 'He's Gonna Step On You Again' (covered as 'Step On' by Happy Mondays), both with an African rhythmic influence. This was long before 'world music' became fashionable. Glam rock picked up on the 'tribal' vibe, as heard on songs such as Gary Glitter's 'Rock And Roll', Suzi Quatro's 'Devilgate Drive', Queen's 'We Will Rock You', Hello's 'New York Groove' (in a Bo Diddley style), and Cozy Powell's 'Dance With The Devil'. Alan Stivell's electric folk on *From Celtic Roots* drew on unusual rhythms from traditional Celtic music. Further on in the 1970s there was Fleetwood Mac's 'Tusk'. Peter Gabriel and Phil Collins both pursued a different drum approach, temporarily banning cymbals from their recordings. On the 1981 album *Ju-Ju*, Siouxsie & The Banshees imitated non-Western drumming patterns; the band's single 'Slowdive' is not much more than a rhythm track. The influence of world music in the 1990s has increased the variety of rhythms heard in popular music, and even heavy rockers like ex-Led Zeppelin Jimmy Page and Robert Plant used Moroccan drum loops for their *No Quarter* project.

The elements of rhythm: time signatures

Music is written in a time signature. Just as the key signature tells you which notes to sharpen or flatten in a given key, so the time signature tells you how many beats there are in a bar. This is the pulse of the music. Here is a diagram of basic note values and rests.

		NOTE VALUES		
Symbol	Rest	Trad name	Modern name	Duration
o	–	Semi-breve	Whole note	4 beats
♩	–	Minim	Half note	2 beats
♩	‰	Crotchet	Quarter note	1 beat
♪	‰	Quaver	Eighth note	½ beat
♪	‰	Semi-quaver	Sixteenth note	¼ beat
♪	‰	Demi-semi-quaver	Thirty-second note	⅛ beat

Simple time

The most common time signature in popular song is 4/4, a form of what is known as 'simple time' where the beats are marked by quarter-notes/crotchets. Other 'simple' times include 3/4, typified by the waltz dance form, and 2/4. Well-known songs in 3/4 include 'Amazing Grace', 'Mull Of Kintyre', 'America',

'Annie's Song' and 'Only Love Can Break Your Heart'. 'It's All In The Game' was originally in 3/4 but The Four Tops turned it into 4/4. Even a hard-rock song in 6/4 tends to have a languid feel – witness Soundgarden's 'Fell On Black Days'. The difference between a bar of 6/4 and adjoining bars of 4/4 and 2/4 is one of emphasis. The first beat of any bar has more stress than the remaining beats in that bar, so the 4/4 + 2/4 combination is *one* two three four *one* two and the 6/4 bar is *one* two three four five six.

A 6/4 bar is useful if you want to heighten expectation for the start of a section by making the listener wait another two beats:

I	/	VI	/	V	/	IV	/	/	/

It is difficult to write a song in an odd-numbered time signature such as 5/4 or 7/4. It can be done, though, and hit singles in 5/4 include Jethro Tull's 'Living In The Past' and The Dave Brubeck Quartet's instrumental 'Take Five'. (Note that these two came from the jazz and progressive rock fields.) The 1960s TV theme for *Mission Impossible* is also in 5/4 time – but when it was re-recorded for the 1990s film version, it was changed to 4/4, losing the memorable asymmetry of the original. Pearl Jam's 'Last Exit' has a 5/4 verse and Sufjan Stevens combined bars of 5/4 and 6/4 for 'The Tallest Man, The Broadest Shoulders'. Pink Floyd used 7/4 for 'Money'. Led Zeppelin's 'Four Sticks' is a fine example of a hard rock tune in 5/4 and 'The Ocean' has bars of 7/8 (4/4 minus an eighth-note). Although they did feature the occasional odd time signature, some of Zep's weirder timings were made in 4/4 by shifting the accent. This can be heard in 'Black Dog' and in the link from the guitar solo back to the guitar riff in 'Over The Hills And Far Away'.

Radiohead did this with 'The Pyramid Song', probably one of the most rhythmically off-kilter songs ever to be a hit single. Notated in 4/4, 'The Pyramid Song' nevertheless manages to sound uncountable by the way it places the chords in the bar. Radiohead's 'Go To Sleep' alternates bars of 4/4 and 6/4 (or two bars of 6/8, depending how you count it), and there are 4/4 + 6/4 effects in 'Everything In Its Right Place' and 'Let Down'. '2+2=5' uses 7/4 as a time signature. Classic examples of odd numbers include the seven-bar verse of The Beatles' 'It Won't Be Long' and the 3/4 bars in the verse of 'Strawberry Fields Forever', the chorus of Mott The Hoople's glam hit 'All The Young Dudes', the chorus of Joan Jett's 'I Love Rock'n'Roll', and the slow vocal section of Mountain's 'Tired Angels'.

Compound time

In compound time a dotted note marks the beat, allowing it to be subdivided into three instead of two. This creates an immediately recognisable 'swing' feel. Like 4/4, 12/8 has four beats in a bar, but each one is a dotted quarter-note/crotchet. This is the most popular compound time signature, especially in blues and blues-influenced songs. After this, 6/8 is sometimes used, and others are possible. Notable songs in 12/8 include Dusty Springfield's 'You Don't Have To Say You Love Me', Sonny and Cher's 'I Got You Babe', Bob Dylan's 'Just Like A Woman', The Pretenders' '2000 Miles' and 'I Go To Sleep', and The Beatles' 'Yes It Is' and 'This Boy'.

At slower tempos, it's often difficult to distinguish 6/8 from 3/4. In 6/8, there should be a feeling of two beats to a bar with each divided into three. Whether 6/8 or 3/4, the 'three pulse' is felt in songs such as The Animals' 'House Of The Rising Sun', The Moody Blues's 'Nights In White Satin', Tom Jones's 'Delilah' and Cilla Black's 'Anyone Who Had A Heart'. It can also be hard to hear the difference between two bars of 6/8 and one of 12/8, as in the case of R.E.M.'s 'Everybody Hurts'. Jimi Hendrix gave us 'Manic Depression' in churning 9/8. Time signatures like 5/8 and 7/8 are rarely heard.

Contrasting time signatures

Just as changing the key can inject new dimensions into a song, so can contrasting time signatures. This is not popular in dance-orientated music because it tends to embarrass the dancers, who may suddenly lose the beat. It was delightfully mischievous of R.E.M. not only to start 'Shiny Happy People' in 6/8 and then go to 4/4, but to drop back into 6/8 for an instrumental bridge halfway through. The Thrills' 'Big Sur' is another track that makes effective use of a change of time signature.

Changing time has never been common in popular music, and the advent of the drum machine / loop has made it even less so. One time-change effect you can use relatively easily with a drum machine is 'half-time' or 'double time', where instead of treating the quarter-note as the beat you take the quaver (eighth-note) or the minim (half-note) as the beat. Note that the tempo does not change, only the rhythmic emphasis and the interpretation of the pattern the drum machine plays. This is even more effective if 4/4 becomes 12/8. The machine maintains tempo, but each quarter-note beat is divided into three. Therefore you have 'slowed' the tempo by playing against it.

Lulu's 'Shout' and Elvis's 'Suspicious Minds' mix 4/4 with 12/8. 'Dedicated To The One I Love' mixes 6/8 and 4/4. Cream's 'White Room' has an intro and bridge in 5/4 while its verses are in 4/4. Seal's 'Kiss From A Rose' mixed 6/8 and 9/8. Mary Hopkin's 'Those Were The Days' has a verse in 4/4 and a chorus in 2/4.

Other rhythmic options

Rhythm can be altered without a change of time signature. In simple time, beats can be temporarily divided into triplets or 16th-note triplets (grouped in six). Quarter-notes can be played three in the time of two, allowing six to be played in a 4/4 bar. This is a common effect in Latin American music, and Madonna used it in 'La Isla Bonita'. Springsteen has one of these on the word "edge" in the chorus of 'Darkness On The Edge Of Town'. Conversely, you can force compound into simple time by having four eighths (a quadruplet) on a beat – think of the chorus of The Mamas & The Papas' 'Dedicated To The One I Love' after "baby" and before "whisper". Either of these can be melodically arresting or at least hold up the relentless march of 4/4 for a bit.

Tempo

Don't confuse tempo and time signature. A time signature does not specify a speed – the fact that a song is in 4/4 doesn't tell you whether it is slow or fast; only the tempo does that. Tempo is measured in beats per minute. This is indicated on sheet music by the sign of crotchet/quarter-note = 120bpm. Anything under roughly 90bpm can be thought of as on the slow side; 90–130 is medium tempo; anything above 130 is fast.

Decide on a tempo early in the songwriting process. Often a musical idea comes with an implicit tempo. Make a note of this, either by using a drum machine or a metronome. Once you have planned your song, count the number of bars in each section and add the total. Establish the tempo and if the song is in 4/4 divide that number by four which gives the number of bars per minute. Here's an example:

Song
i (4) + v (16) + ch (8) + v2 (16) + ch (8) + b (8) + v3 (8) + ch (8) + ch (8) = 84 bars

At a tempo of 100bpm it takes a minute to play 25 bars, so this song will last just over three minutes. This is handy for checking if you want the song to be a certain length. It is also a helpful 'early warning system' if you tend to write songs that are too long (a common fault in amateur songwriting). Shortening songs is good discipline. Always ask yourself if you, your listener, the record company, the bitstream or the world, really need that fourth verse or fifth chorus. "Leave 'em wanting more" is a sound adage in many areas of entertainment. One of the best comments people can make about a song is, "It's great but it's too short."

Here's another tip: after you've finished writing a song and are ready to record the first tracks of drums and rhythm guitar, always try playing it faster first. Increase the tempo slowly and see how far you can go before the tempo is incompatible with the mood of the song. It is surprising how often a song benefits from being played slightly faster than the speed at which it first came to you. Tempos are bound to be slower than they might be when you first write and play a song because you're still learning how it goes. This principle is often true of ballads, where slow tempos increase the risk of boredom.

Tempo Performance Variation

Tempo Performance Variation or 'TPV' – meaning slowing down or speeding up – is the kind of numbskull term that might have been dreamed up by the sort of misguided producer who believes everyone should record to a click track.

Before the advent of click tracks in studios, it was perfectly normal for band performances to speed up slightly, especially through excitement. Rock music is supposed to be exciting, after all. This effect can be approximated when recording with a drum machine by increased the tempo setting by 1bpm at the start of a given section. Don't increase by too much or such a change will be noticeable. When you record instrumental tracks against this, you must listen carefully for this point and adjust your playing in response to the machine. On a computer recording system tempo increases can be written in.

The mechanisation of rhythm

It is true that drum machines and sampled loops are wonderful for home recording. You may be lucky enough to know a drummer with the invention of Stewart Copeland, the power of John Bonham or the explosive force of Keith

Moon. Unfortunately, though, if you stick this drummer in your home studio/front room/flat, the neighbours are not going to be very happy.

That said, click tracks, drum machines, and sampled loops are among the worst things ever to happen to popular music. First, drum machines – like all machines – are expressionless in a true and precise sense. No human being is behind the sound at the moment that sound is made. Of course, the technology is a human artefact, and the programming carries human intention that may contain aesthetic expression. But it is the machine that executes the actual music. The essential link in the moment of performance between the soul and sound waves is not there. You may think that doesn't matter, but this is a dangerous position. The music is literally 'soul-less'. It is a huge irony that 'beatboxes' came to dominate a type of music that once termed itself 'soul'.

Second, both click tracks and drum machines put music in a straitjacket. Some prejudice against popular music in the field of 'serious' or 'art' music is misplaced, but with regard to tempo, the reaction of the classical musician is right on the money. If you suggested to an orchestra that they could improve their performance of a Beethoven symphony or a Rachmaninov piano concerto with a click track – "Oh but guys, you'll all be perfectly in time …" – they would fall off their chairs laughing. Then they would insist to a man and woman that your click track idea would, at one digital stroke, remove the expression from the music. For music to 'breathe' and be fully expressive, performers must be free to pause slightly before a chord or modulation or phrase. Classical scores are full of terms like accelerando, ritenuto, rallentando, a tempo – which indicate departures from strict time. In other words, 'TPV' is an essential element of music performance. Why should popular music be any different?

Since the mid-1980s, popular music has become increasingly mechanised. It has lost the beautiful rhythmic effects achieved in a song such as The Beach Boys' 'Wouldn't It Be Nice'. If you want an example of the potential beauty of TPV, listen to Dusty Springfield's 'I Close My Eyes And Count To Ten'. It starts at approximately 106bpm, quickens to 111bpm and then, at 0:53 and again at 2:06, the instruments pull up sharply. Notice the emotional 'weight' this gives the music, much like the mild G-force you feel standing up on a train as it brakes in a station.

One effective rhythm technique is to have an opening section in a kind of 'free time' where the performer dictates the length of phrases, as with Don McLean's 'American Pie'. Some records speed up deliberately, as with Adam & The Ants' 'Goody Two-Shoes'. Siouxsie & The Banshees' 'Sin In My Heart' starts at 120bpm, reaches 144bpm just before the vocals enter, moves up to 150bpm in the verse and by the end is hurtling along at 162bpm. The Faces' 'Stay With Me' starts at a fast tempo of approximately 164bpm, drops to 89bpm for its verses and choruses and then returns to the faster tempo for the coda. There are tempo changes in Them's 'Here Comes The Night', The Moody Blues's 'Question' and The Yardbirds' 'For Your Love'.

The principle of rhythmic asymmetry
Inserting 3/4, 5/4, or 6/4 bars into a song can be an effective way of resisting the 'tyranny of four', which in rhythmic terms usually means the predictable symmetry of 4/4. As mentioned above, such inserted bars can support the

SIMPLE UPWARD PICK

↓ strum down   (↕) = percussive hit of
↑ strum up   dampened strings

development of the lyric, the melody or the harmonic progression, and to arouse or deflate expectation. A bar of 3/4 on the end of a verse makes a 4/4 chorus arrive one beat earlier than expected.

Here are some examples of songs with 'insert bars': Mott the Hoople's 'All The Young Dudes' has a chorus that ends with a bar of 3/4; this was copied by Oasis for 'Stand By Me'. Joan Jett's 'I Love Rock'n'Roll' has a 3/4 bar in its chorus. The Scaffold's 'Lily The Pink' includes a bar of 6/4 to illustrate a stammer. Manfred Mann's 'Ha! Ha! Said The Clown' drops a beat in the verse. There are 2/4 bars in Pink Floyd's 'See Emily Play', Fairport Convention's 'Farewell, Farewell', and Marvin Gaye and Tammi Terrell's 'Ain't Nothing Like The Real Thing'. Two bars of what rock critic Ian MacDonald vividly dubbed "hard-braking" 3/8 end The Beatles' 'I Wanna Hold Your Hand', and 'Blackbird' has 2/4 and 3/4 bars in a 4/4 meter. The Indian influences on 'Within You Without You' show up in its mix of 2/4, 3/4, 4/4, and 5/4 bars. Chicago's 'If You Leave Me Now' and Roy Orbison's 'Pretty Woman' have 2/4 bars. The choruses of Abba's 'Knowing Me, Knowing You', Roxy Music's 'Jealous Guy' and Argent's 'Tragedy' have bars of 2/4. Jimi Hendrix's 'All Along The Watchtower' has been notated with a bar of 9/8 as the first complete bar where there is lead guitar because of an anomaly in the rhythm. Whether this was deliberate or an accident is unknown – but try counting 4/4 through the song's opening and you will find it does not work.

In folk music and some blues there is a recognised practice of making the gaps between phrases an irregular length. This would create chaos in an ensemble because the other musicians wouldn't know what you were going to do. For solo performers, though, it's an option. It can be heard in performances by singers such as John Lee Hooker and the early Bob Dylan. You sing a line, wait however many beats you feel like and then sing the next line.

Rhythm on the guitar: strumming

Most guitarists learn to strum without thinking about what they're actually doing. A strummed guitar fulfils two functions: one is rhythmic, the other harmonic. The harmonic function is to supply a 'wash' of sound relating to a chord, the equivalent of holding a chord on a keyboard. But the guitar lacks sustain, so the notes die unless they are struck again. Repeated striking sustains the presence of the chord. The relationship between strumming technique and sustain can be vividly heard on the mandolin, where rapid strumming is required to keep the notes audible. Violinists solved this problem by using a bow drawn across the string, continually exciting it to vibrate.

The rhythmic function has two components: the rhythm with which the chords are produced and the percussive attack (usually produced by a pick) on the guitar strings. Both aspects are important for solo performers accompanying themselves on the guitar. Guitarists working with a rhythm section or recording with a variety of instruments need to realise, though, that they no longer have to carry the whole of the rhythm with their strumming.

Effective strumming patterns balance tempo against sustain. At a slow tempo, you hit the strings more frequently because the chords die away. At faster tempos, you might not need to hit them so often, unless like Jimmy

Nolen or Nile Rodgers your guitar part is at least as significant for its percussive as for its harmonic effect.

To experiment with strumming, try first strumming eighths down and up, as in Example 1 in the strumming box left, and then start to subtract some of the strums to produce different rhythms.

Fingerpicking

Fingerpicking is a technique popular in less rhythmic arrangements and styles. It is vulnerable to being drowned out by a loud mix. It is typically used in light arrangements where the notes will be audible, often in ballads. It suits solo performance, since it offers the chance for a single guitarist to play a bassline, a harmony and even a melody, all at once.

Simple patterns are given first, then some in a syncopated style. Some of these can be played in a 'flatpicking' manner with a pick and the second and third fingers. This is handy if you suddenly want to strum in the middle of a song.

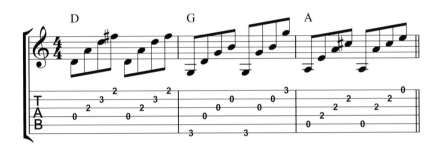

Simple upward pick

Simple reverse pick, changing bass notes

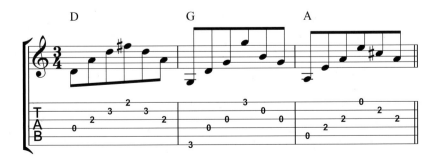

Simple triple-time pick

SECTION 6 | 105

Rhythm variation

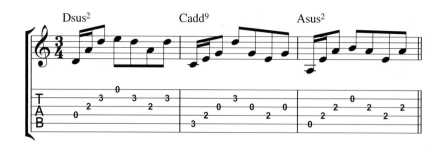

Alternating pick

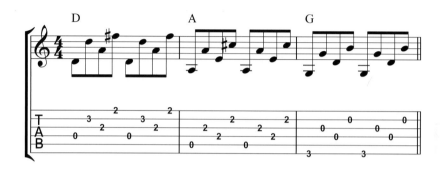

Up and down pick

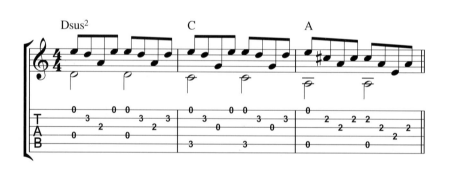

Thickening, ascending

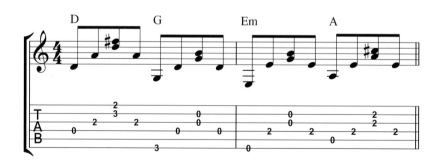

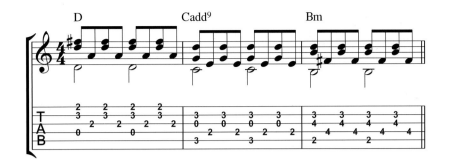

Thickening, descending

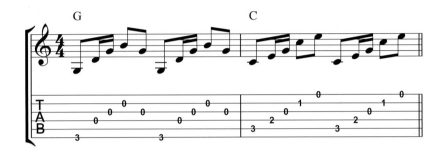

Rhythm variation

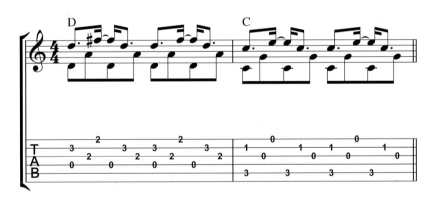

Syncopated, alternating thumb

SECTION 7
MELODY

Great melodies have a certain magic about them. They sound and feel right. They fit the lyric in such a way that it seems inevitable that those notes had to go with those words. Perhaps more than any other aspect of songwriting, writing a great melody is a matter of inspiration. No-one can compose a great melody to order. Even so, an appreciation of the characteristics of melodies – such as their shape, their rhythm, their intervals, and their relationship to the underlying chords – will help you to write better melodies, and to improve the ones that you have already composed.

More than anything else, melody impresses a song into the minds of its listeners. You hear people singing a popular song in the street, taking pleasure in recalling the tune. So what makes a good melody? And what makes a great melody?

How do you know which notes will fit with which chords? Many good songwriters rely on an 'ear' for this, sometimes backed up with no theoretical knowledge at all. For the rest of us, an understanding of a few fundamental principles for harmonising a tune can help, so you don't have to work entirely by instinct.

HARMONISING NOTES
Melody notes have three basic relationships with their accompanying chords. We can categorise these as 'inside', 'outside' and 'alien' notes.

1 Inside
A note is 'inside' when it is the 1, 3, or 5 of a chord. This means that when strumming a C chord, your melody note will be C, E, or G. If the chord is A minor, the melody note will be A, C, or E. A melody note that 'sits inside' blends perfectly because it is part of the chord. If the chord has more than three notes, you could sing the additional note of the harmony. For example, if you sing B against a Cmaj7 chord – C E G B – the note still sits inside, though not so perfectly as 1, 3, or 5. The more complex the chord, the weaker the effect if you sing one of additional notes.

2 Outside

A note is 'outside' when it is one of the notes of the key scale that isn't 1, 3 and 5. In the key of C major and singing over a C chord, you would thus choose D, F, A or B.

Each of these has a slightly different quality in relation to the chord, but they all sound more or less tense. You will feel they want to move to one of the notes of the chord and sit inside the harmony. This tension can be very expressive. If you listen to the end of his cover of 'A Good Year For The Roses', you can hear Elvis Costello come down to the key note (1) and then move off it on to 2 for a tenser, unresolved finish to the melody.

The strength of the tension also depends on how long you hold that note. Melodies consist of a mixture of notes that belong to a chord and those that don't. The notes that sit outside often occur as brief passing-notes lasting only a beat or less; their tension is momentary. If you stayed on such a note for more than a beat over a chord that did not change, then the tension increases.

If a melody were written using only the notes of the major and minor triads in the harmony (ie, all the melody notes fell into the category of 'sits inside'), it would run the risk of sounding bland and too comfortable. Music needs tension to give it drama and make it capable of fully expressing the range and complexity of human feelings. Tension, asymmetry, and dissonance are essential to this. That's why the notes of many good melodies move constantly from 'inside' to 'outside'.

3 Alien

A note is an 'alien' when it is not part of the key scale. In any given key there are always five alien notes. The technical name for them is 'chromatic'. In C major, they are C#/Db, D#/Eb, F#/Gb, G#/Ab and A#/Bb. These are dissonant (try singing F# against a C chord), but the flattened third and flattened seventh notes (Eb and Bb in C major) are very common in popular music. These are the so-called 'blue notes'. Singing them against C major is permitted if the music has a blues/soul influence. The harmonic discrepancy between them and the scale creates an effect that our ears interpret as 'blues'. This can be over-used in a predictable attempts at being 'soulful', when it is merely the exploitation of a formula.

Used with taste, these notes can be evocative. For a non-blues example of an alien note, Bjork's 'Army Of Me' implies the key of C minor (C D Eb F G Ab Bb), but the main melodic phrase has a recurring Db that fits the threatening mood of the song.

The classification of such notes is key and scale dependent. For example, here's a summary of the three melodic categories of note related to a C chord if the key is C major. (I = inside; O = outside; A = alien)

Scale degree											
1	b2	2	b3	3	4	#4	5	#5	6	b7	7
Note pitch											
C	Db	D	Eb	E	F	F#	G	G#	A	Bb	B
Category											
I	A	O	A	I	O	A	I	A	O	A	O

But in the key of G major, where C is chord IV, the Fs change category because F♯ belongs to the scale and F doesn't.

Scale degree											
4	♯4	5	♯5	6	♭7	7	1	♭2	2	♭3	3
Note pitch											
C	D♭	D	E♭	E	F	F♯	G	G♯	A	B♭	B
Category											
I	A	O	A	I	A	O	I	A	O	A	O

You may be thinking at this point, does this mean that composers sit down and think about this stuff when they write a tune? Did Lennon and McCartney have exchanges when they were writing 'Ticket To Ride' in which Lennon said (imagine the Liverpool accent), "Yer can't sing that note, Paul. It's an 'inside' note … it's too dull. Yer want a note that's an 'outside'"? Of course not. Most melodies are written instinctively, following words or chords or both, or by just humming something the songwriter 'hears' internally. But having the ability to focus on a couple of notes or a phrase and then apply some of these concepts is good craft. It can add polish to the finished song.

Knowledge of other melodic tricks and approaches can also be helpful for starting a tune. It is possible to write a two-bar melodic fragment and then develop the rest of the melody from that initial idea. Much of this you will do intuitively. But sometimes awareness can be brought to bear on a melody to get a better result. Knowledge of the craft of melody really pays off when it comes to developing melodic ideas and getting a feel for their potential.

OTHER MELODIC FEATURES
Contour
It is important to cultivate an aesthetic sensitivity to melody. Listen to melodies that really please you. What is it about them that does this? Listen for the rise and fall of a melody, the use of intervals, step-wise movements, rhythm, repetition, arpeggio figures (moving up and down the notes of a chord), and so on. Melodies combine these elements in innumerable ways. There are many more potential melodies than there are potential chord sequences.

Linear melody
Some melodies lie within a narrow range. Imagine writing a song in C major in which you used only the notes C, D, E, and the B below C. The entire melody would be spanned by no more than two-and-a-half tones (whole steps). This might work, but it runs the risk of not sustaining our interest because there won't be room for much melodic contour. Narrow-pitched melodies are sometimes the result of vocal limitations. Partly for this reason they are more common in male singer-songwriter material: Bob Dylan, Jackson Browne, and Bruce Springsteen have written many songs that exhibit linear, narrow-range melody. In Springsteen's case, it comes as a shock when he does a non-linear melody, as on 'Sad Eyes', where the chorus has what is for him an unexpected and beautiful melodic leap. It might be argued that The Verve's 'History' and 'This Time' are both flawed by melodies that spend too long on a single note.

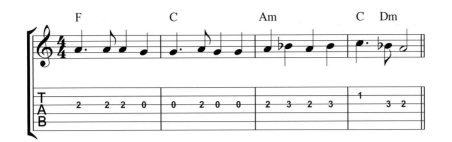

Linear

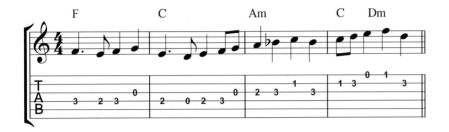

Stepwise, rising

Narrow-range melodies can be used in songs where the emphasis is on a satirical lyric, especially if the rate at which the words are delivered is fast. If Dylan's 'Subterranean Homesick Blues' were set to a melody with soaring intervals it would sound comic, and Dylan would have found it difficult to sing. The same is true of R.E.M.'s 'It's The End Of The World As We Know It', and their 2008 songs 'Living Well Is The Best Revenge', 'Accelerate', and 'Man Sized Wreath'.

Linear melodies that remain on one note for a long time can sound 'trippy' with the right backing; The Beatles' 'Tomorrow Never Knows' and 'I Am The Walrus' are good examples. 'Helter Skelter' and 'Sgt. Pepper' both stay for quite a while on a single note within each chord change. All About Eve's 'Infrared' has a melody largely on one note for many bars at a time, in imitation of Syd Barrett-era Pink Floyd songs such as 'Astronomy Domine'. Songs such as John Lennon's 'Give Peace A Chance', Kate Bush's 'The Sensual World', and Elvis Costello's 'Pump It Up' feature a verse sung almost entirely on one note for a punchy effect. The T. Rex hits 'Ride A White Swan', 'Get It On' and 'Telegram Sam' use a narrow range of notes like the Chuck Berry songs on which they were modelled.

For a different perspective, listen to the chorus of The Jackson Five's 'I Want You Back', where the second line of the chorus lyric is sung almost entirely on the note C. This works because each note is harmonised with a different chord, and so the harmonic value of the note C changes with each chord:

Melody note:	C	C	C	C	C
Chord:	Fm	Cm	D♭	A♭	B♭m
Chord In A♭:	VI	III	IV	I	II
Chord note:	5	1	7	3	2 (9)
Note type:	I	I	O	I	O

(I = inside note, O = outside note)

SECTION 7 | **111**

Vertical melody

Vertical

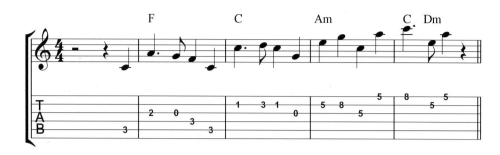

Vertical melodies feature frequent large interval leaps and span an octave or more. These are often composed by female singer-songwriters such as Joni Mitchell, Kate Bush and Tori Amos, who have more vocal range to exploit than many of their male counterparts (though there are exceptions, such as Sting, Robert Plant, Smokey Robinson, Leo Sayer and Colin Blunstone). The Beatles' 'Penny Lane' and 'In My Life', The La's 'There She Goes', The Casuals' 'Jesamine' and Cilla Black's 'Alfie' are songs with strong vertical melodies.

Melodies built on the notes of a chord (arpeggios) tend to be vertical. Burt Bacharach's melodies often develop chordal melodic ideas. Think of the opening of The Carpenters' 'Close To You', with its leap of notes E-G-D against a C chord. The first two notes are inside notes, but the last one (D) is an outside note and creates an expressive tension.

Chordal

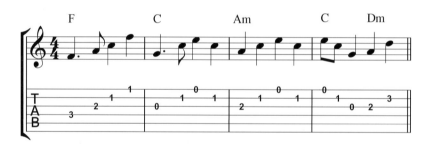

One effective way to start a melody is with an interval leap – anything bigger than a fourth. The most dramatic is the octave, as in the Rodgers and Hammerstein tune 'Bali Hai' from the musical *South Pacific* and Led Zeppelin's 'Immigrant Song', where Robert Plant turns the octave figure into a Viking war cry by going up an octave, down a semitone (half-step) and back to the octave.

Falling intervals

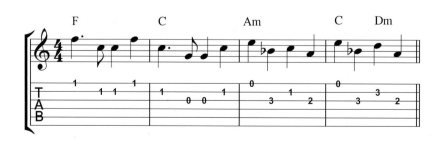

Table of intervals

Number	Degree	Interval	Distance	Name
1	Tonic	C to C	0	Unison
♭2		C to D♭	1	Minor second
2	Supertonic	C to D	2	Major second
♭3		C to E♭	3	Minor third
3	Mediant	C to E	4	Major third
4	Sub-dominant	C to F	5	Perfect fourth
+4		C to F♯	6	Augmented fourth
-5		C to G♭	6	Diminished fifth
5	Dominant	C to G	7	Perfect fifth
+5		C to G♯	8	Augmented fifth
-6		C to A♭	8	Minor sixth
6	Sub-mediant	C to A	9	Major sixth
-7	Sub-mediant	C to B♭♭	9	Diminished seventh
♭7		C to B♭	10	Minor seventh
7	Leading note	C to B	11	Major seventh
8 (1)	Tonic	C to C	12	Perfect Octave

Using chromatic notes

'Alien' or chromatic notes used as frequent passing notes between others that belong to the scale can create some intriguing effects. They spice up a melody and can sound jazzy and sophisticated. If you linger on a chromatic note, you may need to support it in the harmony with an unusual chord of some sort. Listen to Andy Williams's 'Can't Get Used To Losing You' and many of Elvis Costello's later songs for chromatic notes and other unexpected twists.

Chromatic

Rhythm and timing

Remember that a melody also has rhythm, and this rhythm needs to be appropriate for the words and the overall rhythm of the song. Listen for how long or short a melodic phrase is, and which notes are emphasised by the rhythm. Many Michael Jackson hits have melodies in which the rhythm of the melody is more noticeable than the harmonic value of the notes. Consider the rhythm of melodies such as Sacha Distel's 'This Guy's In Love With You', The Kinks' 'All Day And All Of The Night', Marshall Crenshaw's 'Laughter' or Kate Bush's 'Suspended In Gaffa'. Be aware of the beat you use to start a phrase. Watch out that you don't put unimportant words such as prepositions in prominent places – like having 'the' on the first beat of a bar.

Smooth rhythm

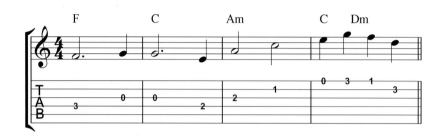

Staccato rhythmic

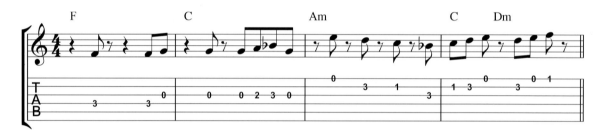

Maximising a melodic phrase

A melodic phrase can be transposed by the same interval with which a chord sequence is moved up. In other words, when you change chords, simply sing the same tune but higher by the same distance. This way of developing melodic material is called 'sequential repetition'. You can hear this in the climbing sequence of the verse in Queen's 'Now I'm Here', and in Beach Boys songs like 'Good Vibrations' and in the chorus of 'California Girls'.

Reharmonising

The same melodic line will sound different if you vary the chords underneath it. In the verse of The Beatles' 'Yes It Is', the same melody is used for two lines of lyric. The first time it is harmonised I-IV-II-V, the second time I-IV-♭VII-V. The third chord, F♯m in the original key of E, is replaced by a chord that is major, D. The switch from minor to major makes the melody sound different, even though its notes are the same. (The vocal harmony changes in keeping with the substituted chord.) In the first and second verses of Scott MacKenzie's 'If You're Going To San Francisco', the first four bars are:

VI	IV	I	V
Em	C	G	D

114 | SECTION 7

In the last verse, this is reharmonised as:

VI	II	IV	I	III	V
Em	Am	C	G	Bm	D

The additional minor chords add a poignant twist. Other examples of this device include the choruses of Meat Loaf's 'Paradise By The Dashboard Light' and Bryan Adams's 'Cloud No. 9', where the chorus has a substitution of VI for chord I (Bm for D). In the chorus of U2's 'Stuck In A Moment You Can't Get Out Of' the hook melody is reharmonised when a first inversion chord I (E/G♯) is replaced by III^ (G♯).

Counter-melody

One of the most powerful devices for making a song commercial is the counter-melody. A counter-melody is sung by a second voice (or backing vocalists), sometimes using different words. A good counter-melody can not only liven up the repetition of a verse but lend devastating strength to the chorus by effectively multiplying the number of hooks. This can be heard on The Casuals' 'Jesamine', The Fortunes' 'You've Got Your Troubles, I've Got Mine', The Beatles' 'Help' and 'Hello Goodbye', The Beach Boys' 'I Get Around', Amen Corner's 'If Paradise Is Half As Nice', Manfred Mann's 'My Name Is Jack' and 'Fox On The Run' (last ch), and the R.E.M. songs 'Near Wild Heaven', 'Fall On Me', and 'It's The End Of The World As We Know It' (ch). The early R.E.M. albums have many inventive shared vocal parts.

One individual can happily sing the tune of a hit song. But not so with a hit that has a counter-melody – a single voice cannot sing both parts at once. Therefore, the only way of satisfying the need to hear the song is to play the track again.

Personal style in melody

Singers and songwriters often develop, sometimes unconsciously, certain melodic, harmonic, and rhythmic habits, which lend their compositions a certain 'fingerprint'. It could be a favourite tempo or chord sequence or key change, or a habit of building the tune around certain notes. If you've been writing songs for a while, can you identify any things you tend to repeat? Do these fingerprints create a strong musical identity? Or do they make all your songs sound the same? If so, more awareness enables you to change whatever needs to be changed. For example, check to see if you are always starting a melody on the same note of the chord.

When Morrissey came to fame as vocalist of The Smiths, I often heard or read the opinion that the band's songs sounded too similar to each other. One major reason for this was Morrissey's use of certain step-wise movements in his melodies, regardless of what the chord sequences were doing. He was fond of starting tunes on the fifth note of the scale and moving step-wise down: 5, 4, 3 and then to 1. He also excluded any blue notes and blues-influenced phrasing. This gave The Smiths a more English sound. Around the time of the albums *Green* and *Out Of Time*, Michael Stipe of R.E.M. repeatedly moved from scale degrees 1 to 4 and 3, exploiting the tension of the 4. Joni Mitchell often ends phrases on the blue ♭7 note and then rises slowly to the 1. Her melodies are also full of unpredictable leaps and descents. Paul Rodgers of Free (now singing with Queen) established an immediately recognisable style with heavy use of blue notes, especially the ♭3 and ♭7. Many classic Beach Boys tunes have phrases that end with a decorative 5-4-3 flourish, a trick copied by 1990s bands like Supergrass in 'Alright' (bridge) and Foo Fighters in 'This Is A Call'. Natalie Merchant's melodies with 10,000 Maniacs were often similar to each other. During the mid-1960s Dylan often created tension in his melodies by singing the fourth note of his underlying chord.

Singers

A melody can be given a certain amount of spontaneous decoration. This is called 'melisma' and is frequently heard in blues, gospel and soul and their derivatives. Soul singers such as Aretha Franklin, Sam Cooke, Otis Redding, Wilson Pickett, and their white counterparts and admirers – Dusty Springfield, Janis Joplin, Joe Cocker, Rod Stewart – decorate melodies by extending notes in various ways at the end of phrases. In the 1990s, this was taken to hideous extremes by Whitney Houston, following the example of Michael Jackson and Stevie Wonder. She often seemed to use a melody to show off her vocal technique with rapid downward and upward scales at the end of a word. For the past ten years or so this has been endemic in chart hits with any soul/hip-hop connection. This can be as witless and redundant as a heavy metal guitar solo. Don't over-decorate a melody – let it speak for itself.

SECTION 8
HOW TO WRITE A LYRIC

It's not unusual (to quote Tom Jones) to meet songwriters who find the hardest part of songwriting is not the music but the words. Sometimes this difficulty arises from having too high expectations, with the consequence that everything you write seems terrible. Another problem is trying to write words that have impact even without the music. But listen to many contemporary Top 40 hits and you will realise that the current standard of lyric writing is pretty poor. The sheer banality of many hit singles (especially in dance music) is striking. From this you can take heart. Maybe your words are not so bad after all – maybe they will still do the job, commercially, even if they wouldn't cause Bob Dylan to lose sleep.

Like melody and harmony, lyric writing is a subject that deserves a book in its own right (so to delve deeper than this section's overview, get a copy of my book *Lyrics*). That said, here we will look at a few tips and points of craft. If you have never written or completed a lyric, the next few pages will provide some ideas. If you have already written some song lyrics but are frustrated because you seem to write the same thing over and over, or feel you lack inspiration, then here's food for thought.

Are lyrics poetry?

This confusion of two distinct crafts often leads to a good deal of trouble for people in the early stages of writing songs. The answer is simple, though: do not confuse poetry and song lyrics. Muddling the two is not helpful when it comes to practical songwriting.

It is true that some lyrics read interestingly away from the music, and might have a poetic quality in their imagery or phrasing. The idea that lyrics are a kind of poetry has been encouraged in recent years by the publication in book-form of lyrics by songwriters such as Sting, Dylan, and Springsteen. But poetic qualities alone do not make a song lyric a poem. The language of poetry is often too complex to be set to music (though art song has a long tradition of setting shorter poems). Poetry is intended to convey meaning and emotion purely through words. True poetry has much less tolerance of cliché than lyrics. There are images you can get away with in a song lyric that you could never use in poetry.

A song lyric is a set of words whose effect depends upon, and is symbiotic with, music. The music can supply whatever profundity is not there in the words. A banal phrase delivered by a great singer like Levi Stubbs or Aretha Franklin can sound fresh and full of meaning. In the same way, great music can excuse or even temporarily revive clichéd words and images.

Music is such a powerful modifier of meaning that a lyric essentially saying "I hate you" could end up leaving the listener with the impression that although the singer *says* he hates her (or she hates him), actually he still loves her. Take 10cc's 'I'm Not In Love'. In this song, the speaker is at pains to insist that he does not feel strong emotion for the addressee, yet the poignant music is undermining all his denials and turning them into excuses. He is saying that he's not in love to the very end. In the end, though, the speaker never comes clean and admits it. In Dylan's 'Just Like A Woman' the music seems to be almost rebelling against the acid disdain of the lyric. Other songs that have a marked tension between lyric and music include The Police's 'Every Breath You Take', Blue Oyster Cult's 'Don't Fear The Reaper' and Elvis Costello's 'Oliver's Army'. The respective themes of possessiveness, suicide and imperialism are deliberately presented in musical disguise, the bitter pill sugar-coated. And all three were big hits.

If you do happen to have a notebook of poems, some may well lend themselves to being abbreviated and re-written as song-lyrics.

THE SEARCH FOR A THEME: WHAT SHALL I WRITE ABOUT?

How often have you dreaded the moment when you had to put down the guitar, face a blank sheet of paper, reach for a pen, and be struck by the feeling that you didn't know what to write about. The search for a theme lies at the forefront of the business of penning lyrics. The most common subject in popular song is, of course, romantic love. Adapting the title of the famous psychotherapy book *I'm OK, You're OK*, we can amuse ourselves by grouping love-song lyrics in accordance with which of these existential positions they express.

Existential positions in the love song

Our starting point is simple and straightforward:

I love you, you love me (the bliss song).

Happy songs are harder to write than unhappy ones, as most songwriters know. Happy songs that celebrate fulfilled love are apt to rub listeners the wrong way – because they're often sentimental, banal, over-simplified, liable to arouse envy, or seem unrealistic.

Happy love lyrics benefit from an element of drama. This could be adversity or a problem of some kind – some kind of 'but' that clouds the picture. So let's introduce some complications. How about qualifying the happiness with a time factor:

I love you, you love me … tonight (but maybe not tomorrow).
I love you, you love me … forever (so let's get married as soon as …).
I love you, you love me … but I'm so much older/younger than you.

Love can be complicated by external factors such as geography and the demands of life and work:

I love you, you love me … but I'm/you're leaving for a while.
I love you, you love me … but we're far apart.

Or by constrictions closer to home:

I love you, you love me … but my/your/our parents don't agree.

Or by moral conflicts, owing to a run-in with The Law:

I love you, you love me … but I've/you've just killed a man/woman (cue 'Bohemian Rhapsody').

Or by the sufferings of mortality:

I love you, you loved me … but you're dead (have a cry in the chapel).

Or by the mysteries of fate:

I love you … I've always loved you (the star-fated-lovers-meeting song).
I love you … wherever you are (the one-day-I'll-find-you song).

Lyrics thrive on trouble of some kind. Songwriters are more often inspired by turbulence and conflict than bliss, peace, serenity, and happiness. Imagine a version of 'Satisfaction' with Mick Jagger singing "Ah've gat lats erf … sah-tiz-fak-shun!" Not quite the same, is it? So here are existential positions for the love lyric where things are not going smoothly:

I love you, you don't love me yet … but you will (the heroic determination song).
I love you, hey! your luck's in! (the how-can-you-resist me? song).
I love you, you don't love me, and I'm going to die (the unrequited love torture song).
I love you but I'm not going to admit it (the exquisite self-denial song).

I don't love you, you love me (the isn't-life-ironic regret song).
I love you, you don't love me anymore, and I give up (or I don't give up).
I love you, you don't love me anymore, but I'll always be here for you
(the Diana Ross Big Orchestra Self-Immolation Special).
I don't love you, you don't love me … any more (the shall-we-be-noble-about-this? song).
I don't love you, but I used to (the free-at-last, move-on-up, I will survive song).
I love you, you say you love me, but maybe you love him (the jealous-guy song).

SECTION 8 | 119

These situations are capable of an infinite variety of lyrical and musical treatments. As the cliché goes, the whole of human life is there.

Triangular existential positions in love songs

If you want to be mischievous, you can generate much more trouble by playing a three-card version of the love lyric – namely, the introduction of The Other Person.

I love you, you love me, and he/she can only watch and regret.

I love you, you love me … tonight (while he/she is away).
I love you, you love me … for ever (so let's get our divorces).
I love you, you love me … but he's/she's taking me away for a while.
I love you, you love me … even though I'm with her/him right now.

I love you … I've always loved you, but why couldn't you have appeared 10 years ago?

I love you, you don't love me yet … but you will because I'll treat you right.
I love you, so does he, but I'm the better bet.
I love you, you don't love me because you love him … but he doesn't love you either.
I love you but I'm not going to admit it because you belong to my best friend.

I don't love you, you love me, but we don't have a future.
I love you, you don't love me any more because you've gone back to her/him.

He loves you, but I love you more.
He doesn't love you so why don't you forget him / come on over to me.

The non-romantic love song

The category of love songs ought to also include love between friends and family. This is not so often dealt with and can be more startling as a result. There are family relationships to write about – with mothers (Kate Bush's 'Mother Stands For Comfort' and 'The Coral Room', Madonna's 'Promise To Try'), fathers (Tori Amos's 'Winter', U2's 'Sometimes You Can't Make It On Your Own'), siblings and other relatives (Sly & The Family Stone's 'It's A Family Affair', Gilbert O'Sullivan's 'Alone Again (Naturally)', The Undertones' 'My Perfect Cousin') children (Kate Bush's 'Bertie', Gilbert O'Sullivan's 'We Will') and also friends, some of whom might be wayward (Free's 'My Brother Jake', John Martyn's 'Solid Air').

A fine example of a friendship song would be Simon and Garfunkel's 'The Only Living Boy In New York', a song which is almost unaccountably greater than the sum of its parts. The lyric describes the speaker remaining in the Big Apple while a friend called Tom, who is praised for his honesty, flies down to Mexico. The lyric is enigmatic – it does not explain the situation – while the music is reverberant, softly spoken, wistful, and ethereal. Unlike romantic songs, where declarations of selfless love often turn out to be anything but (being driven by desire), 'The Only Living Boy In New York' really does glow with a selfless love, like a room lit up by reflected light from snow outside.

Sexual encounters

Needless to say, many times what appears to be a love song is, consciously or unconsciously, really about sex. There are a huge number of songs about sex and sexual encounters, comprising all shades of innocence and explicitness. Songwriters have tried all kinds of ingenious procedures to disguise what their songs are really about in this field. Think of Rod Stewart's 'Maggie May' (the schoolboy and the hooker) or 'Tonight's The Night', Extreme's 'More Than Words' (the persuasion song), Gary Puckett & The Union Gap's 'Young Girl' (illicit love), Abba's 'Does Your Mother Know', Billy Paul's 'Me and Mrs. Jones', Dusty Springfield's 'Some Of Your Lovin'', Roberta Flack's 'Help Me Make It Through The Night', Marvin Gaye's 'Let's Get It On' and 'Sexual Healing', The Beatles' 'Norwegian Wood', The Buzzcocks' 'Orgasm Addict', Frankie Goes to Hollywood's 'Relax', Bad Company's 'Feel Like Makin' Love', The Rolling Stones' 'Let's Spend The Night Together', Wings' 'Hi Hi Hi', Maria Muldaur's 'Midnight At The Oasis', Jane Birkin and Serge Gainsbourg's 'Je T'Aime (Moi Non Plus)', Prince Buster's 'Wet Dream', Pulp's 'This Is Hardcore', Siouxsie & The Banshees' 'Melt' and, of course, vast tracts of Prince's back catalogue.

Given the relationship between pop music, teenagers, and confusion over sexual identity, it's not surprising this should also be an issue in songs such as The Who's 'I'm A Boy' and 'Pictures Of Lily', Blur's 'Girls And Boys', Johnny Cash's 'A Boy Named Sue', The Kinks' 'Lola', Lou Reed's 'Walk On The Wild Side', Billy Bragg's 'Sexuality', Madness's 'House Of Fun', and The Undertones' 'Teenage Kicks'– all of which deal with teenage sexuality. The Shirelles' 'Will You Still Love Me Tomorrow?' looks at this issue from a distinctly female perspective, as do Madonna's 'Papa Don't Preach' and 'Like A Virgin'.

SUBJECTS OTHER THAN LOVE

There are hundreds of possible categories of theme that have been (and will be) the subject of song lyrics. Here are a few categories to get your imagination working. Some songs fit more than one category.

Geography

Write a song about a place, travelling into the unknown, living in a city or in the country, or wanting to live somewhere else. This involves much more than mere description of a place. It encompasses such profound questions as: Where are you? Where have you been? Where do you want to be?

Geography has been highly significant in American song lyrics. There are so many songs named after American places that you could construct an atlas out of them. Sufjan Stevens has released whole albums of songs about states like Michigan and Illinois. The Thrills' *So Much For The City* included songs entitled 'Santa Cruz (You're Not That Far)', 'Big Sur', 'Hollywood Kids', and 'Your Love Is Like Las Vegas'. The USA is so big and varied in terrain and culture that it can seem plausible that a better life waits for you at the end of a long highway. This is a big theme in the blues music of the migrating workers from the South in the early 20th century, and the idea of travelling to the Promised Land is important in the music of Bruce Springsteen.

Here are a few famous songs with American place names in their titles: 'Do You Know The Way To San Jose?', 'Anchorage', 'Wichita Lineman', 'Boulder To Birmingham', 'Sweet Home Alabama', 'Stuck Inside of Mobile With The Memphis Blues Again', 'If You're Going To San Francisco', 'New York, New York', 'No Sleep Till Brooklyn', 'LA Woman', 'Pasadena', 'Viva Las Vegas', 'What Made Milwaukee Famous', 'Yellow Rose Of Texas', 'Don't Go Back To Rockville', 'Witch Queen Of New Orleans', 'Lights Of Cincinnati', '(Is This The Way To) Amarillo', 'California Dreamin'', 'California Uber Alles', 'Californication', 'Mississippi Queen', 'Toledo', 'Baltimore', 'Atlantic City', 'Philadelphia Freedom', 'Please Come To Boston', 'The Night Chicago Died', 'Blue Moon Of Kentucky', 'Night Train To Georgia', 'Kansas City', 'Kokomo', 'Union City Blue', 'By The Time I Get To Phoenix', 'San Bernadino', 'Love Field', 'Nantucket Sleighride', 'Roll Plymouth Rock', 'All The Way To Reno', 'Texarkana', and 'Massachusetts'.

Even if the place is not in the title, it can be in the lyric. Chuck Berry listed place names in 'Sweet Little Sixteen' and The Beach Boys did likewise in 'Surfin' USA' and 'California Girls'. The Beatles returned the compliment in 'Back In The USSR'.

British songwriters aren't as free to use geography because the UK is smaller. There are plenty of place names in the traditional folk songs of the British Isles (think of 'Scarborough Fair'), but they date from an age when the lack of transport made the country effectively bigger. A British songwriter invites ridicule if he or she tries to suggest in the manner of Springsteen that spiritual salvation or a new life lies at the end of a motorway. A British songwriter who starts a song (apologies to Jimmy Webb) with a line like "By the time I get to Plymouth, she'll be waiting ..." is liable to get a laugh. Billy Bragg's wonderful take-off of 'Route 66', 'The A127', had UK audiences laughing as it name-checked the singularly unromantic Basildon, Wapping, Dagenham, and Southend. This didn't stop Kula Shaker from celebrating the 'A303', which is, in fact, a delightful road – but UK audiences are prejudiced against this idea. The English can't see their country as heroic and epic in the way that the Scots and the Welsh do. Maybe it's the lack of mountains.

Popular songs do, however, often mention London and its environs: 'Streets Of London', 'Waterloo Sunset', 'London Calling', 'London, Can You Wait?', 'London Traffic', 'A-Bomb In Wardour Street', 'London', 'Londinium', 'Finchley Central', 'Baker Street', 'West End Girls', 'Portobello Road', 'Wild West End', 'I Don't Want To Go To Chelsea', 'Last Night In Soho', 'White Man In The Hammersmith Palais'. The nearest we get to Chuck Berry's roll-call of place names in 'Sweet Little Sixteen' is The Smiths' 'Panic', which mentions London, Birmingham, Dublin, Dundee, Humberside, Grasmere (in the Lake District), Leeds and Carlisle. There's also been 'Winchester Cathedral', 'Fog On The Tyne', 'Long-haired Lover From Liverpool', 'Solsbury Hill', 'Penny Lane', 'England Swings', 'England Rocks', 'Oh England My Lionheart' and 'Strawberry Fields Forever'. The Isle Of Wight gets a mention in The Who's 'Happy Jack' and The Beatles' 'When I'm Sixty Four', and Salisbury in Kate Bush's 'Sat In Your Lap'.

Telephones and letters

Places often evoke distances, and distances evoke separated people, who need either letters and telephones or transport. Lyrics based on phone calls include 'Memphis, Tennessee', 'South Central Rain', 'Rikki Don't Lose That Number', 'Beechwood 4-5789', 'Telephone Line', 'Telefone (Long Distance Love Affair)', 'Girl On The Phone', 'Baby Don't Forget My Number', 'Just Seven Numbers (Can Straighten Out My Life)', 'I Just Called To Say I Love You', 'At My Most Beautiful' and 'Hanging On The Telephone'. 'Sylvia's Mother' had a protagonist who kept getting asked for another 40 cents by the operator (less likely these days with cellphones). The mail features in 'The Letter', 'Please Mr Postman', 'Return To Sender', 'Dear John', 'Letter To Hermione', 'A Letter To Dominique', 'Paperback Writer', and 'P.S. I Love You'. Mobile phones, email, and video-links will probably feature in pop hits of the 21st century.

Cars

Ever since Chuck Berry and the birth of rock'n'roll at a time when teenagers were obsessed with getting their hands on the wheel, pop lyrics have often revolved around cars: 'Pink Cadillac', 'Little Red Corvette', 'Mustang Sally', 'Drive My Car', 'Day Tripper', 'Cars', 'A Car That Sped', 'Big Yellow Taxi', 'Little Deuce Coupe', 'Mercedes Benz', 'Car Wash', 'Get Outta My Dreams, Get Into My Car', 'No Money Down', 'Baby Driver', 'Racing In The Streets', 'No Particular Place To Go', '2-4-6-8 Motorway', 'Don't Worry Baby', 'Tell Laura I Love Her', and 'Pink Thunderbird'. There are many car songs in Bruce Springsteen's albums. Driving a car often becomes an image for a certain other popular activity, as in 'Radar Love'. 'Convoy' took care of long-distance lorries and made popular the expression "rubber duck". It can only be a matter of time before someone in a pop lyric undertakes a car journey and refers to the "sat-nav".

Trains

Train songs include '5:15', 'Last Train To Clarksville' (which also features a telephone call), 'The Day We Caught The Train', 'Train Kept A-Rollin'', 'Rock Island Line', 'It Takes A Lot To Laugh, It Takes A Train To Cry', 'Morning Train (9 To 5)', 'Mystery Train', and 'Runaway Train'.

Crime and punishment

In songs such as 'Hey Joe' and 'Killing Floor', the singer hopes to escape the Long Arm Of The Law by going down (usually) to Mexico. If you're British and you've just shot your woman down then it's a bit harder because going way down south will only mean you end up in Sussex or Dorset – which is not far enough. If the singer is also in love at this point, we have plenty of drama. 'Indiana Wants Me', 'I've Just Got To Get A Message To You', 'The Green, Green Grass Of Home', 'Last Night In Soho', and 'Gotta See Jane' are further instances. If there isn't an execution and the prisoner is released, you get 'Tie A Yellow Ribbon 'Round The Old Oak Tree'. (On second thoughts, throw that switch, y'all!)

Names

Since so many popular songs have been about love, it's not surprising there are so many songs whose titles include, or are, a woman's name. How many names in this list can you match to the correct artist?

Alison, Amanda, Amelia, Angie, Annie, Barbara Ann, Bernadette, Beth, Betty, Billie Jean, Brandy, Bridget, Candida, Candy, Carol, Caroline, Carrie Ann, Cathy, Cecilia, Cindy, Clair, Claudette, Debora, Delilah, Diana, Dolly, Donna, Eileen, Elaine, Eleanor, Elise, Eloise, Emma, Emily, Gaye, Jackie, Jane, Jean, Jesamine, Jennifer, Jenny, Jessie, Johanna, Jolene, Judy, Julia, Julie, Juliette, Kayleigh, Lana, Layla, Lily, Linda, Lucille, Lucy, Maggie, Mandy, Maria, Marie, Martha, Mary, Mary Lou, Maybelline, Michelle, Natalie, Nikita, Nikki, Pamela, Patricia, Paula, Peggy Sue, Polly, Prudence, Rhonda, Rita, Rosalita, Roseanna, Rosetta, Rosie, Roxanne, Sadie, Sally, Samantha, Sara, Sharona, Sheila, Sherry, Shirley, Stephanie, Sue, Suzanne, Suzie, Sylvia, Tammy, Tracy, Valerie, Virginia, Wendy. (Phew!)

The urban landscape

For decades a large percentage of the world's population have lived in cities. So it is fitting that many popular songs evoke aspects of city and town life, though they don't necessarily refer to specific places: 'Bus Stop', 'Heartbreak Hotel', '59th Street Bridge Song', 'Twenty Flight Rock' (about a girl who lived on the 20th floor), 'No Milk Today', 'Another Day', 'Don't Sleep In The Subway', 'Down In The Tube Station At Midnight', 'Strange Town', 'Ghost Town', 'Babylon's Burning', 'Downtown', 'Disco 2000', 'Want Ads', 'Rent', 'Expresso Love', 'Money For Nothing', 'Walk Of Life', 'Pinball Wizard', 'YMCA', 'Semi-Detached Suburban Mr Jones', 'At The Chime Of A City Clock', and 'Fire Brigade'. There are also songs about leaving the city for the country: 'Take Me Home, Country Roads' and 'I'm Gonna Be A Country Girl Again'.

Answer songs and parodies

If you're stuck for lyric ideas, why not write an 'answer' song? The Silhouettes' 'Get A Job' was answered by the Miracles' 'Got A Job'. The titles of 'Heartbreak Hotel' and 'Hotel Happiness' are obviously linked. Would The Faces' 'Miss Judy's Farm' have existed without Dylan's 'Maggie's Farm'? Similarly, Amy Winehouse titled a song 'Me and Mr Jones' after Billie Paul's 'Me and Mrs Jones'. Brian Wilson wrote 'Caroline, No' and The Kaiser Chiefs wrote 'Caroline, Yes' in reply.

You can do this with your own songs, and in commercial songwriting there has often been pressure on writers to come up with a sequel in the same mould. One label that practised this method was Motown. The title of 'Baby I Need Your Loving', The Four Tops' first hit, started the lyric of the follow-up 'Without The One You Love'. Holland-Dozier-Holland drew attention to this technique with breathtaking honesty in 'It's The Same Old Song' (though if that follow-up is considered a pale imitation, it's one that most songwriters would give their right arm for). The Supremes' 'Love Child' was succeeded by another social-conscience theme, 'I'm Livin' In Shame', and Edwin Starr was reportedly not thrilled when Motown wanted to emulate the success of 'War' with 'Stop The War Now'. In each case, the follow-ups were not as successful.

Try starting a verse with the first line of another song and put a twist on the original's theme. Echoing Cliff Richard's innocent 'Summer Holiday', Elvis

Costello sang Cliff's first line over an arch I-VI-IV-V progression, only to continue with a distinctly un-Cliff reference to being followed by vigilantes in 'The Beat', a song about teenage lust. In 'Possession', he quoted the opening couplet of The Beatles' 'From Me To You'.

Parody

Parody is a special category of lyric that usually involves rewriting the original's lyric but retaining its music. The Wurzels' 'I've Got A Brand New Combine Harvester' parodied Melanie's 'Brand New Key', and Billy Connolly parodied Tammy Wynette's 'D-I-V-O-R-C-E' with a tale of a "wee scabby dog". The legal wrangle over George Harrison's 'My Sweet Lord' and its alleged resemblance to 'He's So Fine' was lent additional colour by The Chiffons then re-recording 'He's So Fine' in the style of Harrison, while Jonathan King, ever the opportunist, did 'My Sweet Lord' in the arrangement style of 'He's So Fine' (doo lang doo lang doo lang, indeed!).

Time

Our relationship to past, present and future is an abiding source of song lyric ideas. The thing we call time has inspired many songs, including 'Time After Time' (Cyndi Lauper, Chris Montez, and R.E.M.), 'Time Is On My Side', 'Time Is Tight', and 'Time Of The Season'.

Time encompasses a huge theme like memory ('Fields Of Gold', 'All Those Years Ago', 'In My Life', 'Those Were The Days') as well as being young ('Sweet Little Sixteen', 'At Seventeen', 'This Used To Be My Playground', 'Summer Holiday', 'In My Room', 'School's Out', 'Almost Grown'), leaving home ('She's Leaving Home', 'The Dean And I'), and broader songs of exile such as 'No Woman No Cry'. Songs about growing old tend to be jokey ('When I'm Sixty Four', 'Your Mother Should Know'), but 'Silver Threads Among The Gold' is a touching lyric.

Some songs have been inspired by the time of day: 'Midnight Hour', 'Stay With Me Till Dawn', 'Quarter To Three', 'Angel Of The Morning', 'All Night Long', 'Afternoon Delight', 'Rock Around The Clock', 'Reelin' And Rockin'', 'School Days (Ring! Ring! Goes The Bell)'. There are songs about days of the week: 'Lazy Sunday', 'That Sunday That Summer', 'Pleasant Valley Sunday', 'Sunday's Best', 'Rainy Days And Mondays', 'Manic Monday', 'Monday Monday', 'Tuesday Afternoon', 'Ruby Tuesday', 'Everything's Tuesday', 'Wednesday Morning 3am', 'It's Friday I'm In Love', 'Friday Night', 'Friday On My Mind', 'Saturday Night', 'Saturday Nite Is Dead', and 'Saturday Night's Alright For Fighting'.

Quite a few songs mention months or seasons: 'January', 'January February', 'April Love', 'April Come She Will', 'First Of May', '4th of July Asbury Park', 'In The Summertime', 'It's Summer', 'It Might As Well Rain Until September', 'Autumn Almanac', 'November Rain', 'December Will Be Magic Again', 'Hazy Shade Of Winter'. Some years have been memorialised in song: Mott The Hoople's 'Late In '58', 'December, 1963', The Stooges' '1969', 'Summer of '69', Ash's '1977', Smashing Pumpkins' '1979', Jimi Hendrix's '1983' and Prince's '1999'. And there is, of course, a whole genre of songs about Christmas.

Or you can write a song about a historical event. 'The Night They Drove Old Dixie Down' is an evocation of the American Civil War. 'Born In The USA' and 'Pull Out The Pin' recall the Vietnam war. 'Cities In Dust' refers to the eruption of Mt. Vesuvius that buried Pompeii. Often such songs have a protest element in them – like Neil Young's 'Ohio' or 'Alabama'. Other historical examples include Joni Mitchell's 'Woodstock' and 'Amelia', 'Enola Gay', and 'The Wreck Of The Edmund Fitzgerald'. History can itself be a source of metaphors, as with Abba's 'Waterloo'.

Famous people

Many songs focus on famous people and celebrate (or criticise) their lives and deeds. Don McLean's two most famous songs celebrated the music of Buddy Holly ('American Pie', re-recorded by Madonna) and the painter Vincent Van Gogh ('Vincent'). Other artists (of various types) who are the subjects of songs include Mozart, Beethoven, Delius, Woody Guthrie, Elvis Presley, Gene Vincent, Levi Stubbs, Smokey Robinson, Scarlet O'Hara, Bette Davis, Marilyn Monroe, John Wayne, Robert de Niro, Michael Caine, Andy Warhol, and Andy Kaufman. Madonna name-checked many Hollywood celebrities in 'Vogue', and Ian Dury wrote about Noel Coward, Van Gogh, Einstein, and Segovia in 'There Ain't 'Alf Been Some Clever Bastards'. It is always hip to drop the name of the British group T. Rex, judging by citations in 'All The Young Dudes', 'You Better You Bet' and 'Wake-Up Bomb' (where Michael Stipe promises to practise his 'T. Rex moves'). The Who's 'The Seeker' mentions references to many 1960s counter-culture figures.

Historical figures as Davy Crockett, Lady Godiva, Robin Hood, Christopher Columbus, Gary Gilmore, Al Capone, St. Augustine, General Custer, Richard III, Henry VIII, Houdini, Nostradamus, and Jack The Ripper have had songs written about them. Political figures who have made it into songs include Steve Biko, Nelson Mandela, and Joseph McCarthy. Eva Peron even got a whole musical, *Evita!* 'Abraham, Martin, and John' paid homage to three assassinated U.S. politicians in John F. Kennedy, Robert Kennedy, and Martin Luther King Jr. Dr King was also eulogised in U2's 'MLK', and John F. Kennedy was memorialised in The Byrds' 'He Was A Friend Of Mine'. JFK is mentioned in an alliterative pairing with Nikita Khruschev in Queen's 'Killer Queen' and appears again in Living Colour's 'Cult Of Personality', which, like The Stranglers' 'No More Heroes' (Shakespeare, Lenin, Trotsky), is an anti-hero song. When writing about a political or historical figure, always take into account your audience. Elvis Costello knew that his song about the 1930s British fascist Oswald Mosley, 'Less Than Zero', would not translate to the USA, so there it had a new lyric about another Oswald – Lee Harvey Oswald, killer of President Kennedy. Many songs, like Dylan's 'Hurricane' (about the boxer Hurricane Carter), have been written about individuals who were the victims of injustice.

Songs have also celebrated fictional characters such as Charlie Brown, Snoopy and the Red Baron, Tarzan, Jane and King Kong, Romeo and Juliet, Captain James T. Kirk, and Mulder and Scully from *The X-Files*. Popular music has its own roll-call of fictional characters, and in some cases these characters seem as real as any from a film or novel. Think of Desmond and Molly ('Ob-la-di, Ob-la-da'), Terry and Julie, Arnold Layne, Emily and Eugene, Lola, Rita the meter maid, Polythene Pam, Mr Mustard, Mr Kite, Bungalow Bill, Rhiannon,

Shorty, Dan and Miss Lucy, Dora the female explorer, Aqualung, the fashion-conscious Carnabetian of 'Dedicated Follower Of Fashion', Dizzy Miss Lizzy, Mr Bojangles, David Watts, Mr Clean, Billericay Dickie, Jumpin' Jack Flash, Mrs Robinson, Ernold Same, and that Mrs Jones who had a thing going on. Incidentally, what rank was 'Fernando', was he deaf and was that why she kept asking him if he could hear the drums?

Books and films

You can also base a song on a book or film, and in the lyric try to condense the story or at least capture its atmosphere. Elvis Costello's 'Watching The Detectives' conjured up the whole world of pulp crime fiction. Jefferson Airplane's 'White Rabbit' was a counter-culture tribute to *Alice In Wonderland*. Kate Bush wrote about 'Wuthering Heights', and 'The Sensual World' was inspired by the closing 30 pages of James Joyce's *Ulysses*. Led Zeppelin's 'Ramble On' and 'The Battle Of Evermore' were both shaped by J.R.R. Tolkien's *Lord Of The Rings*.

Put-down songs

You will find plenty of these in the punk rock repertoire, such as The Sex Pistols' 'Satellite', 'Liar', 'No Feelings', and 'New York'. Elvis Costello had plenty among his early songs, including 'I'm Not Angry' – a title that contrasts ironically with the content. After he went electric, Dylan had a phase of what he called "finger-pointing" songs. Probably the most elegant and cleverest put-down song is Carly Simon's 'You're So Vain', with its booby-trapped chorus, pointing out that the person the song was about was so vain they would probably think it was about them.

What's on the radio?

Another option is to write a song about what's on the radio – or what's *not* on the radio. Since rock has always had a thing about disco and poppy dance music, it's not surprising that Bryan Adams ('Kids Wanna Rock'), The Smiths ('Panic'), Elvis Costello ('Radio Radio'), and R.E.M. ('Radio Song') wrote songs to criticise what they were hearing over the airwaves. 'Oh Yeah', 'Radio Free Europe', 'Yesterday Once More', and '29 Palms' are four of many songs that mention the emotional effect of hearing music on the radio. Joni Mitchell used the radio as a metaphor in 'You Turn Me On (I'm A Radio)'. You could extend this theme by going to television, as in Springsteen's '57 Channels'. It won't be long before someone has a hit with a song that mentions the internet.

Articles of apparel

Sometimes it's clothing that sparks a story or a mood: 'Blue Suede Shoes', 'Blue Jean Bop', 'Wherever I Lay My Hat', 'Famous Blue Raincoat', 'Homburg', 'Hole In My Shoe', 'These Boots Are Made For Walkin'', 'Venus In Furs', 'Raspberry Beret', 'A White Sport Coat (And A Pink Carnation)', 'Hi Heel Sneakers', 'Red Shoes', 'Lady In Red', 'Bell Bottom Blues', 'Chantilly Lace', 'New Shoes', 'Girls In Their Summer Clothes', 'Dedicated Follower Of Fashion' – and from the opposite view, 'It's Still Rock And Roll To Me', where Billy Joel decided that fashion didn't matter.

Dances

Some lyrics offer instructions for how to do a dance: 'Resurrection Shuffle', 'Let's Twist Again', 'Hey Let's Twist', 'Monster Mash', 'Hippy Hippy Shake', 'Agadoo', 'Do You Want To Dance', 'Mickey's Monkey', 'Dance To The Music', 'Land Of A Thousand Dances', 'Harlem Shuffle', 'Do The Funky Chicken'. Thousands of other songs, like 'Peppermint Twist', 'Boogie Fever', 'You Should Be Dancing', '(Shake Shake Shake) Shake Your Booty' and 'Dancing Queen' just mention dancing. Sometimes dance lyrics are really a metaphor for sex. Siouxsie & The Banshees' 'Slowdive' sounded like a lyric of dance instructions but was actually auto-erotic.

Fantasy

In fantasy lyrics, you can let your imagination run riot – though whether your listener will be inspired or confused is something to be considered. The words may obliquely refer to the 'real world', as in 'A Whiter Shade Of Pale', or not. With The Beatles, John Lennon wrote a number of outstanding fantasy songs, including 'Lucy In The Sky With Diamonds', 'Come Together', and 'I Am The Walrus', and he parodied the genre with 'Glass Onion'; 'Being For The Benefit Of Mr Kite' was a fantasy inspired by a Victorian theatre poster.

You will find many fantasy lyrics in Jimi Hendrix's output (such as 'Spanish Castle Magic') and 1970s progressive rock, where David Bowie, Marc Bolan (Tyrannosaurus Rex and T. Rex), Genesis, Hawkwind, Rush (see *2112*), Wishbone Ash (see the *Argus* album), and Yes all featured fantasy. Gothic horror was mined by Alice Cooper and later Michael Jackson, on *Thriller*. Keane have titled songs 'The Frog Prince' and 'Crystal Ball'. There have been plenty of sci-fi lyrics involving aliens and UFOs, such as Neil Young's 'After The Gold Rush', Hendrix's 'House Burning Down', and Graham Parker & The Rumour's 'Waiting For The UFOs', and end-of-the-world scenarios like Nena's '99 Red Balloons' and David Bowie's 'Five Years'. Within fantasy writing lies the realisation that words can make some sense even when they don't logically, as with the famous line about movement and shoulder in 'Hey Jude', which Lennon rightly told McCartney not to change.

A special sub-section of fantasy might involve songs based around the mind-expanding properties of certain drugs. Psychedelia helped to create lyrics such as The Move 'I Can Hear The Grass Grow', The Temptations' 'Cloud Nine', and 'I Can See For Miles'. More general drug songs run the gamut from Velvet Underground's 'I'm Waiting For The Man' and Fleetwood Mac's 'Green Manalishi' to Neil Young's 'The Needle And The Damage Done', Supergrass's 'Caught By The Fuzz', Amy Winehouse's 'Rehab', and the hilariously (and deliberately) mis-titled 'Feel Good Hit Of The Summer' by Queens Of The Stone Age.

Songs about writing songs

When all else fails, songwriters write about what they do. Herein lies a cautionary tale, because the self-referential song-about-writing-a-song has a greater percentage of turkeys than probably any other category. Love-obsessed singer-songwriters who grapple with being tongue-tied in the presence of their beloved are notorious for perpetrating these. Nothing is guaranteed to make you sound more like a self-obsessed egomaniac who ought to get a life than starting a lyric with "I'm sitting here writing a song, / I'm waiting for chords to come along …"

This rogues' gallery includes 'Pop Muzik', 'I Write The Songs' (… and we hate 'em), 'Gonna Write A Classic' (… I don't think so), 'Thank You For The Music' (… but we prefer 'Dancing Queen'), 'I'd Like To Teach The World To Sing' (… in atonal harmony, preferably), 'Silly Love Songs' (… but we've *not* had enough of 'Maybe I'm Amazed'), Bono trying to find a melody he can sing in U2's 'Stuck In A Moment', and the pompous 'Music' (music is our first love, too, aarghh!). Odd references to songwriting within a song, if the song is about something else, are acceptable, as in 'Romeo And Juliet', 'Sunflower', and 'Your Song', but not in the case of Spandau Ballet's 'True', where the question of why the speaker found it hard to write the next line invited a whole series of err … *colourful* … replies. By contrast, 'Killing Me Softly With His Song' provides an interesting perspective from the recipient's point of view.

Sarcasm and humour are welcome here, as with George Harrison's sarcastic 'Only A Northern Song', Noddy Holder singing about how his singing might be imperfect but it makes him money ('Cum On Feel The Noize'), and in 'Hallelujah', where Jeff Buckley spells out part of the chord sequence.

There is a whole genre of songs that deal with the music business and music itself including stardom ('Lady Stardust', 'Hang On To Yourself', 'Bennie And The Jets', 'King Of The Mountain') the fate of rock ('Long Live Rock', 'Whatever Happened To My Rock'n'Roll', 'Indie Rock and Roll', 'Rock And Roll'), managers ('Death On Two Legs', 'So You Wanna Be A Rock'n'Roll Star'), touring ('Homeward Bound', 'All The Way From Memphis'), record labels ('Mercury Poisoning', 'EMI') and groupies ('Sick Again'). BoyzIIMen made a hit title out of their two favourite record labels: 'Motownphilly'. The two coolest lyric couplets ever written about rock are of course the reference to the drummer who relaxes between shows in Neil Young's 'Cinnamon Girl' and the reference to a Gibson Les Paul and Jimmy Page in Wings' 'Rock Show'. And there are, of course, zillions of songs with "rock" or "rock and roll" in the title – but you don't want to add to them, do you? You do? Oh, all right then … but make it snappy!

Politics, religion, spirituality, and protest

With these themes, the song lyric turns outward to much bigger issues. This raises the question of whether a popular song is the best place to do this. How much credence are you willing to give to the views of someone who can strum a few chords on the guitar or play a handful of pentatonic scales at ear-splitting volume? Each topic area (politics, religion, protest) has its own problems and challenges.

Outside of gospel ('Oh Happy Day'), hymns, carols and the songbooks of fundamentalists, religious songs are difficult – especially in rock (traditionally "the devil's music"). If artistically done, religious rock numbers can be highly effective because rock's earthy energy keeps religious expressions from becoming sentimental and woolly. The rock lyricist's abiding challenge is to find a theme weighty enough to justify the high-volume posturing of rock music, and ironically spiritual/religious themes would fit the bill. Think of Who songs about Meher Baba, such as 'Bargain', some of U2's songs and, in reggae, Bob Marley. Biblical themes inspired 'Turn, Turn, Turn', 'Sire Of Sorrow', '40', 'Rivers Of Babylon', 'Song Of Solomon', and 'Heaven Help Us All'. The Waterboys' 'The Glastonbury Song' is impressive because, despite the broad-ranging imagery of the lyric, the poignancy of the music suggests the human cost and struggle that faith entails. The title of R.E.M.'s 'Saturn Return' alludes to an important 29 year transit in astrological thought.

Political songs are sometimes merely sloganeering or preaching to the converted. They become more interesting as they move beyond a black-and-white situation. 'Shipbuilding' is a wonderful political song that examines the human realities of the relationship between war, economics, and employment. 'Sunday Bloody Sunday' is another notable peace-sentiment song. 'Orange Crush' is about defoliants in Vietnam. There's always room for humour here, as in 'Fixin' To Die', the famous anti-Vietnam War song by Country Joe & The Fish.

Other notable songs with political and social themes include 'Invisible Sun', 'Give Ireland Back To The Irish', 'Night Rally', 'Pills And Soap', 'Stand Down Margaret', 'Love Child', 'War', 'Bring The Boys Back Home', 'Young, Gifted And Black', 'Indian Reservation', 'Woman Is The Nigger Of The World', 'Power To The People', 'Ebony And Ivory', 'Candy Man', and 'A Thousand Trees'. The Mission's 'Amelia' is about child abuse. Charity songs such as 'Do They Know Its Christmas?', 'Bangla Desh' and 'We Are The World' are a specialised form of this genre. Dystopian warnings about the future can be heard in songs such as 'Eve Of Destruction' and 'In The Year 2525'.

Ecology has always been a safer bet: 'Big Yellow Taxi', 'Silvery Rain', 'Crazy Horses', 'Cuyahoga', 'Breathing', 'Mercy Mercy Me (The Ecology)', and with rising concern about global warming this topic has become more relevant.

THE TECHNIQUE OF LYRIC WRITING: HOW YOU WRITE

Having considered some theme categories and *what* you can write about, let's look at *how* you write. In other words, it's time to review some techniques. First, I recommend that lyric writers equip themselves with three books: a thesaurus, a book of proverbs and famous quotes, and a rhyming dictionary (and no, a rhyming dictionary is not cheating).

Point of view

Fundamentally, consider the point of view. When you write your lyric, through whose eyes are you looking? With whose voice are you speaking / singing. How does this affect the feelings, events, places you describe?

First person

Song lyrics predominately use 'I', the first person, as the main point of view. This is popular because a lyricist may be writing from experience, and it is certainly popular with singers because it allows them to identify with the speaker (and for their audience to make this identification). Alternatively you can also write in the voice of someone else, such as an invented character. Suzanne Vega's 'Luka' is sung from the point of view of an abused child. In 'Wuthering Heights', Kate Bush voiced the feelings of Cathy Earnshaw from

Emily Bronte's 1848 novel. In 'The Intruder', Peter Gabriel impersonated a psychotic, and Simon and Garfunkel's 'The Boxer' features a down-and-out character.

Second person

This is where the lyric speaks of 'you'. To disguise the personal nature of a lyric, sing it in the second person. This can make it seem as though you are talking about someone else, when in fact it might be yourself. This is used in 'You Should Hear How She Talks About You' and 'Tell Her About It'.

Third person

To grasp how significant point of view is, think of some famous songs and imagine them sung from a different one. 'My Way' sung from the third person would be absurd – it wouldn't be anywhere near as dramatic. Imagine the climax as Sinatra sings "And he did it ... his way!" The audience would wonder why the singer is so worked up over someone else's trials and tribulations.

But the third person can offer an excellent way to distance yourself from material that may be too personal, or to tell a story from more than one person's perspective. Many of The Beatles' mop-top period hits were in the first person, but with 'She Loves You' they tried something different. The lyric tells how the speaker tries to reconcile two lovers who have quarrelled. The song not only celebrates the reunion of the lovers but, implicitly, the generosity of the person who did the patching-up. That's part of the reason the song is so uplifting.

Combined points of view

Consider the lyric of David Bowie's 'Space Oddity'. Passages of first-person reflection by Major Tom in space are combined with the voice of a technician at Mission Control doing the countdown and last checks, and another earth-bound voice telling the astronaut of his new-found celebrity. Compare its treatment of the astronaut subject matter with Elton John's 'Rocket Man'.

Duets

Differing points of view are made explicit with the duet, where two voices are literally present. 'Don't Go Breaking My Heart' and 'Don't Give Up' are variants on the love duet, with the female voice reassuring the male. In most pop love duets, the two voices are in blissful agreement, as in 'It Takes Two', 'Ain't Nothing Like The Real Thing' and 'You're All I Need To Get By', but in 'Fairytale Of New York' the two characters insult each other. Bryan Adams, Rod Stewart and Sting came on like three romantic musketeers with 'All For Love'.

Narrative

A song can be cast as a story, whether true or invented. The folk ballad is a good historical precedent. Stories can be told from a variety of perspectives. 'Leader Of The Pack' and 'Tell Laura I Love Her' were early 1960s teen hits that played on a morbid fascination with death in an automobile accident. 'Don't Stand So Close To Me' is about the relationship between a schoolteacher and a student; 'Down In The Tube Station At Midnight' tells of violence in a subway; 'She's Leaving Home' relates the story of a daughter breaking away from her parents with commentary from both sides. 'In The Ghetto' is a fine compressed narrative of a young man who grows up in poverty, takes to crime and gets shot by the police. 'Someone Saved My Life Tonight' is a revealing narrative about a relationship that engenders suicidal feelings. 'Chestnut Mare' is a story of seduction dressed up as a man pursuing a horse. 'Cut Across Shorty' is the tale of a young woman who helps the man she loves to cheat and win the race against a rival for her affections. 'Meeting Across The River', a story of two small-town crooks, is one of many Springsteen songs with a novelistic quality and where the lyric is sung by one of the characters. For an imaginary tale of maritime mystery check out Procol Harum's 'A Salty Dog'.

ASPECTS OF LANGUAGE

Writing good lyrics is easier when you develop awareness of particular aspects of language and features of writing. If you also happen to write poetry some of this will be familiar.

Rhyme

Lyrics don't have to rhyme but often they do. In contrast to poetry, where rhyme schemes can be complex, song lyrics are often rhymed in couplets or in alternating rhyme. Couplets are punchier. Rhymes don't have to be exact, because the last syllable of a word often gets lost in the pronunciation. Pop lyrics tend to use the same obvious rhyme sounds. To make the whole business of rhyming easier and less predictable, be sure to consult a good rhyming dictionary.

Poor rhyming makes the rhyme itself predictable, forces you into a nonsense line to complete it or makes you distort the syntax (word order) of a statement. Therefore, avoid ending a line with a word for which there is no easy rhyme. Two common examples are "world" and "love". If a line ends with "world", then something is likely to be "unfurled"; if with "love", then something is coming down from "above" or is like a "dove" (a punk song might give it a "shove"). Don't allow a rhyme to trap you into an archaism, as in "I give my love for free, I give it all to thee" or rhyming "before" with "days of yore" (yore?). Even the great are sometimes guilty of this. Dylan, in 'Don't Think Twice, It's All Right', uses "know'd" instead of "knew" for the sake of a rhyme. In 'Play Me' Neil Diamond used "brang" as a rhyme for "sang" instead of "brought". Polysyllabic abstractions generate plentiful rhymes but need to be used sparingly, unless you plan to make the lyric revolve around them, as with 'Give Peace A Chance' and 'The Logical Song'.

As an exercise, find a few interesting rhymes and write a lyric to fit them.

Type of statement

What type of statement do you use in your lyrics? Are the lines declarations, questions, replies, descriptions, or actions?

Imagery

Primary imagery consists of descriptive elements that denote actual things. In

'I Get Around', the "strip" is the place where the speaker is getting bored racing his car. If a song lyric said that something was "like a road", you have secondary imagery, which is conveyed by similes and metaphors. The problem with most similes and metaphors in pop lyrics is that they are too predictable. I mean, complete the following: "beats like a …", "cuts like a …", "sweeter than …" (isn't hard to guess, is it?). Sometimes a great vocal can overcome a cliché. Images can work as titles, as with 'Love Is Like A Battlefield' and '(Love Is) Thicker Than Water'. 10cc deliberately poked fun at pretentious metaphors in 'Life Is A Minestrone'.

The truly poetic moments in pop lyrics occur when a writer disregards cliché and finds something fresh. The line referring to a cat drowning in a bag in The Verve's 'The Drugs Don't Work' is inspired in this respect, as is the face kept in a jar by the door in The Beatles' 'Eleanor Rigby'. Effective language is not always about an image. In 'Man With The Child In His Eyes' Kate Bush's character says that before she goes to sleep she focuses on the day now gone; the word "focus" in the lyric is crucial for evoking the reality of what is described. Similarly in The Beatles' 'In My Life' the singer says he will often "stop" to think about the places he's known. The crucial word is the verb "stop": it is not only that he will think about the past – he will *stop* and think about it.

The most common imagery in popular song is meteorological: the weather. This is where lazy lyric writing goes every time. Think of clichés like "winds of change", "my tears fell down like rain", "swept away by a flood", "like a raging sea", "life is a ray of sunshine with you", etc. And a great many songs have weather in their titles: 'The Sun Ain't Gonna Shine Anymore', 'Heatwave', 'Good Day Sunshine', 'You Are The Sunshine Of My Life', 'I Wish It Would Rain', 'Blame It On The Rain', 'I Love A Rainy Night', 'Raindrops Keep Falling On My Head', 'Here Comes The Rain Again', 'I Wish It Would Rain Down', 'Rain', 'Just Walking In The Rain', 'It Never Rains In Southern California', 'Only Happy When It Rains', 'Laughter In The Rain', etc. It rains more often than it shines in the popular song lyric. As a universal experience, the weather is something to which everyone can relate. Amateur song-lyrics tend to be dominated by weather images. If this is true of your lyrics, try banning them for a while. If you must use weather images, then find a new angle or twist on them.

The other common group of images is drawn from nature: sun, moon, stars, seas, rivers, oceans, lakes, deserts, woods, forests, rocks, sand, stone, jewels, fields, fire, etc. 'Annie's Song' somehow gets just about all of them in. This kind of imagery occurs in numbers such as 'I Still Haven't Found What I'm Looking For', 'Ain't No Mountain High Enough', 'In A Big Country', and 'Fields Of Fire'. Such images tend to go with generalised and often exaggerated emotions – we're talking MOR ballads and stadium rock. If the music and/or the performer is not suitably larger-than-life, then it can be unconsciously funny. The sceptic's response to the thunderously titled 'Where Were You When The Storm Broke?' is going to be facetious, like "phoning a plumber instead of hiding under the table".

In terms of their overall style, lyrics such as 'Both Sides Now', 'MacArthur Park', 'If You Could Read My Mind', 'Windmills Of Your Mind', and

'Unchained Melody' either aspire to be poetry or use words and imagery in quite an extravagant way. At the opposite extreme are songs whose imagery is drawn from the mucky detail and nitty-gritty of everyday life. Lyricists like Jarvis Cocker (Pulp), Morrissey (The Smiths), and Paul Weller (with The Jam) consciously seek out the everyday and find poetry in the unheroic. Sting's image describing a character looking like something that the cat brought in ('Invisible Sun') is effective because it is drawn from colloquial speech. In songs such as 'That's Entertainment', 'Suzanne', 'Kayleigh', and Dylan's 'Sara', images can be specific yet somehow, paradoxically, attain universality. Lyrics fail more often by being too generalised than by being too specific.

Try applying a set of images to a theme that would not normally be thought of in those terms – this can be especially effective in a love song, where less obvious 'cooler' imagery can imply a depth of passion beneath. See the discussion of Dire Straits' 'On Every Street' in Section 14.

A mini-dictionary of pop clichés

These words and phrases are threadbare through over-use and should be deployed with caution, humour or irony:

> *little girl, little miss, blue jeans, forever, body, fantasy, reality, hearts that beat like a drum, sorrow that cuts like a knife, winds of change, love deep as the ocean, all night long, angel, baby, fire/desire, no matter what (they say), set me free, swallow my pride, right from the start, out on the streets, standing in the rain, end of time, shines like the sun, walk the line, going round my head, just about to go insane, it's all in my mind, heaven above, deep inside, I give it to thee, turn to stone, cold as ice, by your side, sweeter than/taste like wine, get me through, get on down, heart like a stone, catch me/you if I/you fall.*

In pop lyrics, prediction is an easy business: mountains tend to crumble into the sea, rivers always flow to the sea, stars fall from the sky, and rain comes down from up above (ever known it to travel in any other direction?). Try to avoid filler words – well, baby, just, really. These add nothing to the sense and only occupy space in a line.

Redeeming clichés

One way to redeem a cliche is to exploit its latent meaning. This requires looking at it with a fresh eye to see how it might be developed in an unexpected direction. In 'Clubland' Elvis Costello played with the "long arm" of the law and the "outskirts" of town, and in 'Possession' he combined "lack lust" with "lacklustre". Robert Plant's 'Heaven Knows' plays with pumping iron and irony, and The Who's 'Substitute' has a memorable line where the expression that someone born in privileged circumstances is born with a 'silver spoon' in their mouth is changed to a plastic spoon. In this category one might also put Radiohead's '2+2=5'.

First lines

A good opening line is valuable. Not only does it set you, the writer, up for the rest of the lyric, but it grabs the listener's attention. A first line might:

- supply one evocative fact about one of the characters
- give a memorable image
- say something provocatively unexpected
- say something enigmatic and mysterious
- describe a dramatic event
- pose a question
- signal the start of a story
- make a declaration
- present a problem
- plunge us immediately into something happening
- say something defiant
- say something paradoxical.

Word-play and titles

Titles themselves can be inspiring. Part of my own songwriting technique is to keep a list of possible titles for songs. A group of related titles can give an album of songs a particular identity. Sometimes they fix a mood long enough for you to get to grips with it. It is satisfying to come up with a title that no one else has used – so be aware that some of the most popular first words in a title are:

can't, dance, don't, give, good, I, I love, I want, I'll, I'm, just, let, little, love, more, my, never, one, only, rock, she, some, take, that's, too, walk.

Some titles are memorable because they feature wordplay: 'Maid In Heaven', 'If I Said You Had A Beautiful Body Would You Hold It Against Me?', 'Aladdin Sane', 'Animal Nitrate', 'High Fidelity', 'I Came, I Saw, I Conga'd', 'Money, Money, Money', 'I Do, I Do, I Do, I Do, I Do', 'The Only Thing That Looks Good On Me Is You', 'Mellow Yellow', 'Yester-me, Yester-you, Yesterday', 'Eight Days A Week', 'Function At The Junction', 'Bummer In The Summer', 'Seven Deadly Finns', 'Love On The Rocks With No Ice', 'Holding My Own', 'Illegal Tender', 'Alone, Together'.

You can also take common phrases and twist them: 'Don't Get Mad Get Even', 'Fifty Ways To Leave Your Lover', 'When The Going Gets Tough, The Tough Get Going', 'Shoplifters Of The World Unite'. This can include proverbs and other well-known sayings: 'Needle In A Haystack', 'Beauty Is Only Skin Deep', 'Plenty More Fish In The Sea', 'The Other Man's Grass', 'Knock, Knock, Who's There?', 'Something Old, Something New', 'Alive And Kicking', 'Another One Bites The Dust', 'Head Over Heels', and 'Objects In The Rear View Mirror May Appear Closer Than They Are'.

Some titles are intriguing because of what they don't say: 'Because The Night' is grammatically incomplete. In the mid-1960s, Dylan had a penchant for adverbs in titles such as 'Queen Jane Approximately' and 'Positively 4th Street'. Other intriguing titles include 'Over Under Sideways Down', 'I'm Left, You're Right, She's Gone', 'I'd Do Anything For You (But I Won't Do That)', 'There! I've Said It Again', 'Sometimes When We Touch', 'Suddenly', 'Till', and 'Truth, Rest Your Head'. Titles with "if" arouse curiosity. 'Wedding Bell Blues' seems contradictory; 'A Punch-Up At A Wedding' sounds all too human. Elton John's 'This Song Has No Title' leaves it up to you.

Repetition

Some lyrics are constructed on a repeated word or phrase: 'Blowin' In The Wind' ("how many" statements), 'Where Have All The Flowers Gone' ("Where have all the … gone?"), 'It's Impossible' (to start so many verses with this phrase, it's just impossible), 'I Believe', 'Every Breath You Take' (count the number of times 'every' appears), 'Ironic', 'This Old House', 'Plastic Man', 'King Of Pain', 'Just An Old-Fashioned Girl', 'Wonderful World' ('Don't know much about … '), and 'Forever Young' ('may you … '). The repeated word could reveal the deeper meaning and/or be the title. Some lyrics are constructed as lists, as with 'Reasons To Be Cheerful' and 'Inside Out'.

A good way to test how you're doing with your lyrics and titles is to imagine what the lyrics will look like printed on the inner sleeve or pasted up on the web, and what impression the titles will give on the back of a CD to the casual browser. Are they likely to intrigue and make that person buy your album?

SECTION 9
CHORD DICTIONARY PART 2
ADVANCED HARMONY

Before we venture into more complex, exotic chords, it is worth considering whether there is something more you can do with the basic chord shapes presented in Section 2 to create song ideas.

Voicings

Sometimes the simplest chord sequences can be made more effective by using different shapes ('voicings') of the same chords. Here are some ideas for such alternate shapes. Some of them feature unison strings (where two notes are at the same pitch) to give a ringy, '12-string' tone on a regular six-string guitar. This effect is one which is available on the guitar but not, for example, on the piano.

Moving an open-string chord

One favourite songwriting trick of guitarists is to take an open-string chord and move it up the neck without turning it into a barre chord. The result is an unpredictable series of new chords. The fretted notes in the shape retain their

ABBREVIATIONS

Roman numerals **I–VII** indicate chord relationships within a key.

m=minor

maj=major

SONG SECTIONS:

b bridge; **c** coda; **ch** chorus; **f** fade; **hk** hook; **i** intro; **pch** pre-chorus; **r** riff; **s** solo; **v** verse

Most of the chord-sequence examples are standardised for comparison into **C major** or **A minor**. The famous songs are therefore not always in the key of the original recordings.

Open-string chords

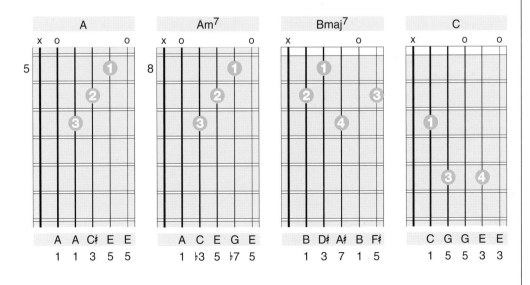

A					
A	A	C#	E	E	
1	1	3	5	5	

Am⁷					
A	C	E	G	E	
1	♭3	5	♭7	5	

Bmaj⁷					
B	D#	A#	B	F#	
1	3	7	1	5	

C					
C	G	G	E	E	
1	5	5	3	3	

Open-string chords
continued

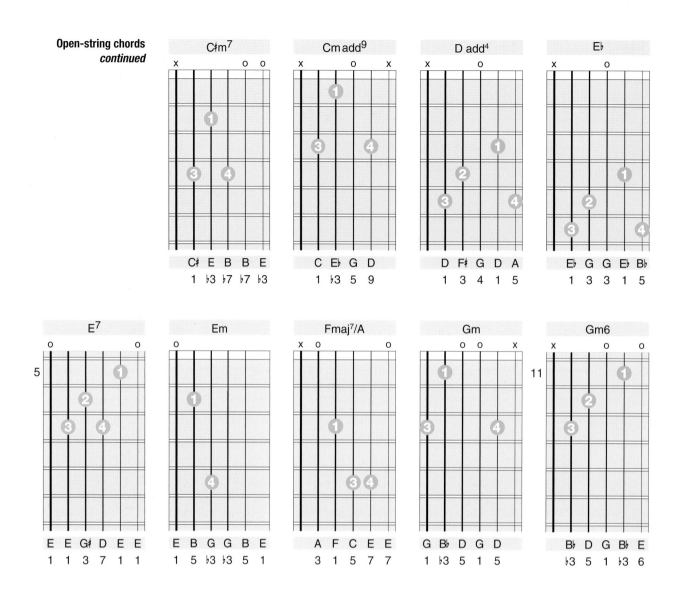

C♯m7	Cmadd9	D add4	E♭
C♯ E B B E	C E♭ G D	D F♯ G D A	E♭ G G E♭ B♭
1 ♭3 ♭7 ♭7 ♭3	1 ♭3 5 9	1 3 4 1 5	1 3 3 1 5

E7	Em	Fmaj7/A	Gm	Gm6
E E G♯ D E E	E B G G B E	A F C E E	G B♭ D G D	B♭ D G B♭ E
1 1 3 7 1 1	1 5 ♭3 ♭3 5 1	3 1 5 7 7	1 ♭3 5 1 5	♭3 5 1 ♭3 6

harmonic relationship to each other (ie, major chord, minor chord), but the open strings change theirs in relation to the fretted. The table opposite illustrates this. The root note needs to be fretted, or you will be moving chords over a pedal note. The effect of such shapes is heard in songs such as R.E.M.'s 'Man On The Moon', Neil Young's 'Sugar Mountain', Mice's 'Miss World', The Red Hot Chili Peppers' 'Under The Bridge' (toward the end), and Joan Armatrading's 'Love And Affection'.

Moving chords over a pedal note

A pedal note is an effective compositional device. It's a note in the bass register of the guitar that remains the same while chords change above it. This creates a more ambiguous sequence than if the bass note changed to the root note of each chord. If the pedal note is the same as the key note, it is called a 'tonic pedal'; if it is named after the fifth note of the scale, it would be a 'dominant pedal'.

Songs that use a tonic pedal include 'Alright' (Cast, v), 'One To Another' (The Charlatans), 'Peaches' (The Presidents Of The USA), 'Gimme Some

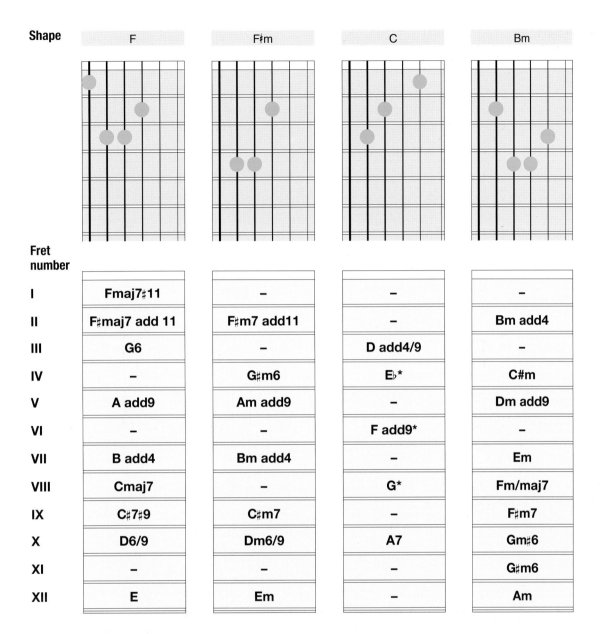

Shape	F	F#m	C	Bm
Fret number				
I	Fmaj7♯11	–	–	–
II	F♯maj7 add 11	F♯m7 add11	–	Bm add4
III	G6	–	D add4/9	–
IV	–	G♯m6	E♭*	C♯m
V	A add9	Am add9	–	Dm add9
VI	–	–	F add9*	–
VII	B add4	Bm add4	–	Em
VIII	Cmaj7	–	G*	Fm/maj7
IX	C♯7♯9	C♯m7	–	F♯m7
X	D6/9	Dm6/9	A7	Gm♯6
XI	–	–	–	G♯m6
XII	E	Em	–	Am

Lovin'" (Spencer Davis Group), 'We Don't Talk Anymore' (Cliff Richard, ch) 'Everything I Do' (Bryan Adams, first v), 'Everybody Wants To Rule The World' (Tears For Fears, v), 'Express Yourself' (Madonna, ch), 'Dancing In The Street' (Martha Reeves & The Vandellas, v), 'The Sun Ain't Gonna Shine Anymore' (The Walker Brothers), 'You've Got Your Troubles' (The Fortunes), 'Everlasting Love' (Love Affair), 'Substitute' (The Who) and 'Let Me Entertain You' (Robbie Williams). Minor-key examples include 'I Know I'm Losing You' (The Temptations), 'Green Manalishi' (Fleetwood Mac), 'I've Never Met A Girl Like You Before' (Edwyn Collins), 'Sweetness Follows' (R.E.M.), 'Running With The Devil' (Van Halen), and 'Out Of My Hands' (The Darkness). 'I'll Never Fall In Love Again' (Bobbie Gentry) has a dominant pedal, where the bass note is the fifth of the scale, not the first.

One of the most unusual pedals I've ever encountered is in Siouxsie & The Banshees' 'Nightshift', where over an A pedal the chords change from Am to

Asterisk means add little finger to top string at same fret as third finger

SECTION 9 | **139**

G#m, creating a sinister atmosphere. Stephen Stills' 'To A Flame' has a Cmaj7-Fmaj7-Cm-Am sequence over a C pedal.

The problem for the guitarist is that changing chords over a static bass note can create fingering difficulties – unless the pedal note is the open E, A, or D string. This is one instance where triads can be made to work on the guitar. You can form triads on the top three strings and have a D pedal, or strings 2-3-4 with an A pedal, or strings 3-4-5 with an E pedal. The key could be either major or minor. In guitar music, pedal notes are almost invariably on one of these three open strings. Triads often feature in the intros to songs. Examples would include Argent's 'Hold Your Head Up', Led Zeppelin's 'Over The Hills And Far Away', and Wishbone Ash's 'Blowin' Free'. For more information see page 17 for the triad boxes.

Inversions

A songwriter can get more mileage out of simple chords by using inversions. A simple major or minor triad has three notes, 1 3 5 or 1 ♭3 5 (C E G or C E♭ G). Most guitar chords are in root position, with the chord-name note lowest in

First inversion chord shapes

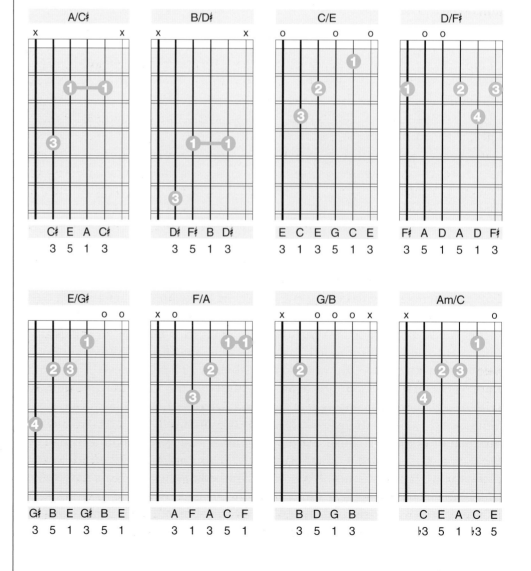

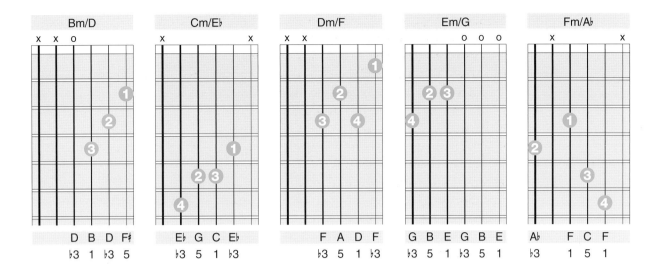

Bm/D	Cm/Eb	Dm/F	Em/G	Fm/Ab
D B D F#	Eb G C Eb	F A D F	G B E G B E	Ab F C F
b3 1 b3 5	b3 5 1 b3	b3 5 1 b3	b3 5 1 b3 5 1	b3 1 5 1

pitch. But what happens if one of the other notes is lowest? An 'inversion' is a chord whose root note is not the lowest. The first inversion puts the third at the bottom: C E G becomes E G C, and is written C/E. In the second inversion, the fifth of the chord becomes the bass note: C E G becomes G C E, and is written C/G.

First inversions

Compared to root chords, first inversions sound mobile. The bass note wants to either rise or drop back. First inversions are therefore useful in descending or ascending sequences, as can be heard in the chorus of The Verve's 'Numbness' which ascends Em-D/F#-G-G/B-Cmaj7. They increase the possibilities for using only three chords in the harmony since each chord in a major three-chord trick could be played as root, first inversion, or second inversion. Minor chords can also be inverted. C minor is C Eb G, so we can play it as a first inversion by making Eb the lowest note. It is written C/Eb. Inversions are usually notated as 'slash chords', with the bass note written after the root: C/E or A/C#.

To get a feel for the 'tentative' sound of first inversions, compare a C to D chord change with C/E to D/F#. Also compare Em to F#m with Em/G to F#m/A. To hear what they sound like played forcefully listen to '2-4-6-8 Motorway' by The Tom Robinson Band where they colour a I-V-IV-V riff. R.E.M.'s 'Hollow Man' has an inversion colouring its three-chord I-bVII-iIV (E D A/C#) verse.

Major chord first inversions that are easy to play on guitar are C, D, F and G; for minor chords they are those for Am, Bm, C#m, Dm, Em, F#m and Gm.

Second inversions

Rarer than first inversions, second inversions have something of the fluid nature of the first inversion but are more diffuse. Jimi Hendrix's 'The Wind Cries Mary' is introduced by an Eb-E-F progression, played initially as second inversions and then as first inversions. There is a striking second inversion in the chorus of The Band's 'The Night They Drove Old Dixie Down', where the chords move between iiI and IV, and a descending link to the last choruses which also depends on inversions. A second inversion (such as C/G) is often played as a substitute for a root chord purely because it has one more string in it than the standard root shape and is therefore more resonant.

SECTION 9 | 141

Second inversion chord shapes

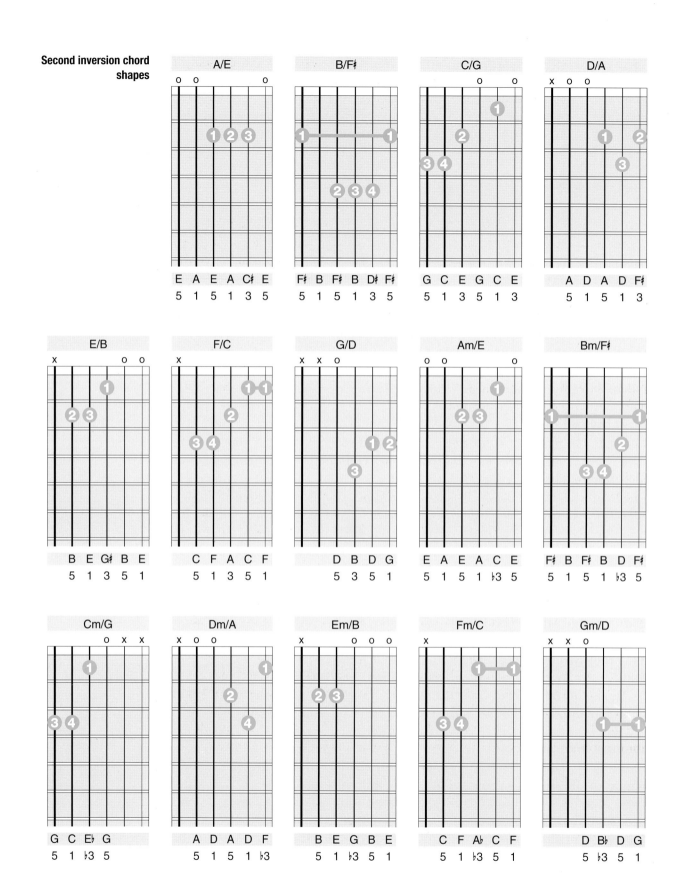

The number of possible inversions is always one less than the number of different notes in the chord. If a chord has more than three notes in it – C7, for example – then a third inversion is possible, with the additional note in the bass.

Third inversions usually occur as passing chords. In the verse of Air's 'Remember' we find this:

I	iiiI7	iIV	V
E♭	E♭/D♭	A♭/C	B♭

Inversions are not often used by songwriting guitarists. They can be difficult to finger, or it may be hard to find one that sounds as good as the equivalent root chord. One way round this problem is to have the bass guitar play the appropriate note to create the inversion while the guitar plays a root chord, as in the verses of The Kinks' 'Waterloo Sunset'.

Inversions are more frequently heard in the songs of singers associated with the piano, such as Elton John and Kate Bush. On a keyboard, an inversion can be created easily by moving the left hand up a few keys. Kate Bush's 'This Woman's Work' gains much of its expressive power from its inversions; for example, a IV-V-I-II progression becomes iIV-iV-iI-II (D♭/F-E♭/G-A♭/C-B♭m). There are plenty of inversions in songs like Bryan Adams's 'Everything I Do (I Do It For You)' and 'Heaven Can Wait'. They also turn up in mid-period Dire Straits and in the verse of Madonna's 'Cherish'.

Using inversions

Inversions can enliven a simple three-chord trick: try E-B-A as E-B/D♯-A/C♯. Inversions also allow you to stretch a three-chord turnaround: C-F-G becomes C-C/E-F-G over four bars. The verse of Razorlight's 'America' has a IV-V-iI-IV turnaround in which the first inversion G delays the appearance of a root position chord I until the chorus. The Hold Steady's 'Party Pit' also has a verse turnaround in which there is a first inversion chord I: G-D-G/B-C (I-V-iI-IV), and two first inversions make an important contribution to the chorus of their 'Hot Soft Light' (A-G/B-A/C♯-D-G-D/F♯-A). U2's 'Stuck In A Moment You Can't Get Out Of' is coloured by the accented first inversion in the main sequence. In 'Anchorage', Michelle Shocked extends a three-chord change in a similar manner: G-D/F♯-C-D. In Eels' 'Novocaine For The Soul', there is frequent use of a I-IVm chord change; toward the end of the song, this alternates with a I-iIVm change, a first inversion of the F♯m. The change is audible and expressive – a good example of attention to detail. Another example is the main theme for the film *Wag The Dog*, written by Mark Knopfler. The basic sequence is:

I	VII	IV^	VI	VII
Am	G	D	F	G

But the third chord is inverted to create a descending bass line:

I	VII	iIV^	VI	VII
Am	G	D/F♯	F	G

Inversions play a significant role in the eight-bar verse of Gabrielle's 'Give Me Just A Little More Time':

I	iV	VI	V	IV	iI	iII^	V
B♭	F/A	Gm	F	E♭	B♭/D	C/E	F

Inversions play a significant role in Percy Sledge's 'When A Man Loves A Woman', The Equals' 'Baby Now That I've Found You', Judie Tzuke's 'Stay With Me Till Dawn', Edie Brickell's 'Circle', Jimmy Ruffin's 'What Becomes Of The Broken-Hearted', The Spice Girls' 'Mama', R.E.M.'s 'Perfect Circle', Manfred Mann's 'The Mighty Quinn', the intro of Living Colour's 'Desperate People' and the coda of Dire Straits' 'On Every Street'. It is especially worthwhile studying Jimmy Ruffin's 'What Becomes Of The Broken-Hearted' for a whole series of inversions to hear what they can do. Many of The Beach Boys' songs from the *Pet Sounds* era, written by Brian Wilson, make good use of inversions. The realisation that the bass did not always have to play roots, as demonstrated by these songs, influenced Paul McCartney's bass in The Beatles from the mid-1960s onward.

A songwriting signature of Muse is their willingness to put other notes in the bass than the root note. At times their progressions sound almost baroque. The reason for this is the first and second inversions above bass lines that move in ascending or descending semitones. You can hear this in 'Falling Down', 'Micro Cuts' and the guitar break at the end of 'Cave', which is played over the progression Bm-B♭-D/A-E/G♯-G7.

Listen to the opening of The Kings Of Leon's 'Slow Night, So Long', the lead-off track from their second album, *Aha Shake Heartbreak*. Under the opening chords the bass is initially on A and then moves to D and F♯, so there is a strong impression of the chords being inversions. A second inversion D means having an A in the bass. The fragile atmosphere of that album's 'Milk' is created by delicate finger-picked first inversions on G/B and A7/C♯, and a second inversion D.

Inversions figure in Snow Patrol's 'How To Be Dead' on *Final Straw* which has the progression, F going to F/A then B♭ and then G or Gm. The same F/A crops up in 'Same', the closing track, along with G/B and Gm/B♭. The change F-F/A-B♭ can be heard in 'Grazed Knees', a classic use of a first inversion. The intro and verse of 'Ways And Means' exploit a tonic minor to tonic major change in an inverted form. This is a special form of minor to major change because the root note remains the same; only the third of the chord alters. This emphasises the chilly effect of going from major to minor, or gives a sudden warmth if going from minor to major. In 'Ways And Means' the effect is heightened because the bass line has quite a few thirds – playing C under the Am and C♯ under the A major chords. The overall sound is not of a change of root position chords but of changing inversions: Am/C to A/C♯.

The Thrills' 'Big Sur' has an expressive first inversion Am/C in its verse, as well as a second inversion chord IV in its chorus used in a traditional manner to delay the arrival of chord I.

Ascending and descending chord sequences

Inversions can play a significant role in creating ascending and descending chord sequences. Many popular songs have upward or downward progressions where the bass moves step-wise by a semitone (half-step) or tone (full step): 'Whatever', 'All You Need Is Love', 'I Am The Walrus', 'Our House', 'Bell Bottom Blues', 'A Whiter Shade Of Pale', 'Go Now', 'Pictures Of Lily', 'Accidents Will Happen', 'Dear Prudence', 'Tales Of Brave Ulysses', 'Awaiting On You All', and 'Turn Turn Turn'. The Byrds' 'Chestnut Mare' has two descending chord sequences in the same key; the first starts at I and goes down the scale; the second starts at IV and goes down the scale.

Let's take a look at how this can be done, beginning with the notes of a C major scale: C B A G F E D. If we harmonised this by using the primary chords of the scale and treating each note as a root note, the result would be these chords:

Chord function	I	VII	VI	V	IV	III	II
Chord name	C	Bdim	Am	G	F	Em	Dm
Bass pitch	c	b	a	g	f	e	d
Inversion	r	r	r	r	r	r	r

Try strumming these chords at a medium tempo, two beats to each. This is a little stodgy and predictable, and the awkward diminished chord between C and Am would be horrible to sing over. Instead, by using an inversion, we could play it this way:

Chord function	I	V	VI	V	IV	III	II
Chord name	C	G/B	Am	G	F	Em	Dm
Bass pitch	c	b	a	g	f	e	d
Inversion	r	1st	r	r	r	r	r

This is the most common way of harmonising a bassline using these notes. In fact, by making use of inversions it is possible to harmonise this bassline with just the three major chords:

Chord function	I	V	IV	V	IV	III	V
Chord name	C	G/B	F/A	G	F	C/E	G/D
Bass pitch	c	b	a	g	f	e	d
Inversion	r	1st	1st	r	r	1st	2nd

We could use this technique for a verse and introduce the minor chords for a chorus or bridge. Here's another possibility using just the three minor chords:

Chord function	VI	III	VI	III	II	III	II
Chord name	Am/C	Em/B	Am	Em/G	Dm/F	Em	Dm
Bass pitch	c	b	a	g	f	e	d
Inversion	1st	2nd	r	1st	1st	r	r

In this example, fewer chords are used:

Chord function	I	V	VI	VI	IV	I	II
Chord name	C	G/B	Am	Am7/G	F	C/E	Dm
Bass pitch	c	b	a	g	f	e	d
Inversion	r	1st	r	3rd	r	1st	r

The following is a variation with a chromatic passing note:

Chord function	I	V	♭VII	VI
Chord name	C	G/B	B♭	Am
Bass pitch	c	b	b♭	a
Inversion	r	1st	r	r

Because in C major the B♭ ♭VII chord suggests F major, it may sound good to treat IV as a first inversion:

Chord function	I	V	♭VII	IV
Chord name	C	G/B	B♭	F/A
Bass pitch	c	b	b♭	a
Inversion	r	1st	r	1st

Here's an extended variation:

Chord function	I	V	♭VII	IV	♭VI
Chord name	C	G/B	B♭	F/A	A♭
Bass pitch	c	b	b♭	a	a♭
Inversion	r	1st	r	1st	r

Sometimes you can treat that B♭ as a first inversion:

Chord function	I	V	Vm	IV
Chord name	C	G/B	Gm/B♭	F/A
Bass pitch	c	b	b♭	a
Inversion	r	1st	r	1st

Here's an avant-garde harmony for this chromatic line:

Chord function	I	VIImaj	♭VII	VI
Chord name	C	B	B♭	Am
Bass pitch	c	b	b♭	a
Inversion	r	r	r	r

Here's a static harmonisation using the inversions of the major seventh and dominant seventh chords:

Chord function	I	Imaj7	I7	VI (or IV)
Chord name	C	Cmaj7/B	C7/B♭	Am (or F/A)
Bass pitch	c	b	b♭	a
Inversion	r	1st	r	r

In the bridge of The Beatles' 'The Long And Winding Road', we find this:

Chord function	I	IV	I	II	V
Chord name	C	F	C	Dm	G
Bass pitch	g	f	e	d	g
Inversion	2nd	r	1st	r	r

Here's an ascending sequence from The Hollies' 'I'm Alive':

Chord function	I	V7	I	IV	I	VI	I	VI	♭VII
Chord name	C	G7	C	F	C	Am	C	Am	B♭
Bass pitch	c	d	e	f	g	a	g	a	b♭
Inversion	r	2nd	1st	r	2nd	r	2nd	r	r

Let's try a minor key:

Chord function	I	VII	VI	V
Chord name	Am	G	F	Em
Bass pitch	a	g	f	e
Inversion	r	r	r	r

With inversions:

Chord function	I	III	IV	V
Chord name	Am	C/G	Dm/F	Em
Bass pitch	a	g	f	e
Inversion	r	2nd	1st	r

Here's an interesting variant:

Chord function	I	V	VII	IV^	VI	III	IV
Chord name	Am	E/G#	G	D/F#	F	C/E	Dm
Bass pitch	a	g#	g	f#	f	e	d
Inversion	r	1st	r	1st	r	1st	r

And an ascending progression:

Chord function	II	I	IV	I	VI	V	I	VI^
Chord name	Dm	C/E	F	C/G	Am	G/B	C	A/C#
Bass pitch	d	e	f	g	a	b	c	c#
Inversion	r	1st	r	2nd	r	1st	r	1st

EXTENDED CHORDS

Now we can sample the musical shadings offered by more advanced chords. This is part two of the Chord Dictionary (part one is in Section 2).

Seventh chords with a sharpened fifth

An extended chord can be formed by sharpening the fifth of a dominant or major seventh chord. C7: C E G Bb becomes C E G♯ Bb. Cmaj7: C E G B becomes C E G♯ B. This is like superimposing an augmented triad and a major triad two tones (full steps) above. It has a mildly dissonant sound. There's a 7♯5 chord at the end of each four-bar phrase in John Lee Hooker's 'The Healer'. This chord imparts a mild blues/jazz feel and is used as a passing chord or as a means of changing keys. The raised fifth may lead to either the fifth or the sixth in a different chord. C7♯5 might go to F or Am.

Seventh chords with a flattened fifth

Another extended chord is formed by flattening the fifth of a dominant seventh. C7: C E G Bb becomes C E Gb Bb. The 7b5 is close to a dominant seventh chord. Like the 7♯5, it is used as a passing chord or to change key.

Seventh chords with a sharpened fifth

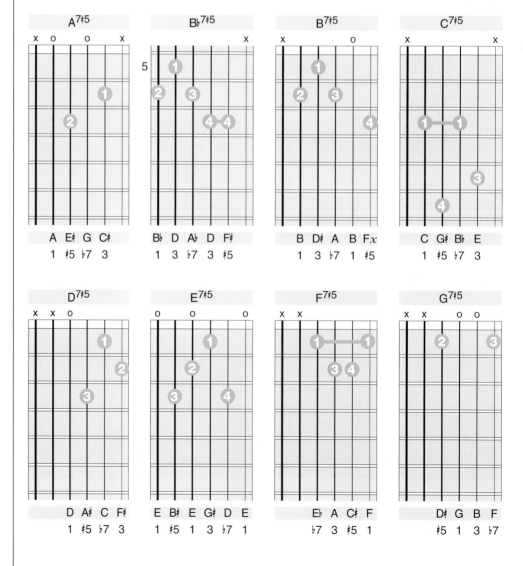

SECTION 9

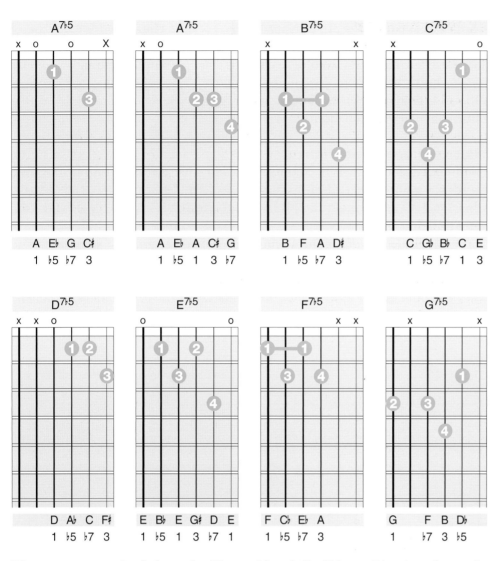

There are several of these in Henry Mancini's 'Moon River' and one in Santana's 'Smooth'.

Chords of the second octave

To create these chords, the scale from which the chord is built is extended over another octave:

C	D	E	F	G	A	B	C	D	E	F	G	A	B	C
1	2	3	4	5	6	7	8	9	10	11	12	13	14	15

Any notes that we cannot distinguish as making any harmonic difference to the chord can be eliminated. Therefore, harmonically 8 and 15 don't exist (because they duplicate the root note); neither does the 10 (which we hear as the third), the 12 (heard as the fifth), or the 14 (heard as a seventh). That leaves the 9, 11 and 13 as additional notes which we interpret as an extra colour to the chord.

C	D	E	F	G	A	B	C	D	E	F	G	A	B	C
1	2	3	4	5	6	7		9		11		13		

SECTION 9 | 149

These extended chords are difficult to voice on the guitar, and in the case of the full 13th, impossible – because it has seven notes and the guitar has only six strings! Their harmonic complexity means they are unsuited to most popular music (unlike jazz, where they are heard much of the time). They are easier to play on a keyboard, where, unlike on the guitar, they can be voiced with the individual notes in sequence.

Major and dominant ninths

Ninth chords are formed by adding the ninth (that is, the second of the scale an octave higher) to a seventh chord. C7: C E G B♭ becomes C E G B♭ D. Cmaj7: C E G B becomes C E G B D. There is also C add9: C E G D, where the seventh is missing.

These ninth chords resemble their respective sevenths, if smoother. The dominant ninth is probably the most significant of the three in popular music. It was used extensively in 1950s rock'n'roll as well as in 1960s rhythm & blues, soul, and funk as well as in jazz. It is not as stark as the dominant seventh. The major ninth, compared to the major seventh, has a less lush sound. The ninth in both cases has a 'diluting' effect. The added ninth (add9) is tenser than

Dominant ninths

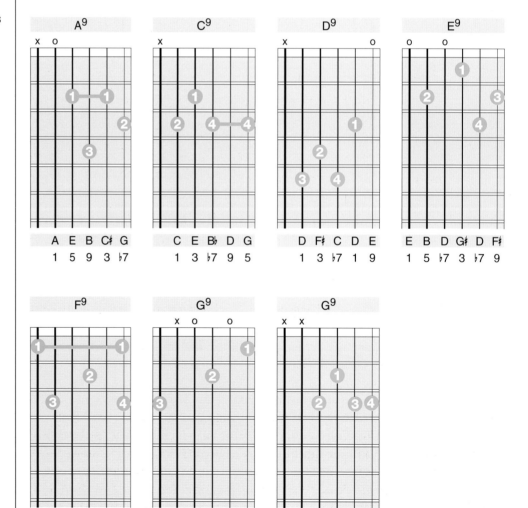

SECTION 9

Added ninths

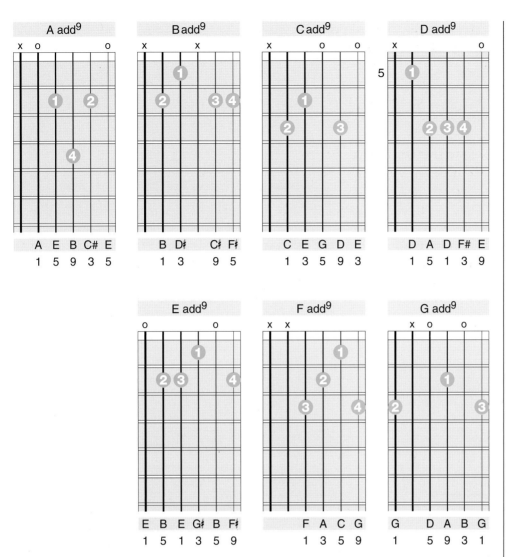

A add⁹	B add⁹	C add⁹	D add⁹
A E B C# E	B D# C# F#	C E G D E	D A D F# E
1 5 9 3 5	1 3 9 5	1 3 5 9 3	1 5 1 3 9

E add⁹	F add⁹	G add⁹
E B E G# B F#	F A C G	G D A B G
1 5 1 3 5 9	1 3 5 9	1 5 9 3 1

either, with more emphasis on the extra note. The add9 can be an interesting variation to a straight major chord, and it is easier to find on the guitar than the others. Both dominant and major ninths can also have altered-fifth forms, in which the fifth is flattened or sharpened. It should also be mentioned that it is possible to add a ninth on top of a fifth on the bottom three strings of the guitar (G D A). This was popularised by Andy Summers of The Police in songs like 'Message In A Bottle' (he also used add ninths on 'Every Breath You Take') and, as he comments in his autobiography, made him for a short while the most imitated guitarist on the planet. One of those imitations was apparently Dubh Chapter's 'Palace Of Dreams'.

Altered dominant ninths: dominant 7 sharp 9, dominant 7 flat 9

The dominant seventh sharp ninth chord is popularly known as the 'Jimi Hendrix chord' because of its use in songs such as 'Purple Haze', 'Stone Free', and 'Crosstown Traffic'. This is sometimes mistakenly described as neither major nor minor because it has both the major third and the minor third in it. This interpretation does not take account of the hierarchy within the chord where the major third low down is the determining factor, and where the sharp

Major ninths

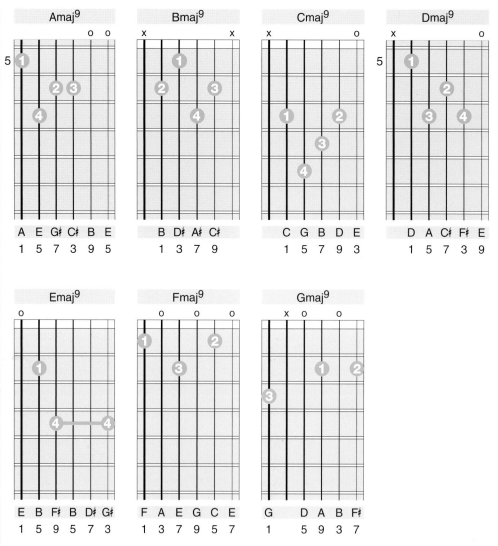

ninth note (it should properly be a flat tenth in a blues context) is clearly an addition to a major chord, not a competing third that has the strength to call the chord's major tonality into question. It should also be noted that what Hendrix is *sometimes* playing (as in the case of 'Foxy Lady') sounds like a 7♯9 but is in fact only a minor seventh.

The Stone Roses used the 7♯9 in 'Love Spreads'. It easily generates baggy-trousered Manchester-type funk, especially if put through a wah-wah. It is also favoured among heavy rock bands for those Spinal Tap-ish thrash endings. It features in The Red Hot Chili Peppers' 'Behind The Sun'. The rarer E7♭9 features half-way through RHCP's 'Dani California' and on the words "open book" in the verse of Wings' 'Live And Let Die'. The lone flat ninth chord, with no seventh, is rare but turns up in blues and slower tempo songs if the harmony is sufficiently sophisticated.

Minor ninths

If you add a ninth to a minor seventh chord, you get a minor ninth (p154). With Cm7, C E♭ G B♭ becomes C E♭ G B♭ D. There is also Cm add9: C E♭ G D, without the seventh. The minor ninth is similar to the minor seventh in sound.

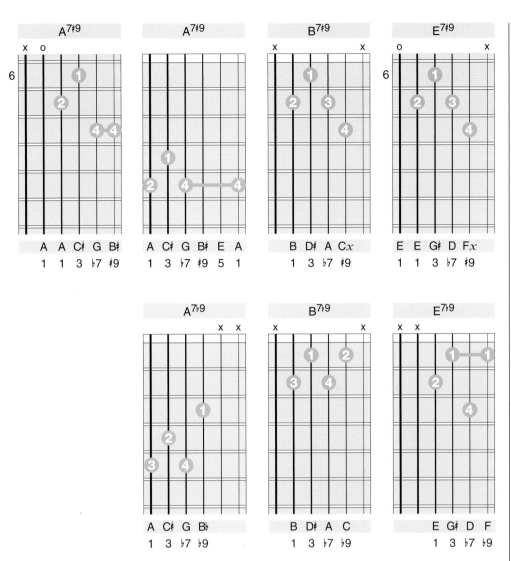

Altered dominant ninths:
Dom 7 Sharp 9, Dom 7
Flat 9, (see page 151)

It is often heard in soul and MOR ballad material as a substitute for the minor seventh, and it intensifies the minor chord. It can be found in some rock and folk. There are wonderful examples of the minor add9 chord in R.E.M.'s 'I Remember California', Cream's 'Badge', Love's 'Alone Again Or', the intro to Led Zeppelin's 'Achilles Last Stand', and in many songs by All About Eve.

Major and minor 11ths

Adding the 11th note (the fourth an octave higher) to a dominant seventh chord or to a major or minor ninth chord produces an 11th chord (p155). C11 is formed when C E G B♭ D becomes C E G B♭ D F; Cmaj11 is formed when C E G B D becomes C E G B D F; Cmin11 is formed when C E♭ G B♭ D becomes C E♭ G B♭ D F. Dominant and major sevenths can also become add11s by the addition of just the 11th. The former can be thought of as two major chords a tone (full step) apart added together; the latter a major chord with a diminished triad on top.

These are complex chords with a subtle colour. Their use on the guitar is compromised by the fact that they are difficult to finger effectively. The more different notes there are in a chord, the harder it is to find a satisfactory

Minor ninths

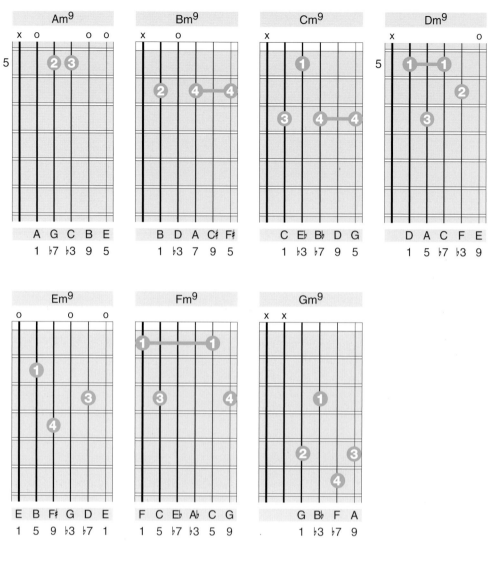

Am^9

x o o o

5

A G C B E
1 ♭7 ♭3 9 5

Bm^9

x o

B D A C♯ F♯
1 ♭3 7 9 5

Cm^9

x

C E♭ B♭ D G
1 ♭3 ♭7 9 5

Dm^9

x o

5

D A C F E
1 5 ♭7 ♭3 9

Em^9

o o o

E B F♯ G D E
1 5 9 ♭3 ♭7 1

Fm^9

F C E♭ A♭ C G
1 5 ♭7 ♭3 5 9

Gm^9

x x

G B♭ F A
1 ♭3 ♭7 9

Minor added ninths

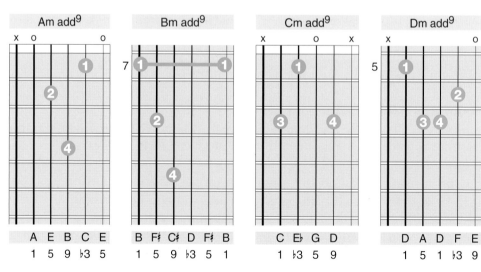

Am add^9

x o o

A E B C E
1 5 9 ♭3 5

Bm add^9

7

B F♯ C♯ D F♯ B
1 5 9 ♭3 5 1

Cm add^9

x o x

C E♭ G D
1 ♭3 5 9

Dm add^9

x o

5

D A D F E
1 5 1 ♭3 9

154 SECTION 9

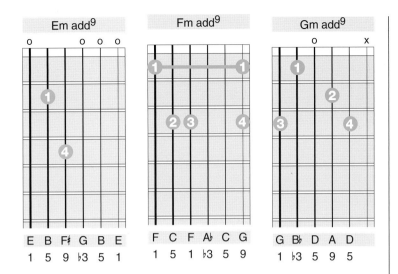

Minor added ninths continued

voicing. On the piano Cmaj11 (C E G B D F) is easy to play. The notes can be voiced in ascending order, three in each hand. If you try to do that on the guitar, look what happens: C is sixth string, fret eight; E is fifth string, fret seven; G is fourth string, fret five. Holding these down will use up your first, third and fourth fingers – but you've got only half the chord. What about B (third string, fret four), D (second string, fret three) and F (first string, fret one)? So often one of the notes has to be left out – usually either the fifth or the ninth – to make an 11th chord playable. They do turn up, though: an 11th is heard at start of 10cc's 'I'm Not In Love', resolving to a straight major chord.

Major and minor 13ths

All 13th chords on the guitar are a compromise. As with the 11th, they are difficult to finger and some notes have to be left out. These chords (p156) are formed by adding the 13th (the sixth an octave higher) to a dominant or a major or minor 11th. C dominant 13 is C E G B♭ D F A; Cmaj13 is C E G B D F A; Cm13 is C E♭ G B♭ D F A. The formation of the minor 13 is affected by which minor scale is used, Aeolian or Dorian. Complex chords such as these have little function in popular songwriting because their tone colour is

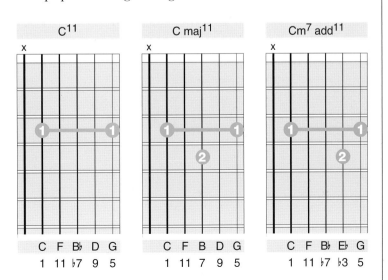

Eleventh chord shapes

Eleventh chord shapes
continued

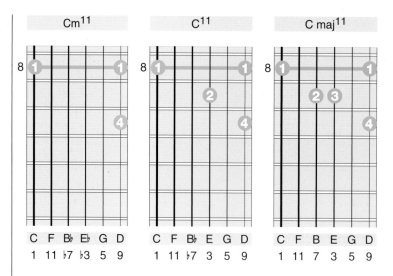

Cm11	C11	C maj11
C F Bb Eb G D	C F Bb E G D	C F B E G D
1 11 b7 b3 5 9	1 11 b7 3 5 9	1 11 7 3 5 9

indistinct. The relationships of the chords are much more important than the types, as long as the ones you're using generally fit the style in which you're writing.

Thirteenth chord shapes

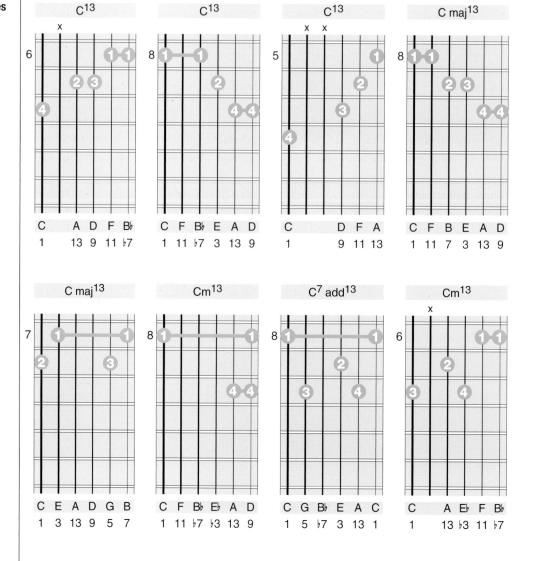

C13	C13	C13	C maj13
C A D F Bb	C F Bb E A D	C D F A	C F B E A D
1 13 9 11 b7	1 11 b7 3 13 9	1 9 11 13	1 11 7 3 13 9

C maj13	Cm13	C7 add13	Cm13
C E A D G B	C F Bb Eb A D	C G Bb E A C	C A Eb F Bb
1 3 13 9 5 7	1 11 b7 b3 13 9	1 5 b7 3 13 1	1 13 b3 11 b7

156 | SECTION 9

Slash chords that are not inversions

Take an ordinary F major, top four strings only: F A C F. If we add the open fifth string, we get F/A, a first inversion; if we hold down C on the fifth string – C F A C F – it's a second inversion. But what happens if we play a G on the sixth string and mute the fifth string, so we have G (x) F A C F? We have F/G. Depending on the musical context, we could stop thinking of the F chord as a chord in its own right and analyse it as if G were the root note. If so, F becomes the flat seventh, A the ninth and C the 11th. (The third, B, and the fifth, D, are both missing.) Strictly speaking, we need a third to tell us whether the chord is major or minor, but context might do that. So this F/G could be used in either a major or minor context as a G dominant 11th. This approach suggests the following:

1 Take a major chord and add a bass note a tone (full step) above its root to make a passable dominant 11th.

2 Take a major chord and add a bass note a fourth above its root to make a ninth chord (C under G B D = 1, 5, 7, 9).

Using extended chords

In most pop, rock and soul songwriting these more complex chords are not used very often. Fascinating as they are, try not to get carried away with them. A fatal habit among keyboard players is to over-use extended chords because they are easy to play. I have known keyboard players who seemed incapable of playing a simple C-Em-Am-G progression without turning it into C11, Em add9♭5, Am7♭5 and G11 (no 3rd). This is as beside the point as guitarists who insist that every song has to have at least two long guitar solos! It may be interesting to play, but songwriting is not about giving yourself interesting things to play. The individual instrumental parts may be dull, or at least not taxing, but the magic of the song is in the whole being greater than the sum of the parts (pun intended).

So use extended chords carefully, just to add a touch of colour here and there. One ninth chord placed at a telling position in a chord progression can add far more than half a dozen. One way to try this out is to take some of the turnarounds in Section 3 and change one of the chords into a more complicated form.

Now it is time to explore one of the most exciting areas of songwriting craft. Got your back-pack, provisions, suncream, and maps? We are going travelling – into the world of key changes.

SECTION 10
KEYS AND KEY CHANGING

To use a geographical metaphor, the chords within a key are like the different districts of your home town, with happy and sad associations. Changing the chord within a key is like making a short journey. By analogy, a key change is like a visit to another county or state, which could be nearby and therefore have similar terrain, or distant and have a very different landscape. Key changes are one of the most powerful song-writing techniques.

What is a key?

A key is a structural device of music. It is derived from a major or minor scale, which in turn creates the chords that belong to that key. In terms of our experience of music, keys are a fundamental aspect of the way we hear and organise music in our minds. A key is a tonal centre, with the key note and key chord at its core. Whenever we land on the key chord (chord I), it feels as though we have reached 'home', or the centre of the music – or, to use a physical analogy, regained our balance. In a major key, this is usually a satisfactory, secure place to be; in a minor key, it feels a place of sadness and regret.

Even within one key, the progression of chords represents a departure from the centre. A key change is called a 'modulation'.

Why is modulation important?

In longer pieces of music, key changes are essential to avoid monotony. Consider a form like the symphony. Most 19th- and early 20th-century symphonies last, on average, 30 to 45 minutes. A symphony that remained in one key would certainly require extraordinary invention to prevent boredom from setting in even during the first of its four movements. That's why expansive forms such as the symphony make extensive use of modulation (key changes), and that modulation itself often expresses meaning or dramatises an inner journey.

Some composers have deployed keys as though they possessed intrinsic extra-musical qualities. In Baroque music, some composers viewed the keys as a sort of metaphysical hierarchy: flat keys were associated with the realms of earth, suffering and hell; sharp keys represented increasing happiness and bliss, culminating in the 'heavenly domain' of E major (the sharpest key in common use at that time). For more on the symbolic possibilities of keys and key changes, read Wilfrid Mellers's *Vaughan Williams And The Vision Of Albion* (1997).

In comparison with a symphony, a song is like a goldfish next to a whale. A song is a short musical form, and therefore modulation isn't essential – though it may be desirable, to add extra interest and contrast. Even in the microcosmic world of the popular song, key changing can be used to excellent effect. Modulation can certainly be found in some popular songwriting, though noticeably less so toward the end of the 20th century, as popular music became increasingly rhythmic and devoid of harmonic colour.

Modulations may be fleeting or more secure. A piece of music might move through several keys in a matter of bars with none of the keys given sufficient time to become established. The home key can be blurred, and it is not always easy to say what key certain bars of music are in – or even *if* they are in a defined key. Franz Ferdinand have a fondness for minor keys, which is unexpected given the overall high-energy feel of their debut album. There are some effective shifts of key, notably in 'This Fire', which goes from Dm to Em for a descending sequence and then returns to its original key. 'Darts Of Pleasure', with its offbeat open disco hi-hat, has a verse based on F♯m and a chorus that's in Em. The transition back at the 1:00 mark on an accentuated, stark B♭ chord is very good if abrupt.

The magic of distance

All major keys have identical internal structures. They are built on the same type of scale which in turn gives rise to the same combination of chords. What differentiates one major key from another is that it is built on keynotes (roots) of differing pitch. But a piece that changes key from C to G subjectively sounds as though it has 'gone somewhere'. From the perspective of C major, G major seems to be a different 'place'. The sense of difference is even more profound if we move from C major to the key of B♭ minor.

Modulation may support the lyrical content – or undermine it. Imagine writing a song about finding new love. Each time you hit the chorus there is a key change upwards. Alternatively, imagine writing a love song in which the speaker sings of the sorrow left behind, in a major key, and the happiness ahead, in a minor key. The keys in this second case are the reverse of what is expected, which suggests that the song is about something more than the lyric makes explicit.

A key change can have a subtle effect that perhaps represents uncertainty or an emotional dislocation. Or it can be crude, as when it is used to heighten the mood of the final choruses for added excitement.

Keys and singing

When you write songs for yourself to sing, take into account which keys suit your voice. Find your lowest and highest notes for comfortable singing, and then any higher notes reachable by pushing your voice, and finally high notes reached by singing falsetto. Relate the highest comfortable note to the scale of the key in which you want to write a song. Check if this note is an important one in the scale, like the root, third or fifth. You may want to plan your melody to take this into consideration.

A well-known producer's recording trick is to pitch a song in a key slightly too high for the singer, so the vocalist's straining for notes becomes indelibly part of the performance. Motown songwriters like Holland-Dozier-Holland sometimes pitched songs in keys that were just a bit too high for Marvin Gaye, or Levi Stubbs of The Four Tops, to bring out more passion in their voices. But if you're going to sing your songs live, don't employ this technique in too many, or you'll never get through a set with your voice intact. The opposite effect is not so common, but worth considering. R.E.M.'s 'Perfect Circle' gains something from Michael Stipe singing at the low end of his range, and as for Lee Marvin's 'Wanderin' Star'....

With age, the voice naturally loses some of its range. This has interesting consequences for a singer-songwriter like Joni Mitchell who relies on altered guitar tunings. Over the years her tunings have had to move down to match the drop in her voice – causing some intonation problems as the guitar strings have got slacker. When the remaining members of Led Zeppelin reconvened in December 2007 to play a concert at the O2 Arena in London, a number of their famous songs – including 'Rock And Roll' and 'Stairway To Heaven', were played a whole tone lower for the sake of Robert Plant's voice. This would have meant re-stringing guitars and bass with heavier gauge strings to compensate for the loss of string tension, but with the advantage of more tone.

Near keys and far keys

Some keys are 'closer' to each other than others – we can speak of 'related' keys, or 'near' and 'far' keys. Adjacent keys (one sharp or one flat away) are close. Each key has a relative minor or major that is three semitones (half-steps) from the root note; that is a near key. These can be seen on this figure, with the relative minor key underneath its paired major:

Flat side									Sharp side					
C♭	G♭	D♭	A♭	E♭	B♭	F	C	G	D	A	E	B	F♯	C♯
A♭m	E♭m	B♭m	Fm	Cm	Gm	Dm	Am	Em	Bm	F♯m	C♯m	G♯m	D♯m	A♯m

If we are in C major, the closest keys are F, G, Am, Dm and Em – chords IV, V, VI, II and III of the key. In each case only one note on the C major scale needs the addition of an accidental (sharp or flat) to create the new key's scale. Next would come C minor, the tonic minor – the minor key that shares the same root note.

Notice that there are 15 major and 15 minor keys on this diagram. If C♭ = B, G♭ = F♯ and D♭ = C♯, that makes the number 12, the same as the number of notes. The range of possible modulations and key-changing effects within this apparently limited number is extraordinary. There are many ways whereby the relative distance of keys can be assessed.

Look back at the Song Chords table in Section 3 and you will notice that adjacent near keys tend to have three or four chords in common, making it easy to change from C major to any of them. The Song Chords table can be utilised to find chords that belong to the key you're in and the one you wish to go to.

Key changing for guitarists

Changing keys is more problematic for guitarists than pianists because of the fingering problems that can arise, which is one reason why songwriter-guitarists modulate less frequently in their songs than songwriter-pianists. For example, take a song whose verse and chorus are in A, with plenty of open-string chords. Raise the key a semitone (half-step) to B♭, and five of the six primary chords turn into barre chords. Guitarists would therefore tend to favour changing to a key that has easier chord shapes.

Instead of it being a problem that trips you up half way through the composition of a song, why not exploit this characteristic of the guitar by reversing the scenario? Start in a key that requires barre chords and then modulate up a semitone (half-step) to a key with open-string chords. The change in the timbre of the chords can be striking. Try B major into C major, or F♯ major into G major, or D♯ minor into E minor. The effect is further complicated by the resonance of certain chords against others – according to how many strings are in the chords. If you write an introduction in an awkward key, at least you won't be stuck in it for long. Your fretting hand will appreciate the break from playing barre chords!

Guitar keys and their associations

On the guitar, A major (three sharps) and E major (four sharps) are both associated with rock, the latter especially with heavy rock, with B major (five sharps) and F♯ major (six sharps) as also-rans. The latter instance might seem implausible because the six primary chords of F♯ major are F♯, G♯m, A♯m, B, C♯, and D♯m – every one a barre chord. But if you drop the minors and bring in some flat degree chords, as is likely if writing a rock number, the six chords would then be F♯, A, B, C♯, D, and E, which is much less of a handful. Sharp keys (without a capo) are much more likely in songs played on electric than acoustic guitars for the simple physical reason that electric guitars have lighter strings and lower actions; it's physically easier. The keys of D, G, and A are popular in indie/'jangle' styles because of the ringing open strings they permit. R.E.M. had a long-standing love affair with E minor for this reason. Oddly, C major has never been a popular rock key.

Some players have marked preferences for certain keys. Mark Knopfler's early songs were often in F and D minor. Blues players who detune a semitone (half-step) end up in E♭ and A♭ by default, as in 'Voodoo Chile (Slight Return)' and some of Stevie Ray Vaughan's songs. Songwriters often establish personal associations with keys – they have 'hot' keys and 'cold' keys, 'summery' keys and 'wintery' keys, or they associate them with colours, or people, or moods.

The keys of B♭ (two flats) and E♭ (three flats) are suited to brass instruments and are associated with 1960s soul/Motown. The Celtic harp is usually tuned to C minor (three flats), so it has Celtic folk associations (listen to the music of Breton harpist Alan Stivell). Several post-2000 indie rock bands seem to have a new fondness for C minor, which is not a great key for guitar because of the barre chords it involves. The Kaiser Chiefs' 'What Did I Ever Give You', Franz Ferdinand's 'Jacqueline', and the 'hymn' section of Radiohead's 'Paranoid Android' are all in C minor.

'Deep' flat minor keys past C minor (three flats) have associations of

CAPO TABLE

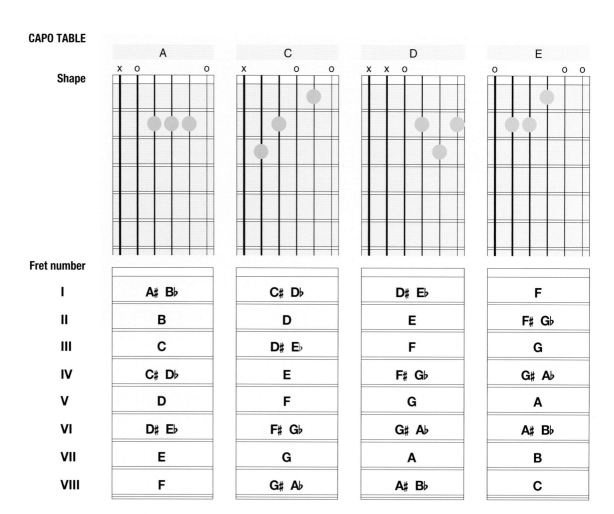

Fret number	A	C	D	E
Shape				
I	A♯ B♭	C♯ D♭	D♯ E♭	F
II	B	D	E	F♯ G♭
III	C	D♯ E♭	F	G
IV	C♯ D♭	E	F♯ G♭	G♯ A♭
V	D	F	G	A
VI	D♯ E♭	F♯ G♭	G♯ A♭	A♯ B♭
VII	E	G	A	B
VIII	F	G♯ A♭	A♯ B♭	C

mystery, coldness, and darkness for some. F minor (four flats) was a favoured key for James Bond film music; session trombonist Don Lusher once said, "If we got a booking for a Bond session with John [Barry], it'd be, 'Oh yes. That'll be another week of F minor then.' It was always F minor. You could bet on it!" This came true yet again with Garbage's 'The World Is Not Enough'. It is an interesting question whether film audiences retain an unconscious memory that Bond music should be in certain keys, and that if it isn't it doesn't sound authentic.

Which keys suit the guitar?

The natural keys for the guitar are those in which the open strings can be maximised. These broadly range from F to E, with their attendant minors. Here are the major keys, with the number of open-string chords in each (this covers chords I–VI plus the ♭VII):

C♭	G♭	D♭	A♭	E♭	B♭	F	C	G	D	A	E	B	F♯	C♯
2	1	0	0	0	1	3	5	5	5	4	3	2	1	0

Guitarists often employ a capo (capodastro, from the Italian *capo tasto*, meaning 'head stop') when playing in flat keys, to make it possible to use open-string

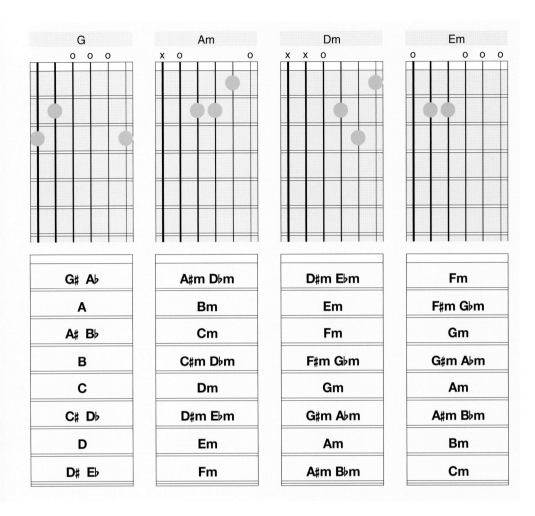

chords. A capo can also be used to lower the action and string tension. Some players like to tune their 12-strings a semitone (half-step) or tone (full step) below concert pitch and then capo at the first or second fret, to lessen the tension on the neck. A capo makes it easy to try a song in different keys with the same chord shapes till you find one that suits your voice. They're great for recording more than one guitar part or in a duo to get a fuller sound.

Here is a table (above) for using the capo. Find the key you are playing in and read up to the shapes at the top and the capo position at the side.

Famous songs that use a capo

I 'Three Steps To Heaven', 'Show Me Heaven', 'Day After Day', 'Kiss Me', 'Changing Of The Guard', 'Jokerman'.

II 'Mrs Robinson', 'Wonderwall', 'Let's See Action', 'Fast Car', 'One Of Us', 'Love Is The Law', 'Julia', 'Norwegian Wood', 'Why Does It Always Rain On Me', 'Run To You', 'And Your Bird Can Sing', 'For No One', 'Nowhere Man', 'Sisters Of Mercy', 'A Hard Rain's Gonna Fall', 'All I Really Want To Do', 'She Belongs To Me'.

III 'Debora', 'By The Light Of A Magical Moon', 'One Inch Rock', 'Homeward

Bound', 'Long Long Long', 'No Surprises', '5:15', 'Getaway', 'Mr Tambourine Man' (Dylan), 'Martha My Dear', 'Hurry Up And Wait', 'More Than Us', 'Every Grain Of Sand', 'I Want You' (Dylan), 'Gypsy Biker', 'Hunter'.

IV 'Catch The Wind', 'Ride A White Swan', 'Holy Mother', 'That's Entertainment', 'Ironic', 'Tumbling Dice' (open G tuning), 'It's All Over Now, Baby Blue', 'All Along The Watchtower' (Dylan), 'Positively Fourth Street', 'Magic'.

V 'I Am The Resurrection', 'Torn', 'It's Only Love' (The Beatles), 'For You Blue', 'Telegram Sam', 'Daisies Of The Galaxy', 'Michelle'.

VI 'Hallelujah', 'Piggies'.

VII 'Here Comes The Sun', 'Blowin' In The Wind', 'Tramp The Dirt Down', 'Driftwood', 'Hotel California'.

VIII 'Girl', 'America' (Razorlight)

How do I change key?

There are many ways of changing key – the choice of route depends partly on whether you are going to a near or far key.

Using chord V

The simplest way is to play chord V of the key you want to get *into*, and from that chord proceed to chord I of the new key. For example, if you wanted to modulate from C major to G major, chord V of G is D (instead of Dm as in C). If this chord V is played as a dominant seventh, the change is strengthened. That gives us this chord progression:

C	F	G	F	C	Dm	D7	G

At the end of this, we are in G major. If that chord then becomes a G7, we can go straight back to C because G is chord V of C major. Remember that any dominant seventh can also take you into a minor key, so G7 is the dominant seventh of C minor as well as C major. The key chord to which you're heading can also be approached from the new chord IV, but the effect is weaker and in the case of going from C to G ambiguous, since C (I in the old key) is IV in the new key (G).

A sequence of dominant seventh chords can create a sense of passing through a series of keys. Take this sequence, starting from A major:

A	F♯m	B	E	A	D	Bm	A

Notice how several of these chords have a dual harmonic function. The fourth chord establishes E as the new key, but the next A takes us briefly into D before returning to A. Try strumming the following version and listen to the difference:

| A | F#m7 | B7 | E7 | A7 | D7 | Bm | A |

After B7, we expect E to be the new key – but E7 (a dominant seventh) suggests that it is chord V of A. But when we land on A, the same thing happens. It's a dominant seventh, suggesting that the new key is D. And then it happens again. D is another dominant seventh, but instead of going to G we go to Bm and then to A as the new key. This features as a bridge in Badfinger's 'No Matter What'; Jimi Hendrix's 'Crosstown Traffic' and the chorus of The Kinks' 'Sunny Afternoon' have similar sequences.

Consider this progression from the verse of Queen's 'Now I'm Here' for the effect of a series of V-I changes in which the sense of a home key is temporarily lost:

V	I	V	I	V	I	V	I
G	C	A	D	B	E	F#	C#

There are many other modulation techniques. Apart from chord V, you can use another chord that is common to both keys, approach it as you would from the home key with a home-key chord, but leave it with a chord that is *only* in the new key. This should either be chord V of the new key or should lead to chord V of the new key.

Same chord, different role

Remember that a single chord can have a different role in different keys, even though its pitch (and its fingering on the guitar) remains the same. The analogy would be with an actor and his or her various film roles. A chord has the ability to play different roles according to whether it is chord I, II, III, IV, V, VI, or ♭VII of the key. Consider the function of C in the following keys:

	I					
C major	C	Dm	Em	F	G	Am	Bdim

			IV			
G major	G	Am	Bm	C	D	Em	Fdim

				V		
F major	F	Gm	Am	B♭	C	Dm	Edim

		III				
A minor	Am	Bdim	C	Dm	Em	F	G

						♭VII
D minor	Dm	Edim	F	Gm	Am	B♭	C

The C chord is always the same in itself, but it appears in different harmonic roles.

Shortcut key changes

Key changes in pop songs usually have to be achieved quickly because the song itself is short. Here are some typical 'shortcuts' to near keys. Remember that in each instance you could end up in the minor key of the last chord if you wanted.

C	Dm	D7	G

C	Em	E7	A

C	Em	D7	G

C	Em	A7	D

C	F	Fm	Bb7	Eb

C	G	A7	D

C	G	Gm	D

C	G	Gm	C	F

C	Am	A7	D

C	Am	E

Notice that II^, III^ and VI^ all have possibilities for modulation. In the verse of The Bee Gees' 'I've Got To Get A Message To You', we have a I-II-V-I progression that becomes I-II-V-VI^ (G instead of Gm) to lead from Bb to a C chorus. This is a strong modulation because V in Bb (F) is IV in C. In the verse of The Supremes' 'Stop! In The Name Of Love', the progression goes:

I	Imaj7	Vm	VI^7	IV	V	IV	V
C	Cmaj7	Gm	A7	F	G	F	G

This is clever because Gm and A7 are chords IV and V in D minor, so we expect to go to D minor, but instead the music turns back to F – chord IV in C. (To hear a song in C major that does have an A7 leading into D minor, listen to the verse of The Supremes' 'Baby Love'.)

Travelling to distant keys
To go to a distant key, choose an intermediary key to help you make the change. For example, imagine going from C major to B major – two keys that have no chords in common. The chart opposite shows various options.

Remember the possibility of enharmonic chords, which may be written as flat in one key but sharp in another – like the Ab/G# in this example.

Key changes with diminished sevenths
The diminished seventh chord is important for key changing. Each note within a diminished seventh can be taken as the leading note (seventh) for a new tonic. Take Gdim7, whose notes are G Bb Db Fb (E). You can get from this chord to any key whose scale includes one of these notes.

- G is the 7th of Ab major or minor
- Bb (as A#) is the 7th of B major or minor
- Db (as C#) is the 7th of D major or minor
- Fb (as E)is the 7th of F major or minor

Therefore, Gdim7 could take you into the keys of Ab, B, D, or F, or their minors. Try changing from Gdim7 to any of these keys, and you will hear that it works.

Old key	I	IV			
Crude semitone shift	C	F	F#	F#7	B
New key			V	V7	I

Old key	I	III		
Abrupt romantic	C	Em	B	
New key		IVm	I	

Old key	I	III		
Crude semitone shift	C	Em	E7	B
New key			IV7	I

Old key	I	IV	II^			
Climbing + secondary key	C	Dm	D7	G	A	B
New key			[V	I]		
				♭VI	♭VII	I

Old key	I	III^			
Intermediate key	C	E	A	F#m	F#7	B
New key		[V	I	VI]		
					V7	I

Old key	I	VI	♭VI^			
Semitone shift + middle key	C	Am	A♭ (G#)	C#m	F#7	B
New key			[V	I]		
				II	V7	I

Classic pop modulation #1: the semitone shift

The most common (and crudest) key change in popular music is executed to avoid monotony in the repetition of the final choruses. Pop songs revolve around the immediate appeal of a repeated chorus, so by shifting the chorus into a new key it can be repeated with a sense of the familiar somehow freshened.

This has tended to be done in two main ways. One is brutally direct: shift up a semitone (half-step).

[C major]	I	II	IV	V					
Old key	C	Dm	F	G	C#	D#m	F#	G#	
New key					I	II	IV	V	[C#major]

Although C major and C♯ major are only a semitone apart, this is a shift to a distant key. What was a scale of seven natural notes (C D E F G A B) has become a scale of seven sharps (C♯ D♯ E♯ F♯ G♯ A♯ B♯) or five flats if we think of the change as C major to D♭ major (D♭ E♭ F G♭ A♭ B♭ C). The chord change from G to C♯ is inelegant, and usually only the speed of the change and the *brio* of the arrangement disguise the dissonance. Even so, the ear accepts the semitone shift as a small step in pitch. And because all the musical material – the melody, the words, the chords, the rhythm, the parts – remain the same, this is enough to make it acceptable.

KEYS AND KEY CHANGING

This key change is an act of musical bravura rather than an approach that is musically smooth. If C is the last chord of the sequence, chord I of C major merely slides up to chord I of C♯ major. If the sequence ends on chord V, G, that could slide to G♯(7) for a V-I into the new key. The problem is that the two keys have no chords in common. Another approach might be via the III^ chord and a temporary modulation to A major:

[C major]	I	III	III^			
Old key	C	Em	E	A	G♯7	C♯
			[V	I]		
New key				♭VI	V	I	[C♯major]

Here's another way of doing it:

Old key	I	III	III^			
	C	Em	E	F♯	G♯7	C♯
			[I	II^]		
New key				IV	V7	I	[C♯major]

Here are some songs that use a semitone shift: 'I Try' D-E♭, 'Glad All Over' D-E♭ (v), 'Baby Love' (v), 'The Onion Song' A♭-A, 'Heaven Help Us All' A♭-A, 'I Got You Babe' F-F♯, 'Always Something There To Remind Me' A♭-A, 'Silence Is Golden', 'Harlem Shuffle' Am-B♭m, 'Don't Stand So Close To Me' (v) E♭ (ch) D, 'The Happening', 'Farewell Is A Lonely Sound', 'For Once In My Life', and 'C'mon C'mon C'mon'.

The Beatles' 'And I Love Her' starts in E major, goes to F major, and ends in D major. This is reached by a sudden dislocating leap from E to Gm at the guitar solo. An unprepared modulation has a dramatic effect of its own. The Beach Boys' 'I Get Around' starts in G, moves to A for the guitar solo and then to A♭ for the last verse and chorus. Stevie Wonder's 'My Cherie Amour' moves from D♭ to D on a swooning "maybe some day", where the key change projects the song into an imagined future. In The Supremes' 'You Keep Me Hanging On', the home key of A♭ contrasts with B and F♯. Marv Johnson's 'I'll Pick A Rose For My Rose' goes from B♭ to B to C and does this shift twice. The change from A to B♭ in The Four Tops' 'Shake Me Wake Me' only serves to pitch Levi Stubbs's agonised vocals to a higher degree of eye-watering anguish.

By the mid-1960s Holland-Dozier-Holland were often willing to exploit the semitone shift to dizzy extremes. The Isley Brothers' 'I Guess I'll Always Love You' starts in C but near the end it suddenly shifts up to D♭ and after only one hook moves up again to D just before the fade. They went further with The Supremes' 'I Hear A Symphony', where the song shifts a semitone (half-step) at least four times and does so somewhat abruptly, causing difficulties for the pitching of the melody (a classic problem of this modulation). It starts in C, moves to D♭, swings wildly to D and finishes in E♭. Diana Ross copes with the first three key changes but is audibly off-pitch for a bar on the last one. The rising modulations, key by key, have significance lyrically in expressing the ecstasy of the lovers. The excessive modulation may also be a nod to the word "symphony" in the title.

Classic pop modulation #2: the tone shift

After the semitone (half-step) shift comes the tone (full step) shift. This is a key change to a closer key than the semitone shift. If a song is in C major, a tone shift will take it to D major, so what was a scale of seven natural notes (C D E F G A B C) becomes a scale of two sharps (D E F♯ G A B C♯).

Like the semitone shift, this key change is usually performed in songs by an act of musical assertion rather than an approach that is musically smooth. In fact, though, there are plenty of common chords with which to make the approach: namely, Em, G and C (as a common ♭VII chord in D) as well as F (as ♭III in D).

Sometimes this modulation is used not only for repeats of a chorus but to contrast a verse and a chorus, giving each chorus a 'lift' in relation to the verse. A IV-I change into the new key can easily do the trick:

						V		
verse:	C	F	G	C	F	G	chorus:	D
						IV		I

Examples of songs with a tone-shift modulation include: 'My Girl' C-D, 'Up The Ladder To The Roof' B♭-C, 'What Becomes Of The Broken-Hearted' (v) B♭ (ch) C, 'Baby I Need Your Loving' (v) B♭ (ch) A♭, 'So Lonely' C-D, 'Going Underground' B-C♯, 'If You're Going To San Francisco' Em-F♯m (partial final v), 'Young Girl', 'Something In The Air' E-F♯, 'Londinium', 'She's Waiting' G-A, 'Fox On The Run' C (ch) B♭ (v) (drops back), 'See My Baby Jive' (v) D (ch) E, 'I've Just Got To Get A Message To You' (v) B♭ (ch) C, 'Don't Worry Baby' E-F♯, 'My Sweet Lord' E-F♯, 'See Emily Play' (v) G (ch) A, 'Dance Away' (v) E♭ (ch) F, 'Anarchy In The UK' (2nd guitar break goes C-D then back), 'God Save The Queen' A-B, 'Instant Karma' (v) A (ch) G, 'Only Happy When It Rains' (Garbage) (v) B (ch) C♯, 'Please Forgive Me' (v) A (ch) B and 'Exhuming McCarthy' A♭-F♯(G♭). Contrast 'Instant Karma' which drops a tone from A to G.

Other modulations

Here are some other modulations. The headings give the interval of the key change, the distance in semitones as a figure (useful for frets on the guitar) and then what it would be as a key-change from C major – but remember these modulations are available from any note.

Major to tonic minor (0): C-Cm or vice versa

'Fool On The Hill', 'While My Guitar Gently Weeps', 'Shakin' All Over', 'Runaway' (v) B♭m (ch) B♭, 'Ha! Ha! Said The Clown' (v) Dm (ch) D, 'Come Round Here' G-Gm, 'Seven Rooms Of Gloom' split between F♯ and D♯m, 'Telegram Sam' A (v) Am (ch), 'December Will Be Magic Again' (v) Cm (ch) C, 'No Milk Today' (v) Am (ch) A, 'Runaway' (v) Fm (ch) F, 'Live And Let Die' (starts in G, riff section Gm), 'Lonely Days' (v) Cm (ch) C, 'Kiss From A Rose' Gm-G, 'Baker Street' Dm-D.

Minor third (3): C-Eb or Ebm

'Children Of The Revolution' (v) E (ch) G, 'Get Ready' (v) D (ch) F, 'Shoplifters

Of The World Unite', 'You're Going To Lose That Girl', 'Don't Sleep In The Subway' (v) C (ch) E♭, 'Goodbye Yellow Brick Road' A-C, 'Pretty Woman' F-A♭, 'Summer Of 69' (br) D-F, 'When You're Young And In Love' C-E♭, 'Tears In Heaven' A-C, 'I Predict A Riot' (v) Cm (ch) A♭.

Major third (4): C-E or Em
'Needles And Pins' A-C♯, 'Message In A Bottle' (v) C♯m (ch) A, 'There's A Place' (v) A (ch) C♯m, 'Bus Stop' Em (br, G-F♯7-Bm, momentarily in Bm).

Fourth (5): C-F or Fm
'Mull Of Kintyre' (v) A (v) D, 'You've Got Your Troubles' (v) A♭-D♭, 'Octopus's Garden' E-A, 'Roadrunner' C-F, 'Sidewinder' (v) C (ch) G, 'I Can See For Miles' (v) E-A (br), 'Yes It Is' E-A (br), 'Wishing Well' Em-Am, 'Candyman' Gm-Cm, 'Badge' (v) Am (br) D, 'Someone Saved My Life Tonight' (v) G (ch) C, 'Everything I Do (I Do For You)' D♭-G♭ (br).

Fifth (7): C-G or Gm
'Make It Easy On Yourself' (v) A (ch) E, 'Crush With Eyeliner' (v) A (ch) E, 'Great Things', 'Yeh Yeh', 'The Sidewinder Sleeps Tonite' (v) C (ch) G, 'Wonderful World' C-G (br).

Minor sixth (8): C-Ab or Abm
'Walk This Way' riff E, C (v), 'Can't Stop This Thing We Started' A goes to F for bridge and part of penultimate chorus.

Major sixth (9): C-A or Am
[To A] 'Pictures Of Lily' C-A, 'Walk On By' (v) Am (ch) F, 'Bell Bottom Blues' (v) C (ch) A, 'Bungalow Bill' (ch + v) in relative minor, 'Something' (v) C (br) A, 'Things We Said Today' (v) starts in Am goes to F. 'Don't Leave Me This Way' (v) D♭, (ch) B♭.

[To Am] 'Blackberry Way' (v) Em (ch) G♭ Am (detuned), 'You Don't Have To Say You Love Me' (v) Dm (ch) D, 'Fool On The Hill' (v) D (ch) Dm, 'Standing In The Shadows Of Love' D-B♭m, 'While My Guitar Gently Weeps', 'Roxanne' (v) Gm (ch) B♭, 'When I'm Sixty Four' C-Am (br), 'I Should Have Known Better' (v) ends on III^, (br) VI. An unusual variation on this key change is Fleetwood Mac's 'Before The Beginning' where B♭ minor plunges down to G minor at the coda.

Using modulation to contrast sections
Modulation is an effective means to contrast sections in a song. The Beatles' 'You Never Give Me Your Money' starts in A minor, goes to C major for the bridge and then to A for the last verse. The contrasts are enhanced by tempo and arrangement features. Other multiple key songs include The Beatles' 'Lucy In The Sky With Diamonds' (A, F, G), The Kinks' 'Days' (D, F, Dm), Wings' 'Band On The Run' (D, Am, C), Bruce Springsteen's 'Jungleland', Catatonia's 'Road Rage' (at least six keys!) and David Bowie's 'Word On A Wing'. Amy Winehouse's 'You Know I'm No Good' has a verse in D minor and a chorus in A minor.

Sting's 'Fortress Round My Heart' has a verse in Gm, E♭, F♯m but the chorus is in Em. Thunderclap Newman's 'Something In The Air' moves from E to F♯ to C to A♭. Catatonia's 'Londinium' goes from A in the verse to B in the chorus to C♯ in the last chorus. The Who's 'Pinball Wizard' has an intro in Bm, goes to B and D and has a final verse in A. A lover's exuberance is depicted in The Supremes' 'The Happening' by a mid-verse jump from G major to B♭ major, a bridge modulation to E minor and a last verse that goes up a semitone (half-step) from the first verse in order to go A♭ major and then to B.

Unsettled or ambiguous key centres

Techniques such as displacing, suppressing or delaying the key chord, or using chords that don't belong to any one key, can create tonal ambiguity. Consider this sequence from the verse of Cilla Black's 'Step Inside Love' (penned by Paul McCartney):

C	Gm7	G♭9	G♭7	F	Fm7	E7	E♭	F	G7	Dm7	G7

There is a chord V to chord Vm that leads to a feeling of ambiguity of key in the chorus of David Bowie's 'All The Young Dudes'.

Using transposition

Transposition can become a song's driving force. The Who's 'My Generation', The Kinks' 'All Day And All Of The Night' and 'You Really Got Me' are songs that use a simple chord change and transpose it into different keys. The chorus of The Beach Boys' 'California Girls' pushes a melodic idea through B to A to G. Semitone (half-step) or tone (full step) shifts often occur with this technique, though its aim is often not to change key but to preserve the melodic material. Madness's 'House Of Fun' starts in D and goes to Em and F♯m on the chorus as the hook line is transposed up a tone.

Of all the techniques covered in *How To Write Songs On Guitar* I would say that currently modulation is the most neglected technique in popular song. It can take planning and a bit more trial-and-error with progressions, but a well-judged key change can greatly deepen a song. For more detailed discussion of the emotional effects of modulation see some of the songs discussed in Section 14.

SECTION 10 | **171**

SECTION 11
GUITAR RESOURCES PART 1

There are many ways that you, as a guitarist, can get the most from your instrument when writing and recording songs. Here are some tips on how to use the guitar effectively in song arrangements.

Get more from one guitar
Try these methods to get a fuller recorded sound from a single guitar part:

■ Use stereo delay recorded onto two tracks.

■ Use stereo delay onto two tracks, with one side also going through chorus, distortion, phasing, or similar processing.

■ When recording an acoustic, put a pickup on it and send that signal to one track; use a microphone to capture the pure acoustic sound and send that to another track.

Make two guitars work together
If you perform live with another guitarist or make multi-track recordings, you have the opportunity to use more than one guitar part. The traditional divide between rhythm guitar and lead guitar doesn't always apply in a song, because the lead will usually be confined to a short break in the bridge or middle eight, unless you play counterpoint to the melody in a disciplined way.

Here are some effective guitar combinations. The trick is not to duplicate a part but to create contrasted guitar tones to get a fuller, more interesting sound (for detail on this aspect of songwriting see my book *Arranging Songs*).

■ Use one guitar with single-coil pickups and another with double-coil pickups – for example, a Fender Stratocaster and a Gibson Les Paul. Take advantage of the recently reissued guitars by companies such as Danelectro and Godin that have lipstick-tube pickups or mini-humbuckers.

■ Try these pairings: electric + electric, electric + semi-acoustic, electric + acoustic, 6-string + 12-string, nylon + steel.

■ Try a clean tone with distorted, standard tuning with open tuning, capoed and non-capoed, standard and detuned standard. Clean guitars provide harmonic definition; overdriven guitars give punch and aggression.

■ Make the guitars dynamic by taking care where you bring them into a mix and where you take them out. Play full chords and triads; balance strumming with arpeggios. Remember that fifths strengthen. Other possibilities include rhythmic interweaving, twin lead, contrasted voicings and low on the neck versus high on the neck.

Part playing

One of the basic principles of making guitars work in a recording is part-playing. If you have played a lot of rhythm guitar or sung your songs solo, you are accustomed to strumming chords constantly to get a full sound. If you like jamming lead guitar, you are accustomed to the freedom to constantly whack out endless streams of notes. Neither of these approaches necessarily works when arranging and recording songs.

Phil Manzanera, guitarist with UK art-glam band Roxy Music, once told me, "We had a very good producer from the second album onwards, Chris Thomas, who had worked with The Beatles, had done *The Dark Side Of The Moon* and subsequently worked with The Sex Pistols. I learned an incredible amount from him about part-playing in recording. With Chris it was: 'Look for the gap, don't play over the vocal, less is more.' You learned how to position things – just as all the great Motown stuff has incredible position and texture. All the parts add up to something greater. It all locks in." You can hear this in, for example, the Roxy Music hit 'Street Life', where Manzanera's guitar often occurs at the end of a vocal phrase, and this approach is especially felt in Roxy Music's 'Avalon'.

To understand part-playing requires, first, the realisation that the overall sound of a mix can generate the harmony, so you don't have to strum chords all the time. Likewise, drums and bass create rhythm, so you don't have to keep strumming for rhythmic reasons either. Sometimes what is needed from a lead guitar during the verses is three or four well-chosen notes to add melodic interest between gaps in the singing. If you find your multi-track recordings start to feature more fragmentary guitar parts, then you're probably on to the right thing. When you come to play the song live you have to re-combine these various phrases into a single, coherent and effective guitar part.

Guitar effects

Modern technology made a vast palette of tones available to the electric guitarist, even before digital modelling appeared on the music scene in the 1990s. Rock arrangements require a touch of overdrive, distortion, or fuzz for an authentic 1960s sound. Remember that distortion tends to soak up frequencies – even on a hard HM track, you may not need as much as you think, let alone as much as is available with most multi-effects processors. Listen to the amount of overdrive Jimmy Page routinely used, on classic Led

Zeppelin tracks like 'The Ocean' – not as much as you might think (nor as many overdubs, either!).

Chorus, delay, flanging and phasing thicken a clean guitar sound and are suitable for rhythm parts. Some of the latest processors offer speaker cabinet, mic placement, vintage amp and guitar simulations to further widen your sound. Synth and MIDI guitars open up a new world of sound triggered from the guitar.

Delay and counterpoint

Fast delays thicken a sound; longer ones lend depth and interest to lead breaks, even if the delay is quieter than the 'dry' signal. Multi-tap echoes will generate rhythms in time with the echo, so it sounds as if there are two guitars playing at the same time. U2's The Edge is a master of this approach. The live recording *Under A Blood Red Sky* gives a good indication of how effective this can be. '11 O'Clock Tick Tock' has a guitar part that acts as counter-melody to the vocal at the same time it outlines the harmony. The Edge's parts often feature open strings ('I Will Follow' and 'Gloria'), and in solos such as the one in 'Sunday Bloody Sunday' he moves up and down a string whilst hitting the adjacent one. 'Pride' also features this sound, along with effective harmonics. U2 songs such as 'Where The Streets Have No Name' and 'I Still Haven't Found What I'm Looking For' are classics of rhythmic guitar playing interacting with delay, where a simple phrase is transformed by the notes bouncing back. Live recordings of All About Eve's Tim Bricheno on tracks like 'Candy Tree' likewise show great use of echo to fill out a guitar sound. Guitarist Nick McCabe's multi-layered stereo delays are crucial to the ambient groove developed by The Verve, as can be heard on their recent album *Forth*.

Working with sustain

Even the finest acoustic guitars have comparatively short sustain, a factor that has shaped guitar technique. Strumming and fingerpicking are techniques that ensure a wash of sound, and, in the case of fingerpicking, a harmonic backdrop for a melody.

To increase sustain, guitarists have experimented with string gauges (heavier strings mean more sound), altered tunings, and feedback. A compressor enhances sustain because it boosts the level of a decaying note. Electric players can get extra sustain with distortion and overdrive, but remember also to work on the quality of the way you hold a note on the fingerboard – that's sustain too. The E-Bow is a hand-held gizmo that, when positioned close to the string, produces a sustained note (R.E.M. celebrated it in their song 'E-Bow The Letter'). The US company Fernandes has developed a guitar with a similar sustain device built into it.

You can use the volume control on an electric guitar to do this trick: turn off the volume pot, play a note and then turn the pot up – the note starts out inaudible and fades up. There's no percussive 'click' when the note is struck, and the ear is more conscious of the sustain in the sound. This technique is favoured by country players because it simulates the sound of steel guitar. How easy it is to manipulate the volume pot depends on the physical layout of your guitar. (If it's difficult or impossible, a volume pedal can be used to do the same thing.) This trick works well with reverb and delay, especially if you come in with a bend, and it can give an expressive quality to chords. Jan Akkerman of Focus deployed this technique to great effect (have a listen to the track 'Focus' from their debut album *In And Out Of Focus*). Fleetwood Mac's 'Dreams', The Smiths' 'Well I Wonder' and Dire Straits' 'Brothers In Arms' also feature it, though in these instances it was probably done with a volume pedal. For a superb amalgam of wah-wah pedal and volume/echo effects seek out the All About Eve track 'Freeze' from their album *Ultraviolet* (1992).

Solos

If you are going to play a solo in a song, think hard about its length and make sure that it serves a musical purpose. Solos should have a strong thematic interest even when they're not melodic. Some songs need something more atmospheric than a few favourite pentatonic blues licks – think of Andy Summers' celebrated solo on The Police's 'Bring On The Night', which amounts to feedback, a fourth and two sixths.

The songwriting guitarist's basic tool kit for lead breaks and fills consists of: the major scale, the natural minor scale, major and minor pentatonic scales, the blues scale, and the Dorian and Mixolydian modes. That will get you through most musical situations (see pages 176-177).

Muse's use of the harmonic minor scale is characteristic of their rock-pomp. You can hear E harmonic minor on 'Sunburn' and 'New Born', F♯ harmonic minor on 'Muscle Museum' (its E♯ clearly heard at 1:54-2:00), and D harmonic minor in the solo on 'Micro Cuts' (2.42-3.06) and in 'Darkshines'.

A quick guitar solo can often be turned out using the pentatonic major or minor scales. The pentatonic major will fit major keys but not minor ones. The pentatonic minor will fit minor keys, and it can also be used in a major key if the song has a strong blues element. In chord terms, this means it will sound acceptable over I, IV, V and ♭VII, or if you use the hard rock formula it's I, IV, V plus ♭VII, ♭VI and ♭III. It won't sound as good over the major key's minor chords (II, III, VI) where you run the risk of sounding positively inept.

It isn't always the case that the lead guitar supplies a distinct solo and that is it. There are songs where the guitar acts as a kind of second voice to the vocal – The Stone Roses' 'Ten Storey Love Song', for example. In Dire Straits' 'Sultans Of Swing', 'You And Your Friend', and 'Brothers In Arms', Mark Knopfler seems to share the vocal part with the guitar. Robert Plant's 'Big Log' is another example – half vocal, half instrumental. The album *Baron Von Tollbooth And The Chrome Nun* (1973), by members of Jefferson Airplane, has many instances of almost continual lead guitar running throughout a track. This was more common during the tail-end of the hippie period, when guitarists were encouraged to solo endlessly while everyone got stoned and when Hendrix cast a long and influential shadow, than in more recent decades. It is the polar opposite of the concept of part-playing. It can sound messy, but this album demonstrates it does have a certain dishevelled (counter-cultural) charm.

Beyond scales: thirds, fourths, sixths and octaves

Guitar breaks and fills do not have to be scale-orientated. You can also use triads, arpeggios, and intervals. These have the advantage of thickening the

SECTION 11 | 175

A SCALES
A major

A pentatonic major

A natural minor (Aeolian)

A pentatonic minor

A blues scale

A harmonic minor

A Dorian

A Mixolydian

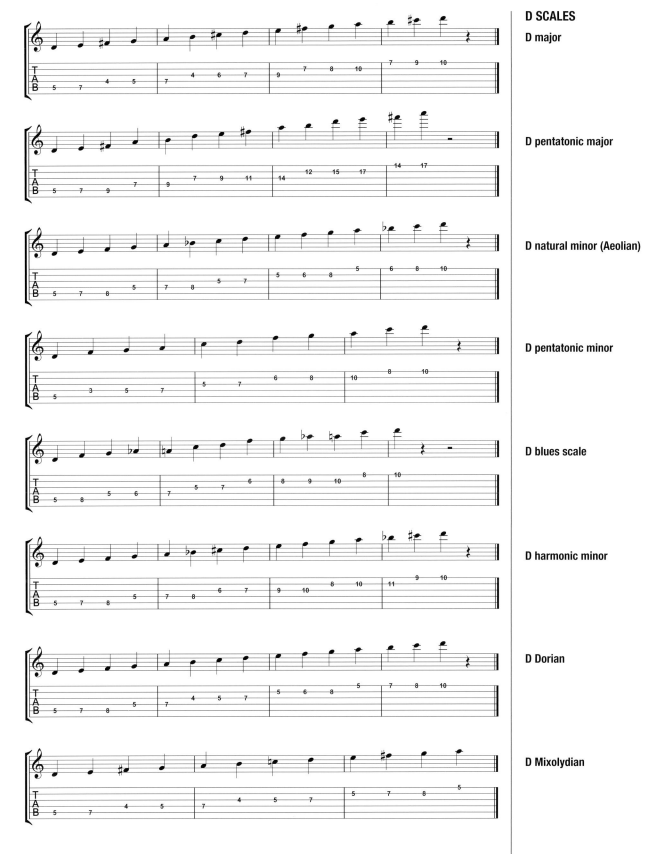

D SCALES

D major

D pentatonic major

D natural minor (Aeolian)

D pentatonic minor

D blues scale

D harmonic minor

D Dorian

D Mixolydian

sound more than single notes, so much so that combined with the right bassline they will imply harmony without the need for any guitar track playing full chords.

Major and minor thirds (C-E, C-E♭) provide a 'sweet' sound. They were used frequently by Johnny Marr with The Smiths – listen to 'This Charming Man'. Marr also showed masterful imagination when he placed dissonant thirds over the main I-♭III-IV chord change in 'How Soon Is Now'. The famous break on The Beatles' 'Twist And Shout' is in thirds. Thirds sound great on strings 1+2 or 2+3, but seem progressively less effective as you go down the strings in pitch (but see what you think of those on The Cure's 'Just Like Heaven'). There is a fabulous guitar break on Tears For Fears' 'Everybody Wants To Rule The World' using thirds and fourths instead of a scale. When moving them up and down, it is important to establish a guide finger to facilitate smooth changes.

When a third is turned upside down, you get a sixth. A minor third (C-E♭) becomes a major sixth (E♭-C), and a major third (C-E) becomes a minor sixth (E-C). Sixths are similar in sound to thirds, though not quite as sweet. They are common for fills, and many blues 12-bars finish with a sequence of sixths. Soul man Steve Cropper used sixths on many classic recordings for the Stax record label. They are usually played on either strings 1+3 or 2+4.

Octaves are mainly deployed in solos for strengthening a phrase. Jazz guitarists like to use octaves, especially to thicken a melody. In his last years, Jimi Hendrix made plentiful use of octaves in songs such as 'Freedom' and 'Dolly Dagger'. Foo Fighters used octaves on some of *One By One*: there are octaves on the intro to 'Overdrive', at the start of 'Low', rapidly strummed octaves on the right at 3:14-40 during a solo, and at the end of 'Times Like These' octaves on the left reinforce the chord changes.

Perfect fourths (C-F) have a distinctive 'bare' Oriental sound. On the top two strings they occur at the same fret, so they can be held down with one finger. Let's say we are playing a sequence of fourths in D major, commencing at fret

Thirds, fourths, and sixths

three. The sequence goes DG – EA – F♯B – GC – AD – BE – C♯F♯. If we treat the top note (G) as the key, you will find one position always sounds wrong. That's because G major does not have a C♯. To adapt the pattern for a key whose root note is on the top string, simply flatten the second-string note when you get to the next-to-last position. If you play the original sequence as DG – EA – F♯B – AD – BE in D major, you have a pentatonic major scale harmonised in fourths.

Fourths can be heard in Chuck Berry's songs and amped up in many of the guitar breaks on The Sex Pistols' *Never Mind The Bollocks*. Their exotic sound is exploited in The Vapors' 'Turning Japanese', The Beatles' 'Don't Let Me Down', Pulp's 'A Little Soul', David Bowie's 'China Girl', The Cranberries' 'Zombie', Led Zeppelin's 'Ten Years Gone', and the intro to Wings' 'Band On The Run'.

Open strings

Open strings generate bigger sounds. Play the right scale for the key or progression up and down one string (instead of across the fretboard) and hit an

Open-string drones

open string above or below it. Treat the open string as the root note of a major or minor chord. If soloing over an E chord (major or minor), the top open E is available as a drone. The open B will work for B major or B minor, and the open G string for G major or minor. The fretting hand then plays the right scale up and down an adjacent string. Since the top three strings make an E minor chord and the second, third, and fourth make an open G, if you are playing in either of these keys you could have two drones sounding rather than one.

The open strings can also function in chords as the third or the fifth: E is the third of C major and C♯ minor; B is the third of G major and G♯ minor; G is the third of E♭ major and E minor. E is the fifth of A major/minor; B is the fifth of E major/minor; G is the fifth of C major/minor.

Droning open strings work well not only as lead ideas but also as riffs. For riffs, try any of the lower three strings (E, A or D) and move a scale or even a sequence of intervals such as thirds on the string above it.

Harmonics

As noted above, the open strings offer two triads – one major, one minor: strings 2, 3, 4 (BGD) make a G major chord (GBD); strings 1, 2, 3 (EBG) make an E minor chord (EGB). With the finger lightly held against the strings over the 12th fret, you can play a G major or E minor triad in harmonics. At the fifth fret, the same harmonics sound an octave higher. At the seventh fret, the harmonic chords become D major and B minor, respectively. In a song with the chord sequence G Em D Bm, you could play the entire sequence in harmonics for an ethereal second guitar part. If you're in a different key, a capo can make the right harmonics available. To strengthen the sound of the harmonics, double the guitar part and/or add echo, chorus, phasing or flanging.

Slide guitar in standard tuning

The harmonics triads also apply to slide (bottleneck) guitar in standard tuning. Much slide guitar is played in open tunings. But by using these triads, you can play a major or minor chord with the slide alone and not have to worry about fretting notes. For a 12-bar in C, chords C, F, and G can be played at the fifth, 10th, and 12th positions with the slide. If there's a minor chord in the sequence, just play the top three strings at the right fret.

12-string guitars

Your first close encounter of the 12-string kind can be a startling experience. The instrument is probably bigger than you're used to, and there doesn't seem to be any room between the strings. Fingerpickers notice this even more, and have the additional challenge of trying to pluck two strings at once. The 12-string acoustic has a bright, shimmering sound with high notes where you don't normally get them. It produces its own 'chorus' effect by never being precisely in tune. (Listen to Dave Mason's 12-string contribution to Jimi Hendrix's 'All Along The Watchtower'.) If you fall for the 12-string's charms, you may feel you will never be able to look a six-string in the soundhole again. Fortunately, this initial impression usually passes.

On a 12-string, the lower three strings alone generate a chord similar to that which you would get on a six-string. Triad shapes become the equivalent of a six-string chord. For example, hold C on the fifth string, third fret; E♭ on the fourth string, first fret; and play the G string open. On a six-string, this produces a C minor triad. On a 12-string, it produces the rough equivalent of playing a standard C minor barre chord at the third fret. Out of the movement of these triads can come different harmonic progressions and ideas. If you want to get really adventurous with a 12-string, tune it so the first string of each pair is a fourth below its partner: bE, eA, aD, dG, f♯B, bE. This produces some wonderful chords, even though it renders the guitar useless for playing anything else!

The music of The Beatles, The Byrds and R.E.M. all benefited from the 'chimes of freedom' of the electric 12-string, which can be a welcome addition to a recording. The classic way to play the electric 12-string is to pick chords in rapid arpeggios. It's unusual to attempt to play a guitar solo on an electric 12-string (though that didn't stop Jimmy Page on the live version of 'The Song Remains The Same'), and string-bending is difficult if you push any further than a semitone (half-step).

The twin-neck electric 6 + 12 has certain unique musical possibilities – and with one neck on and one off, you can explore the wonders of sympathetic resonance. You can hear this effect on the final track of the CD that accompanies my book *The Songwriting Sourcebook*.

Harmonised and non-harmonised lead breaks and fills

Some rock bands, including Wishbone Ash, Queen, Thin Lizzy, Boston, and The Darkness, have used twin-guitar breaks that are carefully harmonised. (Nowadays, intelligent pitch-shifters create harmonised lines from a single guitar part.) The standard intervals for such harmonising are thirds, sixths or octaves, though a few fourths add interest providing that they are in keeping with the harmony. Examples include the guitar lines on Thin Lizzy's 'Whiskey In The Jar', 'Don't Believe A Word', and 'The Boys Are Back In Town', and 10cc's 'The Dean And I'.

Non-harmonised combinations of lead guitars are harder for the ear to keep track of because the focus of attention keeps moving back and forth. As a result, there is built-in unpredictability, and each listen often reveals something never heard before. The effect of two guitars independently soloing can be heard on Wishbone Ash's 'Throw Down The Sword', Janis Joplin's cover of 'Summertime' (part of which is free-form and part of which is arranged), Love's 'A House Is Not A Motel', and on *Layla And Other Assorted Love Songs*.

To try this, set up the track for your solo and record a take. Do another pass without listening to the first take. Play both back and pan left and right. If you retained any ideas from take one for take two, it is possible they may coincide, which gives fleeting moments of reinforcement. Some phrases could be deliberately played a couple of times if you want three or four guitars at once.

The 'telegraph' figure

This is a repeated note played high up (like a pedal note in reverse) and is good for creating a sense of drama. Examples can be heard in 'S.O.S.', 'The Happening', 'Melting Pot', and 'You Keep Me Hanging On'.

SECTION 12

GUITAR RESOURCES PART 2 ALTERED TUNINGS

Sometimes it seems as if people who write songs on the piano have all the advantages. Just think: no barre chords; the ability to play chords with 10 notes; perfectly ordered ninths, 11ths, and 13ths; easy inversions; melody in one hand, chords and bass in the other; weird chord changes at the slip of a finger; a seven-octave range, sustain pedal ... and so on. Well, there is one exception, and that's the wonderful world of the guitar's altered and open tunings.

Many guitarists have written a couple of songs in a tuning that is not E A D G B E; others – like the late, great Nick Drake – did almost nothing else but play in altered tunings. For some, this was a case of necessity being the mother of invention: no-one showed them how to tune the guitar, or they didn't have lessons, so they tuned it themselves until it sounded 'right' – ie, had a musical sound – and what they ended up with was an open chord, the simplest altered tuning.

Purists say the guitar has only one 'proper' tuning. Ignore them. I once took a guitar into a musical instrument shop for repair, and that guitar happened to be in an open tuning. I was told by the bloke behind the counter that guitars were meant to be played only in one tuning. Wrong! What matters is the music you make, not how you make it. When Moses came down from the mountain with the stone tablets, there wasn't an 11th commandment that said, "Thou shalt tune E A D G B E."

Originally, altered tunings were used mostly by folk and blues players, but they have become a popular technique for guitarists in most genres. Well-known songwriters who have made altered tunings integral to their style include Joni Mitchell, Nick Drake, Bert Jansch, John Renbourn, Jimmy Page, Richie Havens, CSN&Y, Sonic Youth, and Soundgarden.

Why altered tunings?

Considered in connection with songwriting, the appeal of altered tunings is not hard to fathom and is clear the first time you re-tune the guitar and suddenly get a song out of nowhere:

ABBREVIATIONS

Roman numerals **I–VII** indicate chord relationships within a key.

m=minor

maj=major

SONG SECTIONS:

b bridge; **c** coda; **ch** chorus; **f** fade; **hk** hook; **i** intro; **pch** pre-chorus; **r** riff; **s** solo; **v** verse

Most of the chord-sequence examples are standardised for comparison into **C major** or **A minor**. The famous songs are therefore not always in the key of the original recordings.

SECTION 12

- Songwriting is driven by inspiration. If you get tired of E A D G B E, an altered tuning is motivating because of the way it changes the sound of your guitar. It takes only a couple of superb chord shapes to spark a song.

- Commonplace chord sequences can sound fresh in an altered tuning. Sometimes you write a song and only later realise what a common sequence it would be in standard tuning.

- Altered tunings facilitate fingerpicking.

- For solo singer-songwriters, altered tunings help to create a fuller sound.

- Open strings can be used for drone effects, consecutive octaves, or playing the melody while you're singing.

- Unison voicings give a '12-string' quality to some chords.

- Altered tunings generate chords that are impossible or difficult in standard tuning. They create more chords with seconds in, for example, which have a distinctive sound.

- Open tunings are better for slide-guitar playing in blues songs.

- To the more devious and image-conscious among you, altered tunings offer an opportunity to puzzle the hell out of other guitarists, who won't be able to figure out what you're doing from the shapes.

Drawbacks of altered tunings

- There's more danger of breaking strings.

- You must re-tune in live performance (unless you have several guitars).

- Chord shapes can be hard to remember. Write them down. (They are hard to transcribe, even from your own demos, after a few years have passed.)

- Key-changing is harder, and you may get trapped in one key. (This shouldn't matter too much if you're making the most of the key to which the tuning gravitates – otherwise, what's the point of being in it?

- Sometimes the open top strings dominate the chord shapes, giving a certain sameness to the overall sound. Learn to include a few shapes that temporarily block out these open strings and that way you avoid the risk of monotony

TYPES OF ALTERED TUNINGS

Altered tunings can be usefully divided into the following groups:

Detuned standard

This is not much of an altered tuning, per se, but it is worth a mention. It is common for guitarists to tune down a semitone (half-step), especially in hard rock/blues and heavy metal. This has the following advantages:

- The lower pitch can make it easier for the singer to pitch a melody.
- The lower string tension makes it easier for the lead guitarist to bend strings.
- It's popular with heavy bands because of the lower frequencies.
- If writing a song in E♭, B♭, or A♭, it can be sensible to detune because you will get fuller open-string chord shapes, especially if you're working with another guitar part.
- It is not uncommon to find 12-string acoustic guitar recordings that are detuned a semitone to ease tension on the guitar's neck.

A detuned guitar can match nicely with a second guitar part at standard pitch and with a capo. Simon & Garfunkel's 'The Boxer' is tuned down a semitone so B major can be played as if it were C major and matched with a standard-tuning guitar capoed at the fourth fret, where B is a G shape:

Chord	I	II	III	IV	V	VI	♭VII
Actual pitch	B	C♯m	D♯m	E	F♯	G♯m	A
Semi-detune shape	C	Dm	Em	F	G	Am	B♭
Capo IV shape	G	Am	Bm	C	D	Em	F

The Move's 'Blackberry Way' and The Beatles' 'Yellow Submarine' are also down a semitone (half-step). Sometimes guitars are detuned by a tone (full step); Paul McCartney did this for 'Yesterday', All About Eve on 'Martha's Harbour', and Jimi Hendrix for the longer version of 'Voodoo Chile', and it has also been used by the late Canadian guitarist Jeff Healey and grunge bands like Nirvana. This detuning creates effective timbral changes in an acoustic guitar that complement a guitar in standard tuning. Let's say you are recording a song in C major. Compare these two guitar parts, one with a capo at the eighth fret and the other standard detuned by a tone:

Chords	I	II	III	IV	V	VI	♭VII
Actual pitch	C	Dm	Em	F	G	Am	B♭
Tone-detune shape	D	Em	F♯m	G	A	Bm	C
Capo VIII shape	E	F♯m	G♯m	A	B	C♯m	D

Conversely, on the first album by The Smiths, Johnny Marr tuned a tone above standard pitch to get a brighter guitar sound. With regard to string tension, this is not a good idea – unless you can afford lots of strings and/or replacement guitars. The frequency changes caused by detuning EADGBE are analogous to changes that result from vari-speeding analogue tape (as heard on the vocals on Beatles songs such as 'Lucy In The Sky With Diamonds' and 'Strawberry Fields Forever').

Single-string alterations
The easiest form of altered tuning involves retuning only one string. Even such a small change can produce stimulating new chord shapes.

The most popular way to do this is to detune the low E to D, which is slightly misleadingly called 'dropped D' tuning. Fingerpickers like it because it provides an octave in the open bass strings (six and four) for an alternating-thumb pattern, leaving the fingers free to play a melody. It gives much deeper-sounding D and Dm chords than standard tuning. Bob Dylan's 'Mr Tambourine Man' uses dropped D tuning. The sixth-string D can be a pedal note, allowing you to move shapes over it, or to play the bottom three strings as a drone and move triad shapes on the top three. This tuning is also favoured by writers who want to play low, heavy riffs. A 'power chord' can be played on the bottom three strings with only a first-finger barre, and the famous 'boogie

DADGBE tuning

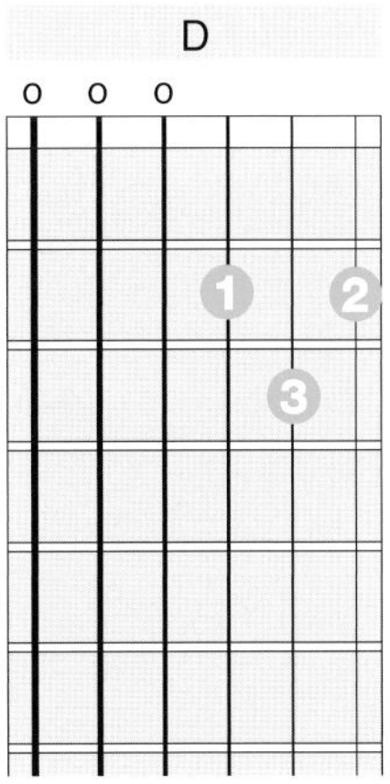

D

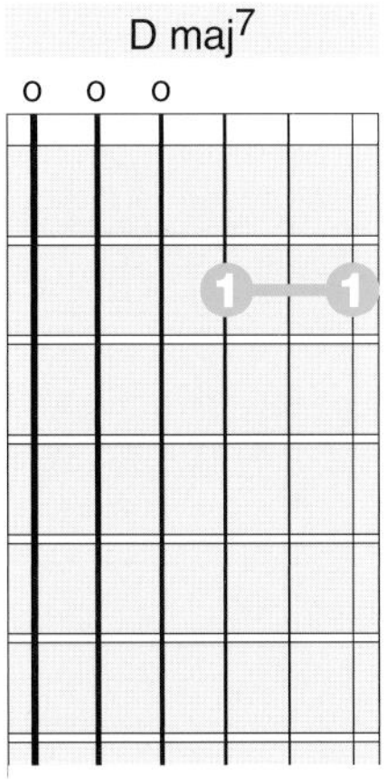

D maj^7

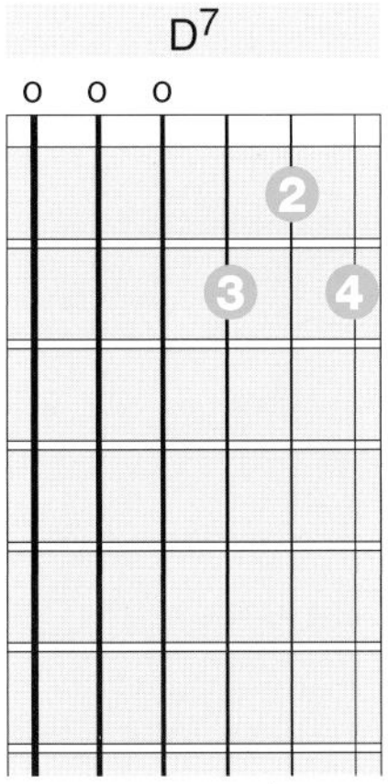

D^7

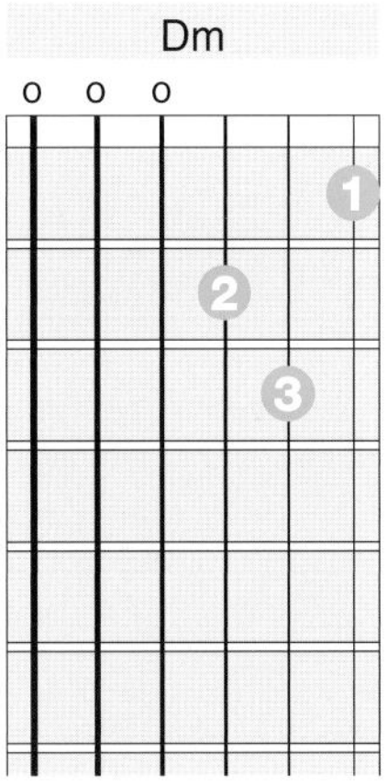

Dm

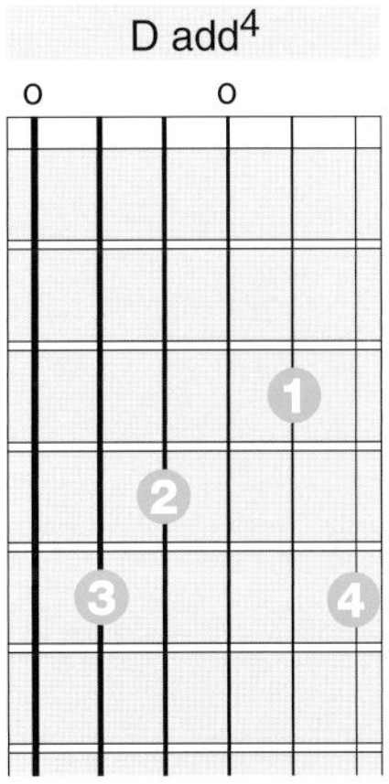

D add^4

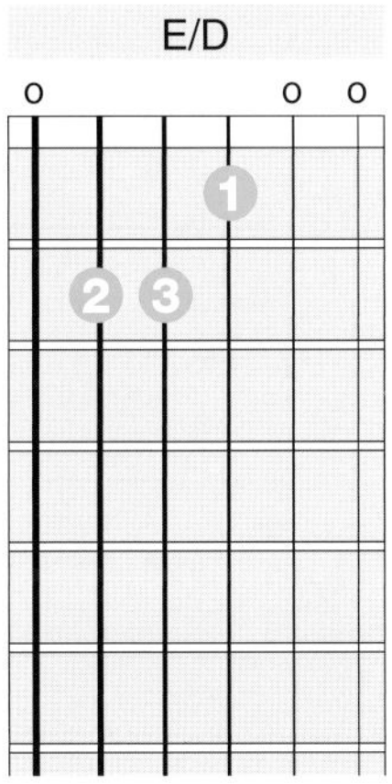

E/D

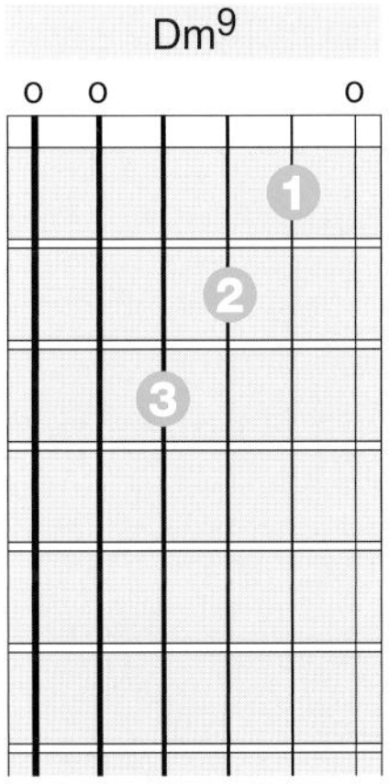

Dm^9

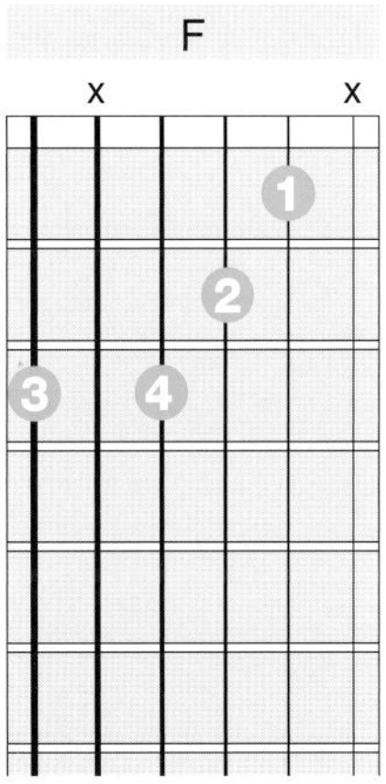

F

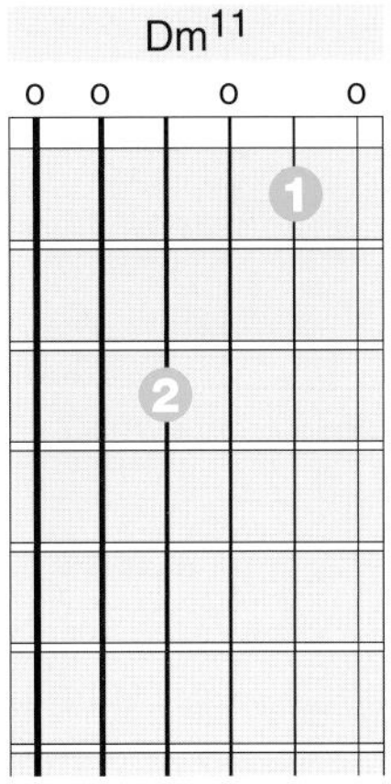

Dm^{11}

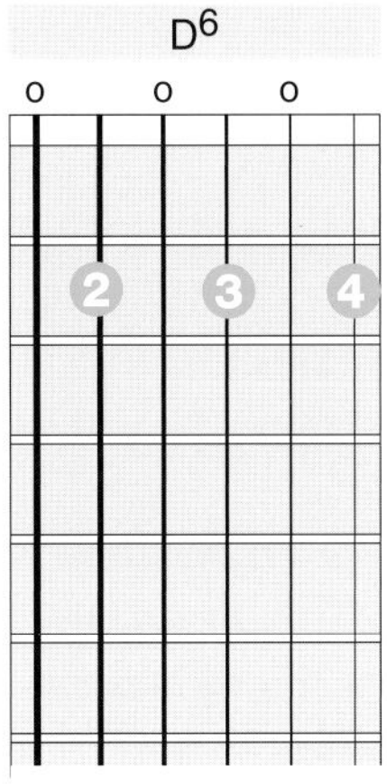

D^6

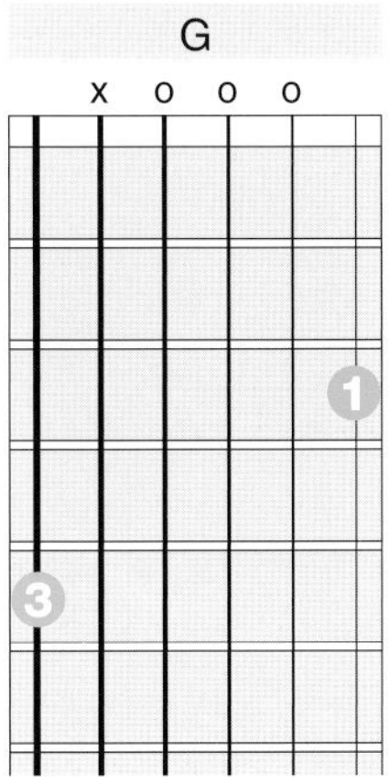

G

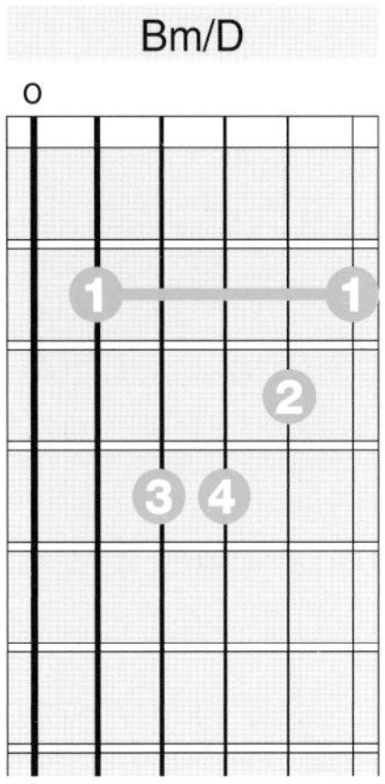

Bm/D

EADGBD tuning

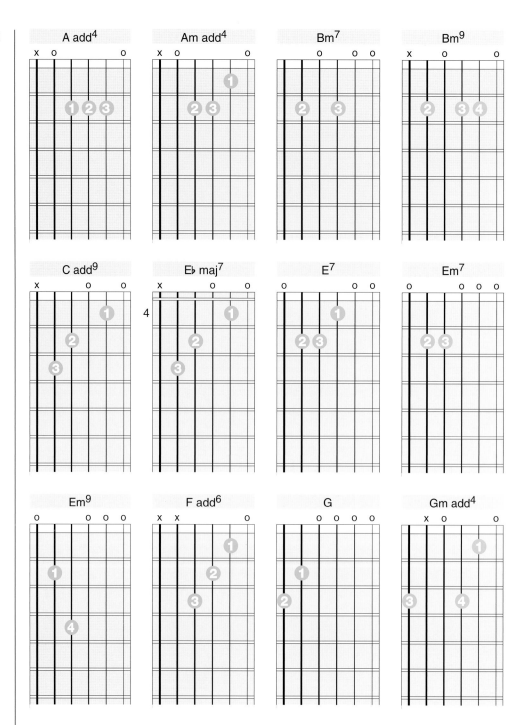

rock' rhythm figure is easier to finger than in standard tuning. The soundtrack to *School Of Rock* features a song titled 'Fight' which provides an example.

Other single-string alterations include detuning the high E string down to D; the G string down to F♯ (so-called 'lute tuning'); and the A string down to G to make E G D G B E, an open Em7 chord.

It's great fun to experiment with single-string alterations. They instantly mess up all your normal chord shapes, but not so drastically that you can't figure out where you are. And if you don't like the sound, it is easy to make a small tuning adjustment and try something different. One way to think your

EADF♯BE tuning

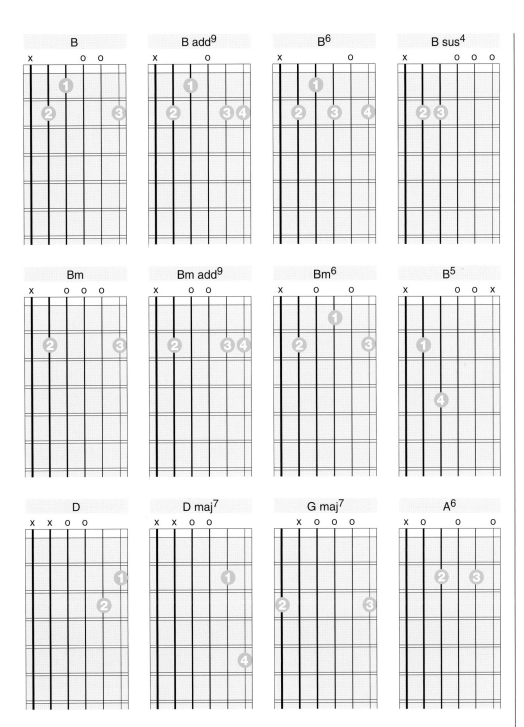

way to a new tuning is to consider the key in which you're playing and re-tune a string to the advantage of that key or one of the chords in it. This may be how Dylan arrived at 'It's All Over Now, Baby Blue' which has a capo at IV and the lowest string tuned two tones down. The song is in C (actual pitch E major) and the tuning gives a root note octave at the base of chord I.

Open tunings

An 'open tuning' is one where the strings are tuned to the notes of a major or minor chord. This means that when you lay a finger across the neck, the barre

SECTION 12 |

EGDGBE tuning

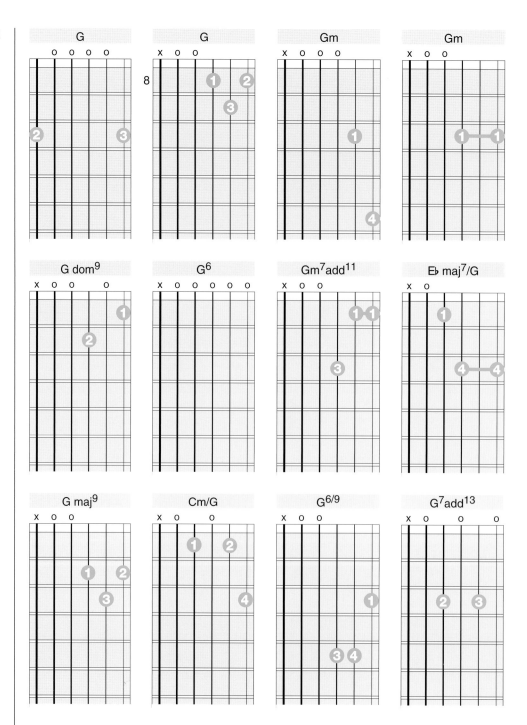

creates another major or minor chord. The other fingers can then add notes to that chord. In an open minor tuning, a major chord can be played by identifying the string(s) tuned to the third and putting a finger on that string one fret up.

Open major and minor tunings share certain characteristics. For example, the chord on which the tuning is based repeats itself at the 12th fret. Chord IV is played as a barre at the fifth fret, and chord V as a barre at the seventh. These, in combination with the open strings, give a three-chord trick. Minor open tunings are the same, except IV and V will be minor. The fifth, seventh,

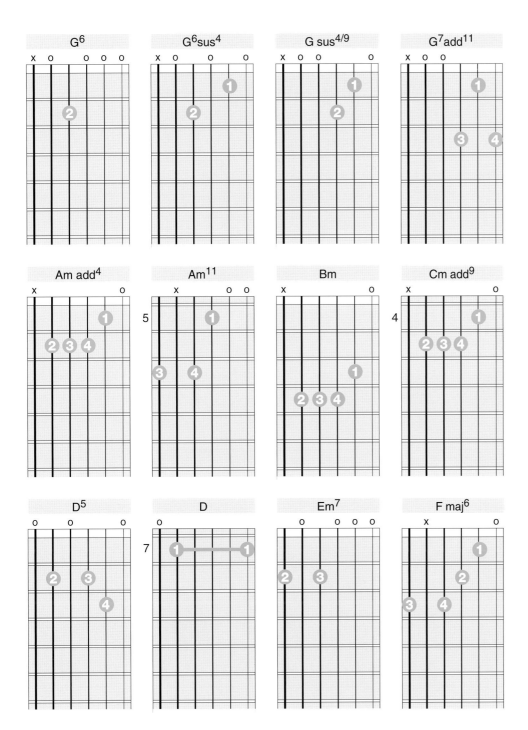

and 12th frets will also provide resonant harmonics. In a major open tuning the hard rock / pentatonic-based formula of I-♭III-IV-V-♭VII mentioned earlier in the book represents frets 0-3-5-7-10 regardless of the precise pitch of the tuning.

Open G – D G D G B D – is a popular tuning, favoured by Keith Richards and suited to both electric and acoustic music. You can also hear open G on The Beatles' 'Blackbird', Led Zeppelin's 'That's The Way' (detuned a half-step as open G♭) and 'Black Country Woman'. Since the root note is on the fifth string, some players don't bother to tune the low E down to D but find it more useful to leave it as is, giving E G D G B D. A tone (whole step) higher, open G

DADF♯AD tuning

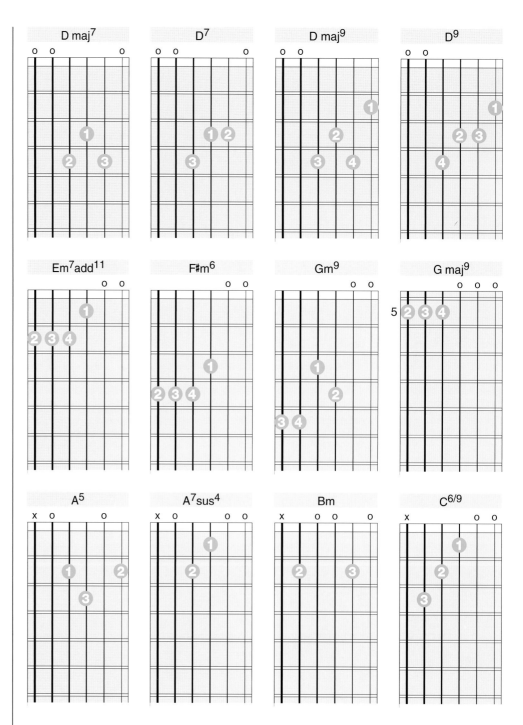

becomes open A – E A E A C♯ E – a tuning favoured by electric slide players. But be careful on acoustic, because this increases tension on the neck.

Open D – D A D F♯ A D – is a tuning used by Joni Mitchell and in its electric version of open E – E B E G♯ B E – by Ron Wood. Open D has a deeper sound than open G because the root note is on the bottom string. John Squire used this for slide on 'Love Spreads'. Open C – C G C G C E – is an even deeper-sounding open tuning, though not as popular as open G or D.

Open *minor* tunings are not as often heard as the majors. In some ways this is surprising, because they can be more flexible when it comes to getting strong

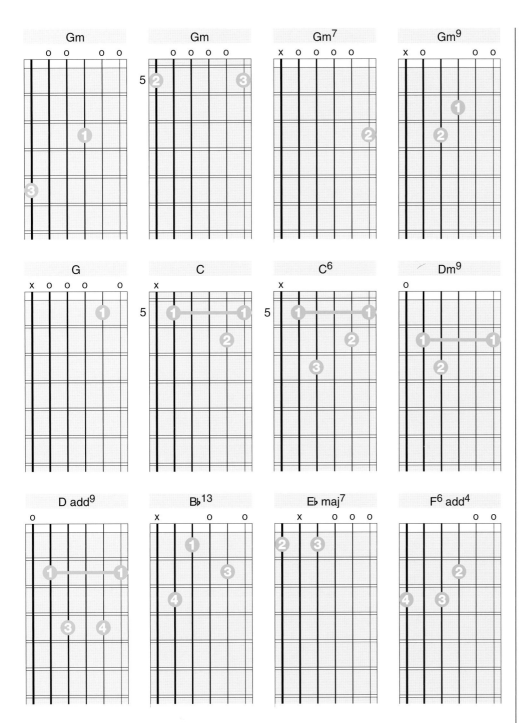

minors and majors. In open major tunings, it is sometimes hard to find a good fingering for a minor chord. Standard tuning requires only two alterations to create open Em – E G B G B E. Folksinger Michael Chapman used open Gm – D G D G Bb D – which is a single-string alteration from open G. Flattening the third string of open D – D A D F♯ A D – makes D A D F A D, which is open D minor.

Remember that putting a capo on an open tuning enables its use for different keys. Keith Richards capoed open G at the fourth fret to play open B for The Rolling Stones' 'Tumbling Dice'. And there's nothing to stop you from writing a song in open G that is actually in another key, say C, as The Rolling

DADFAD tuning

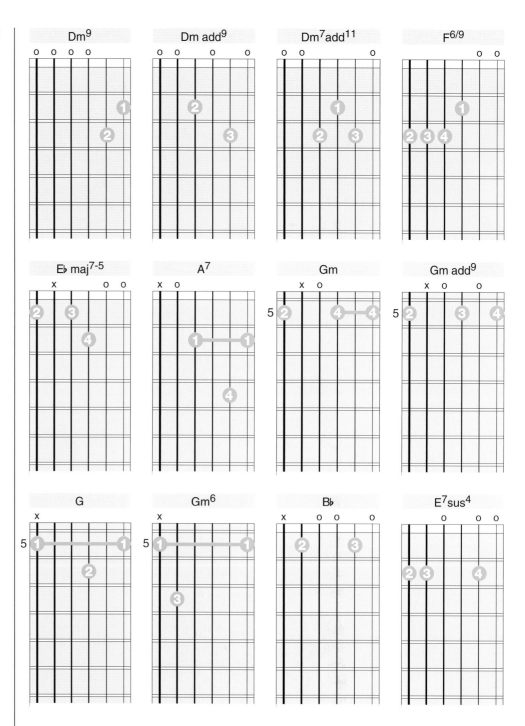

Stones did with 'Start Me Up'. Acoustic singer-songwriter David Wilcox, an expert in alternate tunings, told *Acoustic Guitar* magazine in 1994, "There are some wonderful voicings you get when you play in an open tuning outside of its tonic centre, and I really love using a major key open tuning but playing it so that the song is in the key of the chord that's maybe on the second fret, so it comes out in a sort of modal, minor, fun thing."

Altered tunings

It is helpful to reserve the name 'altered tuning' for any tuning that does not

DADGAD tuning

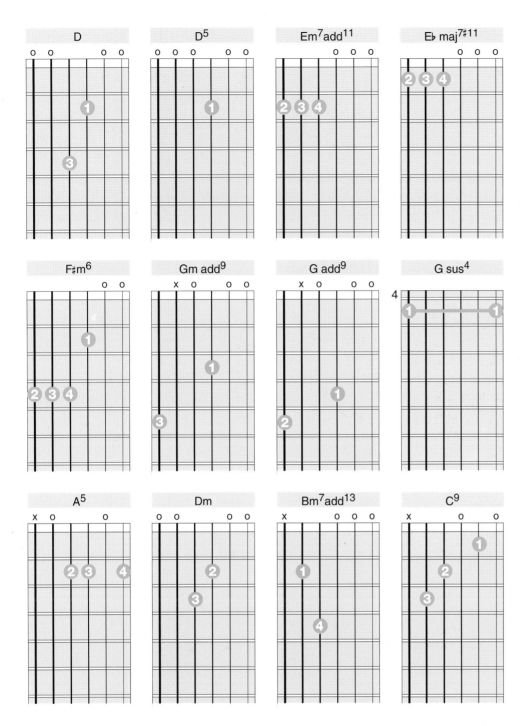

make a simple major or minor chord. Some are seventh chords or are derived from the open majors. These are sometimes called 'modal tunings'. They are not as easy to work with as straight open tunings and are less suitable for slide guitar. It takes a little patience to get the best from these. Here are some examples:

■ D A D G A D can be thought of as Dsus4 and has been used by Davy Graham, Pierre Bensusan, and Jimmy Page. (Beware the misprint B A D G A D which occurs in some early 1970s music articles on Led Zeppelin.)

- ■ 'Double Dropped D' – D A D G B D – was famously used by Neil Young for 'Cinnamon Girl'.
- ■ D A D F♯ B D is D6.
- ■ D G D G C D is Gsus4.

Players have also tuned to a fifth chord: two possibilities are D A D A A D and E B E E B E. The Indigo Girls used DADGBD for 'Chicken Man', DADGBC for 'Galileo' and 'Virginia Woolf', and DADGAD for 'Love Will Come To You'.

Alternative 90s bands such as Sonic Youth pioneered the use of altered tunings (some of them almost atonal) in rock. Another trick is that if you happen to have a double-neck guitar, you could write a song that is played with one of the necks in standard tuning and the other in an altered tuning, so you could play the verse on one and the chorus on the other. Jimmy Page did this on Page and Plant's 'Wonderful One'.

DGDGBD tuning (open G)

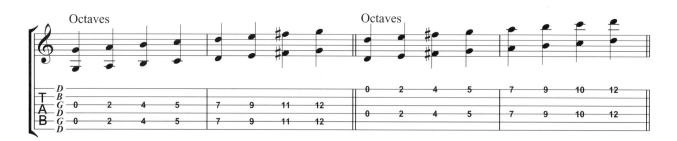

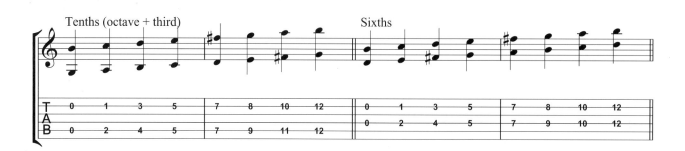

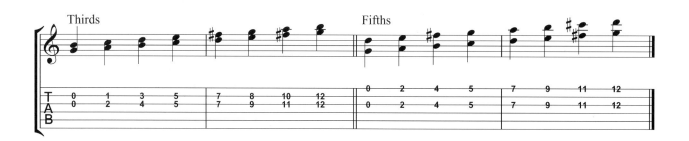

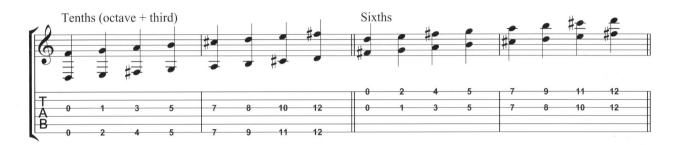

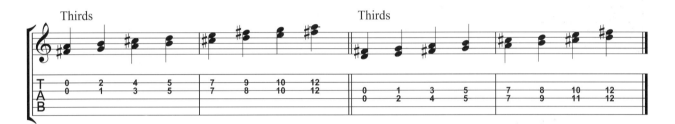

Tips for creating your own tunings

DADF#AD tuning

■ Tune down rather than up, to lessen the risk of breaking strings.

■ Try to retain at least one of the open strings of E A D G B E.

■ The lower the open string to have the root note of the tuning, the better.

■ In an open major tuning, locate any open strings which are the third of the chord. Fret this string at the first fret for a sus4; fret at the third fret for a fifth chord. Lower this string a semitone for an equivalent open minor tuning.

■ Be sensitive to the balance of roots, fifths, and thirds in your tuning, and to the intervals between the strings. One string out of six tuned to a third is enough, and the higher the better.

■ Look for strings tuned an octave, third, or sixth apart. These can be valuable for consecutive interval figures.

■ Movable major and minor shapes are useful in case a sequence requires a chord unavailable as an open-string voicing.

■ Heavier gauge strings will restore lost tension if you detune more than a tone.

■ Write down any good shapes you find in a tuning. They are easily forgotten.

■ The distinctive quality of the chord voicings are vulnerable to being obscured by other harmonic instruments in an arrangement.

SECTION 12 | 195

Some alternative tunings

It is possible to create different versions of the same open tuning by changing the mixture of roots, thirds, and fifths. Let's take E major as an example. The following tables list the string, the pitch, the increase or decrease in semitones, and which part of the triad any given string becomes in this tuning. The standard open E is:

String	6	5	4	3	2	1
Note	E	B	E	G#	B	E
Inc/Dcr	-	+2	+2	+1	-	-
Part of triad	r	5th	r	3rd	5th	r

This tuning increases the tension on the neck. Is there a way of doing it by tuning down instead? Here's a solution I devised:

String	6	5	4	3	2	1
Note	E	G#	B	E	B	E
Inc/Dcr	-	–1	–3	–3	-	-
Part of triad	r	3rd	5th	r	5th	r

The same thing can be done with open A. The standard version (used for Led Zeppelin's 'In My Time Of Dying') is:

String	6	5	4	3	2	1
Note	E	A	E	A	C#	E
Inc/Dcr	-	-	+2	+2	+2	-
Part of triad	5th	r	5th	r	3rd	5th

This is my version:

String	6	5	4	3	2	1
Note	E	A	C#	E	A	E
Inc/Dcr	-	-	–1	–3	–2	-
Part of triad	5th	r	3rd	5th	r	5th

Now let's try open C. The standard version is:

String	6	5	4	3	2	1
Note	C	G	C	G	C	E
Inc/Dcr	–4	–2	–2	-	+1	-
Part of triad	r	5th	r	5th	r	3rd

But it could be achieved like this:

String	6	5	4	3	2	1
Note	C	G	E	G	C	E
Inc/Dcr	–4	–2	+2	-	+1	-
Part of triad	r	5th	3rd	5th	r	3rd

The same principle can be applied to minor tunings. Here's a standard E minor:

String	6	5	4	3	2	1
Note	E	B	E	G	B	E
Inc/Dcr	-	+2	+2	-	-	-
Part of triad	r	5th	r	3rd	5th	r

Here's a variant with a deeper sound and less tension on the neck:

String	6	5	4	3	2	1
Note	E	G	B	E	B	E
Inc/Dcr	-	–2	–3	–3	-	-
Part of triad	r	3rd	5th	r	5th	r

You can build more unusual tunings around one of the open strings of standard tuning. Let's use D: D is the root of D and Dm, the third of B♭ and Bm, and the fifth of G and Gm. So we could construct a tuning for any of these in which that string would not change. In B♭, that would work like this:

String	6	5	4	3	2	1
Note	D	B♭	D	F	B♭	D
Inc/Dcr	–2	+1	-	–2	–1	–2
Part of triad	3rd	r	3rd	5th	r	3rd

Or how about B minor? That would be:

String	6	5	4	3	2	1
Note	D	B	D	F#	B	D
Inc/Dcr	–2	+2	-	–1	-	–2
Part of triad	3rd	r	3rd	5th	r	3rd

With altered tunings the only limit is your musical imagination and your patience at working out the potential of a tuning. But don't forget to put the song first, otherwise you will move into composing guitar instrumentals.

MAKING A DEMO RECORDING

"There are records I love that are not good songs but are great records.... People were making significant records from the beginning of rock'n'roll. Elvis's records, all the Motown records. Motown made those records the way they made the '55 Chevrolet. It's still beautiful and it still drives." – Jackson Browne, quoted by Dave Marsh from Bill Flanagan's *Written In My Soul*.

A great song versus a great record

It is important to distinguish between writing a great song and making a great record. The latter calls for a different set of skills – which is where engineers and record producers come into the picture. Great songs do not always become great records, and some great records have been made of less-than-wonderful songs. The ideal is, of course, to have both.

If you took Madonna's 'Erotica' and played it on an acoustic guitar, you would not think it was a very good song. The recording itself is another matter. Conversely, if you play Crowded House's 'Don't Dream It's Over' on an acoustic guitar, you can hear it's a good song right away. But is Crowded House's recording of it a great record? Personally, I feel the arrangement is adequate but it doesn't add a lot to to the song. It is a testament to the quality of the song that it survived such a plain presentation. Or what about U2's 'Beautiful Day'? A good song which was given an even better arrangement and production. Listening to covers is a good way to get a feel for what an arrangement and a production can do for a song.

Home demos

Most songwriters want to hear what their songs would sound like when played and recorded in a proper arrangement. The advent of the four-track cassette recorder in the early 1980s made it possible to experience the joys of multi-tracking without the expense of buying a reel-to-reel tape machine (or booking studio time). Songwriters could make demos and mix them on a single portable device. Even though the sound quality left something to be desired, the four-

Roman numerals **I–VII** indicate chord relationships within a key.

m=minor

maj=major

SONG SECTIONS:

b bridge; **c** coda; **ch** chorus; **f** fade; **hk** hook; **i** intro; **pch** pre-chorus; **r** riff; **s** solo; **v** verse

Most of the chord-sequence examples are standardised for comparison into **C major** or **A minor**. The famous songs are therefore not always in the key of the original recordings.

track cassette recorder was a wonderful and cheap sketchpad. At the same time companies like Fostex pioneered narrow-gauge recording, which resulted in eight- and 16-track machines using narrow width tape. In the 1990s, the advent of digital hard-disk recording led to the first eight-track digital recorder/mixer. By 2000, for less than the cost of an old eight-track tape machine you could buy a digital mini-studio that combined eight-track recording, CD quality, editing, mixing and sound effects – all in one compact package. At an amazing speed, in the nine years since the first edition of *How To Write Songs On Guitar*, the development of computer hardware and the design of software sequencing and editing programmes, has meant that many musicians now do multitrack recording directly onto home computers and laptops.

If you are seriously interested in songwriting, I strongly recommend that you make your own multi-track recordings in whatever medium – analogue or digital – that suits your taste, financial reach, level of computer literacy, and available space. Two guitars, a drum machine, and an electronic keyboard provide a range of sounds and possibilities. Learning to record multitrack arrangements will improve your musicianship (if you play the parts, as opposed to programming software samples and loops), teach you about production and arrangement, and give a greater appreciation of the finer parts of songwriting. Virtuoso technique on bass or keyboard is not necessary to play simple parts that fit the context of a song. The key here is 'part playing' – more about that in a moment.

If you want to submit your work to publishers, realise that while it is true that a simple piano/guitar accompaniment and a voice will carry a good song, people looking for songs in the music industry these days expect to hear a fuller arrangement. They may even expect you to come up with the finished article.

Instrumentation

The instruments you use on a home recording are determined by what you physically have access to, what you feel comfortable playing, what suits the song and/or genre in which you're working, and also the recording method. Digital recording brings vast numbers of instrumental sounds to a computer set-up in the form of sampled instrument libraries. For rock, you need drums, bass, rhythm and lead guitar, and vocals. If the song has more than one guitar part, try to differentiate them; this can be accomplished with one of these combinations:

- single coil/double coil
- front pickup/back pickup
- distorted/clean
- detuned/normal
- capoed/normal
- standard tuning/altered tuning
- strummed/fingerpicked
- 12-string/six-string
- acoustic/electric

Digital modelling technology puts approximations of the sound of many famous makes of guitar at the press of a computer key. Rock guitar is often played with distortion. Modern effects units have put amounts of distortion at the fingertips of guitarists that, in the 1960s, would have required huge stacks and enough volume to drown out the sound of most aircraft taking off. What's surprising, though, is that even on a hard rock recording a little distortion often goes further than you think, so be prepared to use less on a rhythm part. Distortion acts like a sponge, soaking up frequencies and leaving less space for everything else.

When you add other instruments, consider how they will sound when you come to mix. Highly unusual sounds may detract from the vocal/melody line, so employ them sparingly. Instruments can be divided broadly into those whose main function is to create the harmonic padding and those that have a supporting melodic interest. Strummed guitars, piano chords and sustained string or organ chords provide the harmonic backdrop against which everything else happens. One such instrument either side of the mix is a good approach – and it doesn't need to play all the time. A harmonic background can also be established with pared-down parts whose overall effect is to suggest a chord sequence. Listen to the verse of U2's 'Vertigo' where the song is carried by voice, bass, and drums, with the guitar only adding damped percussive flicks.

When choosing instruments for an arrangement, consider:

- Their natural sustain: are they for stretching notes? Are they for short bursts?
- Their pitch: are they high, middle or low?
- Their tone: are they bright or muted, percussive or smooth?

In commercial music, certain instruments function as 'emotional shorthand' – a harmonica is for downhome sincerity; Spanish guitar indicates organic feeling; Irish pipes and South American pan-pipes say 'World Music'; an oboe might suggest English pastoral. There is more about the emotional signature of instruments in *Arranging Songs*.

If you're concerned about how many tracks to record on a multitrack, then eight-track recording is an ideal compromise in terms of the opportunities it offers. Initially you may feel you have to pile on the instruments, using all the tracks and even sub-mixing (if your hardware limits the number of tracks) to load on even more. Remember, though, that the more instruments you record, the harder it is to mix so they do not get in each other's way. Instruments with similar timbres can be difficult to separate in the final mix.

It is surprising how full a mix can be generated with just a few well-chosen parts. This is not to say that arrangements with plenty of space are any better than full ones. It is partly a matter of taste, and arranging styles tend to go in and out of fashion. During the 1960s and 1970s, as recording technology went from two to four to eight tracks, and then to 16, 24, 32, and 48 tracks, songwriters and musicians often recorded accordingly, to make the most of such capabilities. Think of the production on a record such as The Police's 'Walking On The Moon' and compare it with The Beatles' 'Hey Jude' or a Phil

Spector wall-of-sound single such as 'River Deep – Mountain High'. They are contrasting approaches – but who would want to be without any of them?

Let's look at some typical arrangements that are possible with eight tracks without any 'bouncing'. In these examples, the keyboard part could be piano, organ, strings or any other sound from an electronic keyboard.

TRACKS							
1	2	3	4	5	6	7	8
vcl ——	vcl	r/gtrl ——	r/gtr	dr ——	dr	bass ——	bass

A 'live' four-piece rock band sound, with all instruments and voice in stereo.

1	2	3	4	5	6	7	8
vcl	vcl	r/gtrl ——	r/gtr	dr ——	dr	bass	l/gtr

The same with bass stereo sacrificed for a lead guitar part.

1	2	3	4	5	6	7	8
b/vcl	vcl	r/gtr	a/gtr	dr ——	dr	bass	keyb

Stereo rhythm sacrificed for acoustic guitar.

1	2	3	4	5	6	7	8
b/vc	vcl	a/gtr	a/gtr	dr ——	dr	bass	keyb

A nice combination of two acoustic guitars. Try this with two 12-strings or 12 + 6.

1	2	3	4	5	6	7	8
b/vcl	vcl	a/gtr	a/gtr	violin	violin	viola	cello

A guitar ballad with a built-in string quartet.

1	2	3	4	5	6	7	8
l/gtr	vcl	r/gtr	a/gtr	dr ——	dr	bass	keyb

Lead guitar, acoustic guitar, and rhythm guitar.

1	2	3	4	5	6	7	8
b/vcl	vcl	r/gtr	l/gtr	dr ——	dr	bass	keyb

Acoustic guitar sacrificed for backing vocals.

1	2	3	4	5	6	7	8
b/vcl	vcl	r/gtr	sax	dr	bass	piano	organ

If you use a mono drum sound, then you have one more track to play with. Here's a pattern for a 'soul revue' sound.

1	2	3	4	5	6	7	8
b/vcl	b/vcl	b/vcl	vcl	r/gtr	dr	bass	keyb

If you can sing harmony vocals, try this.

SECTION 13 | 201

Bouncing

This technique is relevant for anyone using a small multitracker device, perhaps limited to four tracks or eight. If you start 'bouncing' tracks, amazing things become possible – as long as you get the sub-mixes nicely balanced. Let's say you want to record a song with a three-part backing vocal but more instruments than in the previous example. The recording process would go like this:

			TRACKS				
1	**2**	**3**	**4**	**5**	**6**	**7**	**8**
					r/gtr	dr	

Step 1: Record a rhythm guitar part with the drum track onto separate tracks.

1	2	3	4	5	6	7	8
					r/gtr	dr	bass

Step 2: Add bass.

1	2	3	4	5	6	7	8
vcl					r/gtr	dr	bass

Step 3: Add a rough 'guide vocal' for the melody.

1	2	3	4	5	6	7	8
vcl	b/vcl	b/vcl	b/vcl		r/gtr	dr	bass

Step 4: Put the three backing-vocal parts on tracks 2, 3 and 4.

1	2	3	4	5	6	7	8
vcl				b/vcl	r/gtr	dr	bass

Step 5: Sub-mix and re-record tracks 2, 3 and 4 onto track 5.

You now have a three-part harmony on track 5 and three empty tracks to add more guitars or keyboard-derived parts. To take an extreme example, you could record another two backing vocal parts on tracks 2 and 3 and then bounce them onto 4, adding as you do so a third backing vocal. This requires care in balancing the three parts – you must sing the last part so it blends with the two that are being bounced. If this works, you have (presumably different) three-part harmonies on tracks 4 and 5, enabling you to place them left and right. That's a lot of vocal power.

Digital recording makes sub-mixing more effective because there isn't the same degradation of signal as with analogue recording. Some of the decision-making involved in this technique is also assisted by the digital facility some machines have of 'virtual tracks' and track-swopping, which permits tracks to be put to one side while other recording takes place, and then assigned a final track position.

The stereo image

The choice of instruments and track alignment is also shaped by your sense of where things will go in the final production. One of the eccentric features of 1960s recordings, to modern ears, is the placing of the drums or vocals exclusively in one channel, left or right. In The Beach Boys' 'Don't Worry Baby', for example, a double-tracked lead vocal is on one side, the vocal harmonies are on the other, and the instrumentation is in the middle.

A standard mix approach puts the main vocal in the middle, along with bass and drums. Even though they are in the same central position, these can be distinguished from each other because they tend to occupy different frequencies. Other instruments can then be panned left or right. If you have more than one guitar part, put them on opposite sides. If you have instruments dropping in and out at various points, be careful that you don't make the mix 'lop-sided' when one drops out. Avoid passages of music where you have either the left or right of the mix unoccupied for any length of time.

Mixing is too complicated an art to discuss here in any detail. For example, there is no set order in which instruments are supposed to be balanced. Try setting the level of the bass and drums first and then the lead vocal against the rhythm section. Then bring in the harmony instruments. Here are some other tips:

- Never mix exclusively on headphones. Use them to check fine detail or to scrutinise the mix for unwanted background noises and glitches. Obviously, when you have what you hope is a final mix it's worth listening to it on headphones as well as through speakers.
- Sit equidistant between the speakers.
- Don't mix at high volume levels. If it sounds balanced and exciting at a domestic listening level then it will sound great louder. High volume levels fatigue the ears and fool you into thinking a mix is better than it is.
- The prominence of a part in a mix is influenced not only by its volume but by its frequency and the amount of reverb on it. Instead of pushing the fader up, try altering the EQ. Remember that EQ can be subtracted as well as added.
- Try mixing in mono first. If the parts sound well-defined in a mono mix, when you pan them out into stereo they will sound even better.
- Test a mix by listening from the next room with the door open, by listening on different speaker systems and in varying locations, and then with other people present. You will be surprised how different a song sounds when you play it back in company.

Unusual arrangements

A song can be presented in many different ways. This is the art of arranging as well as recording. Occasionally, an unorthodox arrangement piques the ear of the listening public and contributes to a record being a hit. Songs such as David Essex's 'Rock On', Colin Blunstone's 'Say You Don't Mind', and The Beach Boys' 'Barbara Ann' are worth analysis for their unusual arrangements. Sometimes, one instrument stamps its sound on a mix and becomes what makes the song memorable. Think of the clavinet on Stevie Wonder's 'Superstition', the harmonica on The Who's 'Join Together', the bass harmonica on Simon & Garfunkel's 'The Boxer' (reprised in R.E.M.'s homage to Brian Wilson, 'At My Most Beautiful'), the wah-wah guitar on Isaac Hayes's 'Shaft', the theremin on The Beach Boys' 'Good Vibrations', the saxophone on Gerry Rafferty's 'Baker Street', the synth on The Who's 'Baba O'Riley', the cimbalom on early Portishead tracks, or the accordion at the start of K. D. Lang's 'Constant Craving'.

Drum machines and drum loops

For many songwriters, the drum machine or sampled loop is a necessary evil. It would be great to have real drums on our songs, but we either can't play drums, don't have the room, or find that recording a kit at home is impractical due to space, expense, and the neighbours. Enter the drum machine – a brilliant piece of kit (pun intended), even if it's no substitute for Keith Moon, Mitch Mitchell or John Bonham. If you write dance music, then the artificiality of the drum machine is part of the sound you want. But if you are writing pop, rock, soul, folk, blues, or jazz songs, here are a few tips on how to make drum programming, from whatever source, sound more 'human':

- Copy real drum patterns from records.
- Don't use the pre-set rhythms, write your own.
- When you select drum sounds, make sure they 'agree' with each other.
- Use quantisation sparingly. Quantisation is a handy technical feature that enables drum machines to move your tapped-in rhythm to the nearest beat or chosen division of a beat. But this is what makes drum machines sound mechanical: they play strict rhythm. Quantisation is especially noticeable on handclaps.
- Use a variety of rhythms within a song, with plenty of small variations.
- Don't program things a drummer can't do. A drummer has only two arms and can, therefore, hit only two things at once. Don't program a snare strike, a crash cymbal, and a side drum all at once.
- Avoid implausible bass-drum patterns at faster tempos. The quicker the tempo, the sillier rapid bass-drum patterns will sound. Intricate bass-drum patterns sound better at slower tempos.
- If you want the drums to stop for a few bars, take care with the way they enter and exit. Use a fill to get in and a fill to get out.
- Don't always put cymbal crashes on the first beat of the bar.
- Change the parts of the kit within a song. For example, use a closed hi-hat in the verse and an open one in the chorus – this gives extra intensity to the latter.
- Flams on the snare – where the sticks hit a split-second apart – sound very 'human'.
- Time changes – going into half-time or double-time – also help to make the sound less artificial.

Sound-processing effects like echo and reverb make drums sound more 'alive'. For a dance groove, write a simple drum pattern and then feed it through a delay until a coherent pattern of delays emerges. You can make the echoes quieter than the main drum part, if you like. When recording drums in stereo, try putting a fast echo on one side to thicken the sound.

Drum pauses
The near-constant presence of a drum kit (real or electronic) in popular music can make us forget that a song could approach rhythm in a different manner. Think about not having a continuous beat. Consider the way percussion is used in an orchestral setting: tympani rolls, snare rolls, and cymbal crashes occur only to mark special moments in the music, such as a crescendo or climax. Marking the beat percussively all the time would be considered vulgar in classical music – that's what the conductor is doing by waving his arms.

Compare the 1947 revision of Igor Stravinsky's ballet *Petrushka* with the 1911 version, and you will find that he took out much of the percussion – presumably on the mature judgement that he had been over-emphatic in the original score. The Beach Boys' *Pet Sounds* album offers a fine example of percussion used in a less obvious way.

Even in a rock song, dramatic effects can be generated by taking out the beat for a few bars. Good examples can be heard in Eddie Cochran's 'Summertime Blues' and 'Something Else', Little Richard's 'Lucille', The Who's 'My Generation', Ash's 'Goldfinger', Dodgy's 'In A Room', Metallica's 'Enter Sandman', Led Zeppelin's 'What Is And What Should Never Be', Razorlight's 'In The Morning', and The Bluetones' 'Slight Return'. There's a wonderful pull-out and re-entry of the drums in The Rolling Stones' 'Tumbling Dice'. The obvious place to delay the entry of the drums is on the intro, as in 'There She Goes' by The La's, The Verve's 'Bittersweet Symphony', and Led Zeppelin's 'Over The Hills And Far Away'. The absence of a snare rock beat gives a mildly exotic and dark sound to the opening of Radiohead's 'There There'. Phil Collins's 'In The Air Tonight' has a long-delayed entry which was the probable inspiration for Preston Hayman's spectacular snare-drum entry on Kate Bush's 'Leave It Open'. You can even bring in the drums on what sounds like a 'wrong' beat, as on The Rolling Stones' 'Start Me Up' and Television's 'Marquee Moon'. When considering alternatives to drums, think of the tambourine that enters with a smack at the start of the verse on Martha Reeves & The Vandellas' 'Dancing In The Street'. Listen to the interruption of a drum loop in Tori Amos's 'Caught A Lite Sneeze', where at 2:46 the drums are suddenly silenced. She sings a line with the piano and then on the word 'closer' the drum loop is back in. Other arresting moments of silence occur in Eels' 'Novocaine For The Soul' (at 1:23), Lush's 'Single Girl', and Radiohead's 'Just' (at 2:22). You can also use a drum loop to carry the early part of a song and bring in live drums later in the arrangement for a dramatic lift.

SECTION 14
GALLERY OF SONGS

To deepen your knowledge of songwriting, it is helpful to listen carefully to well-crafted songs. Here are some to consider. This chronological list is not the 'greatest' of anything, but each of these songs has an important lesson to teach the songwriter who's willing to learn. These brief discussions take us to the edge of what can be described as songwriting technique. At this edge we pass from the measurable nuts and bolts of songwriting to the mysterious domain of musical meaning – of why it is that one song which uses the same chords as thousands of others is far greater in terms of what it communicates. This is the domain that music criticism tries to discuss, of course, but to pursue that road any further would take us outside the remit of a book on songwriting craft. Dave Marsh's *The Heart Of Rock And Soul* and Ian MacDonald's *Revolution In The Head* and *The People's Music* are essential accounts of the deeper meanings of popular songs.

1 Gene Pitney: 'Twenty Four Hours From Tulsa' (1963) This is a fine example of a narrative lyric presented as a letter, as well as a song where ambiguous keys express an emotional conflict. The production has many classic early 1960s touches: high female voices; chopped, high guitar chords; light percussion; low-note guitar with tremolo; and the thrice-played brass motif, taken up twice by the strings for a five-bar intro. In the verse, each lyric phrase goes I-II^ to V, establishing V as the key, only for the next line to take it back to the original key. Chord I represents the emotions he has for "home" (his wife), heard first as Gene sings "dearest darling". The chorus introduces a I-VI-IV-V progression in a stretched form in C major and stops on the dominant, which is the key of the verse.

The coda settles on a C chord, the key of the past rather than the future. So, although he appears to be saying that he loves this new woman, the music insists on his regret that he cannot go home. Notice the dominant ninth chord at the end of the repeated "never", which cancels out the lover's key of G major because it makes it harmonically subservient to the wife's key of C major.

2 Roy Orbison: 'It's Over' (1964) Orbison brought a new drama to pop with his song arrangements, and 'It's Over' is typical of his mini-epics, with its advanced (for the time) approach to arrangement, and romantic lyrics. This is another song where the emotional distress of the speaker is mirrored by the presence of two keys.

A free-time intro announces the subject of the lyric ("Your baby doesn't love you anymore") before the foreboding, martial drum beat leads into the verse. Structurally, there are several different verses at work. The second is more complex and features a classic early 1960s chord change when F-Am-Dm-B♭ is followed by G and then C (IV-II^-V), creating momentary confusion as to whether the music has changed from F major to C major. This key change is accomplished in the bridge, which starts on Em (a chord not found in F major), moves repeatedly from Em to F and then forward to G (chords III, IV, and V in C major). The first climax comes with the establishment of C major at 1:32, the title line, and a bar of 6/4. There are bars of 6/4 in the verse as well at the end of some lines. Notice how the melody creeps higher at the end, as the rhythm intensifies.

3 John Barry/Don Black: 'Goldfinger' (1965) John Barry invented a distinct harmonic language for the James Bond films, full of strange chord changes, melodies with unusual notes and dissonant effects. Songs such as 'Thunderball', 'You Only Live Twice' and 'We Have All The Time In The World' all deserve study. 'Goldfinger' is structured ABABA and opens with a harmonically ambiguous and spacious I-♭VI in E. This becomes the first change of the verse, which then compounds the ambiguity by going from C to Bm (the minor form of chord V in E), leading to a brief change into A major:

Old key	I	♭VI	Vm			♭IV	
	E	C	Bm	E	A	D♯	B
New key			II	V	I	III^	I

The stability of A major as a key is immediately undermined by the D♯, which finds its way to B – which functions as chord V in E for the next phrase. The bridge section further confuses things by going to D♯m, G♯m and A♯. The shifting harmonies express the untrustworthy nature of the villain.

4 The Beach Boys: 'God Only Knows' (1966) 'God Only Knows' may not match 'Good Vibrations' in the experimental stakes, but for sheer perfection of form it is perhaps even better. At a time when many songs seem to take forever to get going, it is a powerful example of how inspiration and songcraft can evoke another world in a matter of seconds.

The short instrumental intro has a soaring horn melody that returns later in the song. A one-bar interruption to the quarter-note rhythm sets off the intro from the first verse. Our attention is immediately caught by the lyric's provocative first line: "I may not always love you." The music has established a romantic atmosphere, and we are not expecting such an apparently *un*romantic statement. We listen to hear if the speaker will backtrack on this pronouncement – and, sure enough, he eclipses this blunt realism with a touching romantic promise.

'God Only Knows' does not have a separate chorus – the hook is beautifully incorporated into the verse itself. Notice the unexpected intervals in the melody (it keeps landing on notes that are not quite what we expect) and the inversions in the harmony. These inversions play a big role in making the progression so expressive. Verse two is prefaced by a one-bar link that is the same as the one that connected the intro and Verse one, except it is played on different instruments. Strings thicken the arrangement of Verse two.

Two verses and two hooks have passed by the time we get to 1:04–12. Here the song surprises us by changing its rhythm. This is a fine example of asymmetry. This makes the resumption of the verse form with 'scat' vocals and the hook seem fresh. The coda is reached at 1:59. There is a brief lull in the arrangement before the snare drum punches in and the ensemble surges at 2:16. The coda itself is a glorious three-way vocal counterpoint echoed by the swooping horn figure. 'God Only Knows' clocks in at a mere 2:45, but it makes us feel as though we have just had a week in paradise. No wonder they call Brian Wilson a genius.

5 The Kinks: 'Waterloo Sunset' (1967) The Kinks had established themselves by 1967 as a first-class singles group with punchy numbers such as 'You Really Got Me' and 'All Day And All Of The Night', and gently satirical songs such as 'Sunny Afternoon' and 'Dedicated Follower Of Fashion'. Neither type anticipated the ethereal 'Waterloo Sunset'.

Musically, the song uses a descending figure under a static V chord to create anticipation. Inversions play a significant part in adding a pastel colour to the I-V-IV progression, for the bass guitar makes it I-iV-iIV with sustained notes. The high melodic motif sung by the female backing vocalists is a striking regeneration of an arrangement technique that had been used conspicuously in pop in the early 1960s. A second descending sequence occurs on the F♯m chord ("but I don't …"). The bridge introduces a more aggressive guitar part for contrast, with the F♯ chord implying that it is chord V of a new key, B major. Notice the quick B-E change on "sha-la", which contrasts with the smoother rate of chord change on the verse. The bridge concludes with the same downward bassline of the intro, having employed another descending line under the F♯-B change. The psychedelic effect of the coda partly comes from the use of an unresolved A7 chord.

Lyrically, there's a fascinating tension between the detached speaker who, expressly unafraid, is mysteriously content to simply gaze at the sunset, and the lovers Terry and Julie, who meet each other every Friday night and "cross over the river". The lyric is deeply consoling because it offers not one but two ways out of loneliness. It is realistic and other-worldly at the same time. Ray Davies gives us details of London – the dirty river, taxis, the crowds, the Underground – and yet the city is transformed into something visionary.

6 The Mamas & The Papas: 'Dedicated To The One I Love' (1967) In 1966–68 the airwaves were blessed with the wind-blown harmonies of The Mamas & The Papas on hit songs such as 'California Dreamin'', 'Monday Monday', 'Dream A Little Dream Of Me' and 'Dedicated To The One I Love'. One member, John Phillips, also has a claim to fame as the writer of Scott MacKenzie's 'If You're Going To San Francisco'. So what has 'Dedicated To The One I Love' to teach us about pop songwriting?

Its obvious virtue is that of melody: 'Dedicated' has a beautiful tune and gorgeous harmonies. The arrangement is blessed by a quirky honky-tonk piano that lends character to what could have been out-and-out MOR. Most important of all, the song is continually inventive in a manner so different from the lazy mentality of much recent pop. It bursts with musical ideas, and you never quite know what is coming next. The delicate intro is almost a lullaby: a double-tracked vocal over two acoustic guitars. A D7sus4 chord takes us into the first chorus. Listen to the way the rhythm plays off four against the triplet swing of the 12/8 before the word "whisper". On the word "all" there's an unexpected chord, E♭7 (♭VI^), which suggests a key change that never happens.

The first verse contrasts two bars of melody with two bars that have plenty of blue notes. The lead-in to the second chorus uses an Am-A7 change that suggests we're going into D, but we actually land on D7sus4. Chorus two has a different last line, musically, than chorus one. After a four-bar honky-tonk piano solo, there's a two-bar phrase of "There's one thing I want you to do" where each beat has a different chord. It's rare for pop songs to harmonise separate beats. The melody going into the last chorus is pitched higher than you expect it over a D♯7, which again creates the expectation of a key change. Chorus three has a different ending than the others do, and the coda features vocal counterpoint over a new sequence of Em-C-A-G. And all of this in only three minutes! Too much variety to be commercial? 'Dedicated To The One I Love' was the 12th best-selling single of 1967 in the UK and a Number Two hit in the US.

7 Jimi Hendrix: 'House Burning Down' (1968) Hendrix tends to be thought of first as a guitarist and second as a songwriter. 'House Burning Down' is, as usual, crammed with incendiary guitar work, and the phased tone of the middle lead break obviously inspired Ernie Isley to emulate it on 'Who's That Lady?' The guitar coda is stunning, as Hendrix's guitar goes whooshing off into the distance before apparently turning around and coming back. But 'House Burning Down' is a remarkable rock song not only for its lyric – a blend of UFO visitation and the smoking American cities of 1968 – but also for the fact that Hendrix had the audacity to link a galloping soul rhythm (in F minor) with a foxtrot (in E♭m).

8 The Four Tops: 'I'm In A Different World' (1968) Few songwriting teams can match the record of Holland-Dozier-Holland. 'I'm In A Different World' was one of the last hits they had with Motown and their last with The Four Tops. It has typical Motown features in terms of the arrangement and a characteristically impassioned, straining vocal from Levi Stubbs, though for once he has a happy love theme, a taste of the final redemption of the seraphic 'Still Water (Love)'. Most of all, it is an object lesson in how to use modulation to express the meaning of a lyric.

It starts without an intro of any kind, Levi's vocal coming in a fraction of a second after the instruments. The verse moves I-IV-II in B♭ but changes to G♭ when the title comes in for the first time over a II-V-I in that key. Stubbs sings that he is in a different world – and so is the music, because it has modulated. This leads to a bridge section ("Each time you call my name …") with a clever single-note guitar line (partly doubled by James Jamerson's bass) that is reminiscent of the guitar line central to 'My Girl'. To get back to the verse and the key of B♭, the four-chord link goes C♭sus4-C♭sus2-A♭-D♭, momentarily making D♭ the key before dropping down to B♭.

'I'm In A Different World' is a song whose musical twists and unexpected turns mirror the shocked delight of the speaker, for whom life itself has turned so unexpectedly from dark to light.

9 Simon & Garfunkel: 'America' (1970) 'America' is a greater song than the more celebrated 'Bridge Over Troubled Water'. The latter plays to the gallery too much. Essentially a song of selfless love, there's something queasy about its implicit glorification of the speaker in such a religiose manner. By contrast, the lyric of 'America' is grounded, working from the concrete to the general. It is full of evocative images: the coach, the place names, the cigarette, the raincoat, the magazine, the moon, the bow tie. The apparent whimsy of the middle eight, where Simon gently evokes the paranoia of 1960s America, masks a deeper pathos. Maybe the man in the gabardine mac *is* a spy after all. And the hook – "All gone to look for America" – gives this song a breadth few popular songs attain. This is not just about lost love or lost lovers but a lost political ideal. This also expresses a truth about America at its best: it is committed to the process of becoming, of the future. To go looking for America is to do the quintessentially American thing.

The song is played with a capo at the second fret, so the following discussion refers to chord shapes rather than actual pitch. In terms of the music, notice that the verse uses the intro's descending chord sequence only once before making an unexpected shift to an A7. The last-line move on the word "moon" to a D and then C/G and G suggests a momentary key change to G, which is immediately cancelled out by a repeat of the descending sequence from C down to F. The D is also made less secure by virtue of being inverted (D/F♯). Verse two has a slightly different form from verse one. The title hook (D-G-D-Cmaj7) reaches for G major without getting a firm hold on it. The middle eight matches its lyrical change with an indeterminate ♭VIImaj7-Imaj7 sequence. Verse three is like verse one, but verse four has some important extra touches, such as the organ entering and the harmonising of the second line as C-Em-Am instead of G/B, which deepens the sadness of the moment where he's lonely talking to her and she's asleep. Notice how the coda develops the intro's descending progression by extending it to a Dm chord.

10 The Carpenters: 'We've Only Just Begun' (1970) There are *considerably* fewer songs that celebrate marriage as opposed to romance. 'Maybe I'm Amazed', 'Wonderful Tonight', and 'If I Should Fall Behind' are three famous examples. Such songs are lyrically difficult, because they risk sounding complacent and thus arousing hostility and envy in the listener. Take Barbara Streisand's 'Evergreen', which opens with the disastrous simile comparing love to a soft, easy chair.

Paul Williams's 'We've Only Just Begun' gets around this in two ways. The lovers' relationship is seen as a journey, so there are references to horizons, roads, ways, flying, walking, and running. It is not a fixed state and is therefore less likely to arouse envy. Change and growth are emphasised through verbs: the couple choose, learn, watch, share, talk, work, and find. Since they are active and at the start of something rather than the end, they win our sympathy.

Many trademarks of MOR are present in the arrangement, such as the block vocal harmonies (sometimes singing major seventh or major ninth chords), the use of orchestral instruments such as the plaintive woodwinds and the poignant minor ninth piano figure on the F♯m chord (as on "promises"). Notice the dynamic contrast of the chorus, which is more rhythmic, with more prominent brass, drums, bass, and tambourine. Here the sense of motion is more palpable. It is as if the verses express the inner side of the relationship and the active choruses its outer expression in the world.

The chorus also benefits from some unexpected key shifts. The verse is in A major (using chords I-VI) but a D-E-F♯ change establishes F♯ major as the new key:

Old key	I	IV	I	IV		
	A	D	A	D	E	F♯
New key				♭VI	♭VII	I

The music changes from F♯ to B (I-IV) several times, establishing the new key, before transposing the I-IV change into the distant key of B♭. A semitone (half-step) slide from E♭ (chord IV in B♭) to E takes us back to chord V of A major. The composer has one last surprise in store. After two A-D changes, the song resolves on a C♯ major chord (III ^ in A), which cancels out the C♯m chord in the verses and establishes a new key – perhaps hinting at some future state of happiness.

Karen Carpenter's vocal perfectionism sometimes led to a fatal discrepancy between the way she sang and what she was singing about. But 'We've Only Just Begun' finds a subject and a form that enable her extreme control and glassy vibrato to signify the optimism and courage of the newly-weds. They have had the "white lace" and made the "promises" of the first line, they are entitled to their hope; they have earned it.

11 The Temptations: 'Ball Of Confusion' (1970) Talk about 1960s protest and people invariably mention Bob Dylan and Joan Baez. Too often Motown's last years in Detroit are forgotten, and if Motown is cited it's usually Marvin Gaye and *What's Going On* that get the plaudits. But the label also released protest records such as Stevie Wonder's 'Heaven Help Us All', Edwin Starr's 'War' and The Temptations' 'Ball Of Confusion'.

'Ball Of Confusion' is a typical Norman Whitfield 'groove' song, with a repetitious two-bar C pentatonic minor bass riff churning beneath the C major harmony. On top, guitars add strange licks with echo, notably on the dramatic intro with Dennis Edwards's arresting count-in (listen to the CD on headphones and you can hear the amps buzzing), and the brass section has the occasional jazzy flourish. Every now and then, there's an arpeggiated bridge using C, F, and G, with a punchy James Brown-type link – but the rhythmic drive of the track is relentless. The music can be simple because of the aggression and the clever division of the lyric among the Temps' contrasting voices.

The lyric is an extraordinary set of snapshots of American society after the riots of 1968, with cities on fire in the summer heat, and the aftermath of the Martin Luther King and Robert Kennedy assassinations. Race, poverty, taxes, back to nature, drugs, politics, religion, education, the moonshots, suicide, population growth, Vietnam … it's all there, with daring combinations best caught in the line contrasting rising unemployment with the comment that the latest Beatles record is a "gas".

12 10cc: 'I'm Not In Love' (1975) 10cc were a musically literate outfit with the ability to pastiche early pop and rock styles to make ingenious, witty singles such as 'The Dean And I' and 'Rubber Bullets'. 'I'm Not In Love' has more depth than any of their other hits and was their boldest musical vision. The lyric was an excellent example of a speaker who is undermining the very thing he claims, as he invents various excuses to hide his love for the woman.

The song has a superb arrangement that defied the technological limitations of the day. The intro features a complex B11 to B change on electric piano and a sparse mix. The verse starts on A. The change from A to a sighing Am perfectly expresses the speaker's attempt to cover up his feelings giving way, as does the melancholy rise to C#m via G#. Notice the surprise when "It's because" lands on E, and the way the second bridge about waiting a long time is in G. For the amazing middle section, the band recorded 240 vocal parts (on a 16-track). The effect resembles the work of the composer Ligeti, whose eerie vocal music was featured on the soundtrack of *2001 A Space Odyssey*. What is also striking is that 'I'm Not In Love' began life as a bossa nova, only later metamorphosing into a Number One hit. This shows that if a song isn't working, don't be afraid to try a drastic change of interpretation. (The same thing happened when George Martin told The Beatles to play 'Please Please Me' faster.)

13 Bruce Springsteen: 'Born To Run' (1975) Springsteen's first three albums offer many insights into lyric writing, production, and longer song structures. 'Born To Run' was the moment when he successfully revamped the best music of the pre-Beatles era. The Spectorish production starts with a six-note Duane Eddy-type guitar motif supported by a barrage of saxes, guitars, and keyboards. The verse moves twice round an E-A-B change before bringing in a couple of minor chords. Listen for the ♭VII chord on the first "oh-oh", played as a sus4 and then resolved. There isn't a separate chorus, as the hook is part of the verse. Since the song is about journeying, it is fitting that the middle section after the sax break travels in harmony terms. From E major we go to a 16-bar sequence of sus4 chords and their resolutions: D, G, A, and C. The sense of key is fluid throughout. We watch possible tonal centres rush by as though in a car seeing the sights. Then, with a crash, F is established as a new key for six bars; after a few bars there, the music ascends and then descends by semitones (half-steps), landing on a drawn-out B chord that thrusts the music back into the final verse. Springsteen repeats the hook several times, reharmonising by adding a VI chord (C#m) before the coda.

At this time, Springsteen was conscious of the effect of a song in concert and shaped his material for the stage. He adapted the old 'soul revue' trick of having many mini-climaxes in a song. 'Born To Run' has a number of these peaks, which play a big part in never letting the energy of the track drop.

14 Bebop Deluxe: 'Maid In Heaven' (1975) Bebop Deluxe were a UK band who enjoyed moderate success at the tail-end of glam rock with a literate version of the Bowie/Queen sound. They were led by singer-guitarist Bill Nelson, and 'Maid In Heaven' is one of their two hit singles. It is a beautiful example of how effective 1970s rock can be when all its self-indulgence is stripped away. It starts with a false intro, an F-D-A progression that implies F is the key. A change to G in bar six, however, leads to the true key of D major and an eight-bar sequence with some fine lead over the top. The verse is a further ten bars – six vocal and four with a guitar arpeggio. After verse two, the song goes to a middle eight that pivots off an Em chord (displacing D and thereby adding interest) and links up with part of the intro (a crescendo on A) before two more verses, the last of which repeats the hook-line "was made in heaven for you". The earlier descending arpeggio figure is then extended down a full octave. The coda is decorated by studio phasing, dynamic drums, expressive lead and a classic rock I-V-IV progression, before the whole thing finishes with a punched-out descending sequence going down the scale to chord I.

A bright, passionate, thumping little world in a mere 2:17, and for all its romance it still has the humanity to say, in the last verse, "take the rough with the smooth".

15 R.E.M.: 'Fall On Me' (1986) This song was voted the best single of 1986 by *Creem* and is taken from the band's fourth album, *Life's Rich Pageant*. The lyrics are as impenetrable as ever (the theme is apparently ecological), though enough of the images come through to carry a variety of emotions. The song is in C major but there's no sign of chord I until the pre-chorus, and there it is present only for two beats, displaced in a II-V-I-IV progression. The verse consists of a melancholic Dm-Am change (II-VI). The middle eight is almost entirely on the minor chords II, III and VI, and there's an extended pre-chorus instead of a third verse to delay the last choruses by a fraction.

The real power of the song lies in the chorus, which is fuelled by a powerful I-II-IV-V turnaround. What lifts it into the sublime is the presence of an increasing number of vocal lines. If you listen carefully you'll hear four different vocal ideas on the final choruses. This is a powerful hook because no single voice can replicate it. The only way to satisfy the desire to hear it again is to play the record one more time.

16 Elvis Costello: 'I Want You' (1986) 'I Want You' is one of Costello's most dramatic arrangements. It has a false intro long enough to be a section in itself, played in a country style using I-IV-V in A major. The second verse comes to an unexpected end on A-G-F♯m. Appropriately for a song about emotional disjunctions, a sudden unrelated D♯m chord on the electric hastens in the first verse proper in a new key. The main part of the song is built on a I-III-VI-V ^ turnaround in E minor: Em-G-C-B(7), occasionally punctuated by the D♯m. The mix comprises a brittle spiky electric, sustained organ chords, an acoustic guitar, bass, and drums. The playing gradually intensifies with the organ seeking higher voicings. At 3:21 there's a demented two-note guitar solo on two deliberately 'wrong' notes. The music subsides, builds up and subsides again at about the five-minute mark. The long coda gradually fades to nothing – a kind of anti-climax.

The lyric obsessively alternates the title with the other lines. Costello's theme is jealousy and its self-torturing focus on the imagined details of a lover's betrayal. 'I Want You' falls short of the last degree of greatness, for there's something melodramatic about it, almost as if the songwriter enjoys the conceit and prolongs the song as a consequence. Would it be any less effective if it were a minute or 90 seconds shorter? The speaker seems too willing to embrace the pain he suffers. His imagination is voyeuristic, and the lyric (reinforced by Costello's close-miked vocal presence) implicates us as voyeurs if we get any pleasure out of this pain. But it's riveting theatre.

17 Dire Straits: 'On Every Street' (1991) Dire Straits were a frustrating band. It's easy to understand why their huge sales and the popularism of songs such as 'Twisting By The Pool', 'Money For Nothing', and 'Walk of Life' led many to dismiss them as incapable of creating anything of depth.

In his vocal delivery, lyrics, and guitar playing, Mark Knopfler is a master of understatement, which in rock is an astonishing thing in itself. 'On Every Street' is a love song that conceals deep feeling behind sometimes offhand, oblique imagery. It has a powerful three-verse-plus-coda structure. The verses are melody driven, with frequent chord changes that rise with effort to C, the apparent key, and an interpolated 2/4 bar, indicating that rhythm does not have the upper hand. The hook has a sombre and unexpected B♭ (♭VII) chord, which lets the suppressed emotion through by shifting to B♭maj7, reaches C with momentary hope and then dashes it with a drop to A minor on a tremoloed 1950s three-note guitar lick. Each verse is followed by a few bars of what will become the driving theme of the coda, the second statement having a rhythmic anomaly in it. Knopfler's trademark mournful guitar supplies tell-tale sighs throughout.

At 2:50, the guitars introduce a four-bar turnaround that is in C but never reaches the key chord and includes a telling D/F♯ inversion to preserve the shape of the bassline. The song rides out on a coda that is in strong dynamic contrast to the verses, with the drums entering for the first time. The use of a turnaround for the coda is more powerful because the verses did not have one. And how many guitarists could have resisted soloing loudly at this point? Knopfler judged rightly that the song did not need it.

18 Ash: 'Goldfinger' (1995) The uninspired and mildly presumptuous title ("There's only *one* Goldfinger, Mr. Bond …") is the only place where Ash's 'Goldfinger' disappoints. It has a good grasp of dynamics, which is essential to rock. It's loud and grungy but there are spaces, so the full sound doesn't get tiresome. In this age of desk-driven punch in/out beatboxes, it has tempo changes and a real drummer who stops playing, counts off two bars and then re-enters with a fill. From an arrangement angle, notice how the backing vocals are kept till the last chorus.

'Goldfinger' creates interesting contrasts with keys. The band detuned by a semitone (half-step), but to keep things simple I'll pretend they didn't, to make it easier to describe the chord shapes. The instrumental chorus at the start is squarely in G, though it ends on an ambiguous B7sus4 (III^). The guitar solo suggests E minor. B is the key for the verse, which is mostly a four-chord turnaround in B: B-G♯m-C♯m-F♯ (I-VI-II-V). I say 'mostly' because there's a harmonically outrageous chromatic change from the F♯ to an F and then B♭, and then a leap back to C♯m. This is topped off with a fine three-note guitar overdub that accentuates the sudden weirdness of the changes. Thousands of songs have been written using a I-VI-II-V sequence, but Ash found a new angle on it.

19 Garbage: 'Stupid Girl' (1995) 'Stupid Girl' is carried by its arrangement. It's built on a I-IV change in F♯, and both chords are dominant sevenths that provide a sulky edge. This change appears in the intro, verse, chorus, and the instrumental bridge; the texture is varied to make the sections sound different.

On the intro, adorned only by a guitar pick-slide and other effects, four bars set the rhythm. The verse adds Shirley Manson's voice and a dancey bass riff with flattened blue notes for an almost R&B feel. An eight-bar pre-chorus cuts in with a couple of minor chords that provide harmonic contrast to the harder-edged strut of the F♯7-B7 change. Listen for the way Garbage overdubbed a distorted vocal sample with reverse reverb, which is guaranteed to make anyone sound like an extra from *The Exorcist*. On the chorus, the title hook is answered by a voice/guitar unison "ah-ah" (maybe a slight nod to 'Smells Like Teen Spirit'). The word "girl" is on a flattened blue note (A instead of A♯ against the F♯ chord). In verse two, Shirley sings lines that answer the main tune and in the last chorus adds a harmony. The bridge guitar figures include a bassy Duane Eddy-type phrase and a 'stab' guitar chord on the opposite side of the mix. Listen for the bass dropping out during the bridge so that its re-entry is felt on the last choruses. 'Stupid Girl' has an effective sudden ending, the sort DJs don't dare talk over.

Sometimes you don't need lots of ideas – you just need to develop the one you've got.

20 Radiohead: 'Paranoid Android' (1997) The first time I heard this track on the radio, the DJ commented, after the abrupt ending, "Hmmm … I'm not sure about that one." At that moment, it was clear Radiohead had done a great job. This track is disconcerting and does the unexpected.

Key-wise, it shifts between G minor, D minor and A minor in an ambiguous way. The opening acoustic Cm-Gm sequence cries out that it must be in some weird tuning, although it's actually standard. The music sounds like it's going into Am, but this happens only after the second verse. Next, a moment of arranging genius: most rock bands would have made the single-note riff a straight pentatonic minor figure. Instead, Radiohead introduce an A♭, implying an Am-A♭ chord change, interspersed with a ♭VI-♭VII-I. When the electric guitars come in the riff's power is unleashed, but the band don't overdo the headbanging – that heavy riff is played only a handful of times. This leaves you wanting more. After the first solo, the music enters its hymn-like third section, which starts on a Cm chord and changes key to D minor via an A7. Notice the feeling of dislocation when the music goes from A back to Cm, as they are distant chords.

The two solo breaks show how rock guitar returned to its roots in the 1990s, rejecting the over-technical widdling of the late 1980s for a less-is-more approach. The first break has what I would call 'cultivated (apparent) incompetence'.

Maybe the whole isn't quite equal to the sum of the parts (the song was apparently pieced together out of three fragments) but it has an impressive variety of emotion by Oxford's finest.

21 Manic Street Preachers: 'There By The Grace Of God' (2002)

Once The Manics put their youthful sloganeering away, along with the mascara, they turned into a potent rock band with a penchant for serious lyric themes. The stand-out track on their debut album was 'Motorcycle Emptiness', which is a great rock song sung beautifully by James Dean Bradfield but spoiled by robotically inflexible drumming. The expressiveness of his voice is evident on 'There By The Grace Of God'.

This song has an impressive, austere beauty. It is the sound of rock music coming up against an emotional frontier beyond which it cannot pass without surrendering everything. Despite its reputation for being 'the devil's music', rock's main problem is that its sheer power – its extremes of volume and dynamic force – are simply too powerful for most lyric subjects (which is why there is something absurdly Neanderthal about most hard rock songs about sex). But in spirituality, in contemplating the divine and human imperfection, rock does find a subject to get worked up about, as here. Musically, the arrangement has many subtle touches, especially the choice of bass notes. I know of few songs where the pathos of the major seventh chord is so achingly felt.

22 The Raconteurs: 'Blue Veins' (2006)

The Raconteurs are Jack Lawrence (bass), Patrick Keeler (drums / percussion), Jack White (vocals, guitars, and synthesizers), and Brendan Benson (vocals, guitar, and keys). Their debut album, *Broken Boy Soldiers* (2006), opens with 'Steady, As She Goes', one of its stronger moments. From a songwriter's perspective, it soberingly demonstrates how little actual music is needed to make a song these days. It comprises a two-bar phrase lasting roughly four seconds repeated about 38 times, a link bar, and a middle eight comprised of four different bars (G to A to B and G to A to E). That makes a total of 15 seconds of music. The repetition of those bits takes the song to 3:35.

For me, the stand-out track is 'Blue Veins'. There's a 'false' intro created by 30 seconds of backward music which rights itself into a blues in A minor reminiscent of Peter Green's Fleetwood Mac (listen to the album *Then Play On*). It features lovely echoed tremolo guitar and spooky piano, with another backward section in the middle instead of a solo. The chorus plays a harmonic trick with two bars of C, then two of B7, which you would expect to lead to E but instead go to Am. In the verse there is a clever time-signature twist. Bar one is 12/8 (four beats counting 1-2-3 on each) with a Dm chord. Bar two is countable as 13/8 (ie, count 123, 123, 123, 1234). An extra quaver is added to the bar. So try adding or subtracting a quaver from a 4/4 or 12/8 bar occasionally when writing a song.

FAMOUS SONGWRITERS ON SONGWRITING

Here are some interesting comments on songwriting from the people who do it professionally. Notice that they do not necessarily take the same view of it, and their opinions concerning how to achieve certain songwriting goals may differ. Nevertheless, these observations will stimulate your own songwriting approach.

Paul Weller

When we finished [The Jam's] *Setting Sons* (1980), I got the engineer to play the whole album backwards for me to listen to on cassette, and there was one little piece of music, of backward vocal, that I really liked the melody of. So I wrote the whole of 'Dreams Of Children' built around that, more or less made up on the spot. (1992)

I suppose in some ways I write in an old-fashioned way because I always have middle eights in my songs and not many people do any more. It's usually just a verse and chorus. Structure is really important. Some I've really had to work at, others come really quickly. Keeping the whole thing interesting – that's what it all comes down to. (1984)

Mike Mills (R.E.M.)

I asked everyone to sing a background part for the chorus [of 'Find The River'] without hearing any of the other guys. Mine was really emotional, and Bill's was totally the opposite, cool and low-key. They really worked together. That's the kind of thing that keeps it from being too processed – that let's you know it's not being machined to death, that there are human beings doing it. (1992)

Peter Buck (R.E.M.)

[On 'Country Feedback'] We didn't have a song. I walked in and I had four chords. I put them down with Bill playing bass. I put the feedback on it. John Keane put the pedal steel on it. Michael walked in and said, "Oh, I've got words for that." The next day he just sang it. The total recording time, not including the mix, was, like, 35 minutes. It's really nice if you can get it to flow like that.

Bruce Springsteen

The only trick to writing a new song is you have to have a new idea. And to have a new idea, you've got to be a bit of a new person, so that's where the challenge is. (1987)

The writing is more difficult now. On this album [*Born To Run*], I started slowly to find out who I am and where I wanted to be. It was like coming out of the shadow of various influences and trying to be me. You have to let out more of yourself all the time. You strip off the first layer, then the second, then the third. It gets harder because it gets more personal. (1975)

Neil Young

I try not to think about the songs that I write, I just try to write them. And I try not to edit them....

I know there's a source where music comes through you and words come through you, and editing is really something you do to something that you've thought about. I think some of the things I write are mine, but I think some just come through me.

My mind is working behind the scenes and puts these things together without me consciously thinking of it, and then when the time is right it all comes out. (1985)

I've written most of my best songs driving on a long journey, scribbling lyrics on cigarette packs while steering. (1990)

Bob Dylan

I just wanted a song to sing, and there came a point where I couldn't sing anything. So I had to write what I wanted to sing 'cause nobody else was writing what I wanted. I couldn't find it anywhere. If I could, I probably would never have started writing. (1984)

Since the late 1960s, maybe since *Sgt. Pepper* on, everybody started to spend more of their time in the studio, actually making up songs and building them in the studio. I've done a little bit of that, but I'd rather have some kind of song before I get there. It just seems to work out better that way. (1985)

Brian Wilson (The Beach Boys)

When I've thought out a theme I go to the piano and sit playing 'feels', which are rhythm patterns and fragments of ideas. Then the song starts to blossom and become a real thing. (1966)

I think that 'Good Vibrations' was a contribution in that it was a pocket symphony.... It was a series of intricate harmonies and mood changes. We used a cello for the first time in rock'n'roll, so I think in that respect it was an innovation. (1976)

Kurt Cobain (Nirvana)

When I write a song, the lyrics are the least important thing. I can go through two or three different subjects in a song, and the title can mean absolutely nothing at all. (1989)

I think of my new songs as pop songs, as they're arranged with the standard pop format: verse, chorus, verse, chorus, solo, bad solo. (1990)

Jimi Hendrix

On 'The Wind Cries Mary', the words came first, you know, the words came first and then the music was so easy to put there. The whole thing just fell in ... it just melted together. (1968)

Paul McCartney

Sometimes I've got a guitar in my hands; sometimes I'm sitting at a piano. It depends on whatever instrument I'm at – I'll compose on it.

Every time is different, really. I like to keep it that way, too; I don't get any set formula. So that each time, I'm pulling it out of the air.

There's not much that takes years and years. If it takes that long, I normally abort it.... The best songs are written in one go. They're just done – inspiration comes quickly, it falls in place. (1990)

John Lennon

I remember in the early meetings with Dylan, he was always saying to me, "Listen to the words, man!" and I said, "I can't be bothered. I listen to the sound of it, the sound of the overall thing." Then I reversed that and started being a words man. I naturally play with words anyway, so I made a conscious effort to be wordy à la Dylan. But now I've relieved myself of that burden and I'm only interested in pure sound. (1980)

Keith Richards

If you try and add a melody to a riff rather than it evolving from it, it always sounds completely false, like the melody's been stuck on the top with a piece of sellotape....

You don't create songs. They're not all your creation. You just sort of pluck them out of the air, if you're around and receptive, and then you say, "I kind of like this" and something about the songs says, "I'm worth the time and the trouble to keep playing me and find out." And if you hang on to their tail long enough, suddenly you get, "Ah, there I am, I'm ready." So you have to listen to the mechanics of the song all the time and be very receptive to what it's trying to tell you while you're making it. (1988)

Brian May

I like to live with the song for a while without touching the guitar at all. Then I can form an idea in my head of what I'd like to play, and then work it out on the guitar and take it into the studio pretty much complete. (1990)

Frank Zappa

Basically, what people want to hear in a song is: "I love you, you love me, I'm OK, you're OK, the leaves turned brown, they fell off the trees, the wind was blowing, it got cold, it rained, it stopped raining, you went away, my heart broke, you came back and my heart was OK." I think basically that is deep down what everybody wants to hear. (1974)

Damon Albarn (Blur)

I did all my grades on piano, but I write all my songs on acoustic guitar, which I can just about play 10 chords on. I do them all on an E shape, and put a finger on the bottom E, so I've always got an E and B drone, whatever chord I do. That's all I do. I've limited myself massively, so the whole thing has become incredibly simple. (1991)

Eric Clapton

It's important for records to be as good as you can make them, you know? When I've written songs and made them into demos – for instance, on the *August* album I had one demo that we did clean up and polish a lot.

Mark Knopfler

Different keys on the guitar suggest different moods. I can't get any height on my voice, so I tend to choose keys that might not suit the song but happen to suit my non-existent range. Sometimes you pick the wrong key when you're recording – 'Why Worry' was recorded in E and you can hear it's in the wrong key. I'm straining to sing it, and I think on the last tour we changed it to D.

Morrissey

My lyrics are only obscure to the extent that they are not taken directly from the dictionary of writing songs. They are not slavish to the lyrical rulebook, so you'll never catch me singing, "Oh baby, baby, yeah." My only priority is to use lines and words in a way that hasn't been heard before. (1983)

Tori Amos

The songs just hang out, you know, they come in and move in. To me the songs already exist, I'm just an interpreter for them. Yes, because of my experiences they're going to come through my filter, and that's going to change how I see them. But they already exist in a certain form, and I'm just trying to take them to the third dimension – maybe the fourth, really, because I'd like to think my work taps into the fourth dimension, not just three dimensions.... I'm always trying to push the boundaries of form, but I don't analyse it when I'm writing. (1996)

Marc Bolan (T.Rex)

I play about for a couple of hours before I move into new dimensions where I'm being very creative. I record everything then. (1971)

I've suddenly tuned into that mental channel that makes a record a hit, and I feel at present as though I could write Number Ones for ever. Let's face it, the majority of pop hits that make it are a permutation on the 12-bar blues, and I've found one that works. (1970)

Matt Johnson (The The)

I think if a song sounds good on just an acoustic guitar, then it *is* good. That's a song as opposed to a track. A lot of modern records are just tracks, and if you take away the production then they cease to exist. (1993)

Glenn Tilbrook (Squeeze)

People often point out that some of our best-known stuff is musically quite tricky; it revolves around a lot of chord changes, but that was actually something I was striving to stop doing. I wasn't really conscious of doing it until other people mentioned it. I personally don't like songs that are too tricky, but it all depends on how it grabs you. The acid test for me is not whether it's tricky or not, it's whether it works when you play it on its own, just guitar or keyboards. I know that's an old chestnut, but it's true.

Joni Mitchell

[On altered tunings] You're twiddling and you find the tuning. Now the left hand has to learn where the chords are, because it's a whole new ballpark, right? So you're groping around, looking for where the chords are, using very simple shapes. Put it in a tuning and you've got four chords immediately: open, barre five, barre seven, and your higher octave, like half fingering on the 12th. Then you've got to find where your minors are and where the interesting colours are – that's the exciting part.

Jack Bruce (Cream)

I had this idea that you could have very heavy, wild, instrumental stuff but a lyrical, gentle vocal. Something like 'I Feel Free' – very rhythmic backing, very smooth voices on top. It would've been easy to scream something, but then it's one dimensional. (1993)

Kristin Hersh (Throwing Muses)

It's immature to think you're smarter than the music. For me, the only time I can write is when I see really clearly – and I'm so unselfconscious for that reason, I can hear what the songs are saying, and I let them say whatever they want regardless of how much it has to do with my situation. Not that you should make things up – it should resonate with you. You shouldn't pretend. (1995)

Toni Iommi (Black Sabbath)

I'd pick up the guitar, come up with a riff and go, "That sounds a bit evil." The words had to fit the mood. (1995)

Elvis Costello

Recently, I've started changing the keys. Steve [Naive] and I have been doing a version of 'Veronica' that brings back the feeling that was somewhat submerged by the brightness of the pop arrangement, by shifting the key. The verse is higher in register, in E♭, but then drops instead of ascending at the chorus, which closes the song into a more emotional feeling. (1996)

Kate Bush

How I wrote at least the last two albums was to go into the studio and write ideas onto tape – dump stuff onto tape, as it were, forget about it and then move onto the next area. But when I first started, I always used to write on the piano, and just the last couple of months I've felt at home again writing on the piano. It's such a different process, I find it quite shocking. It's like suddenly you've become the memory banks; instead of dumping it onto tape, it's staying in you. And each time you play the song, it changes. The sense of transformation is very subtle; each time you play it, something will change.

Richard Fairbrass (Right Said Fred)

We took a tea break, and the computer was playing this loop round and round, and right out of the blue – I can't tell you where it came from – I started singing "I'm too sexy for my shirt" and we all fell about laughing.

John Barry (film score writer)

It's quite an art to write a good bridge, 'cause it lifts you into another area. It's got to be a variant on what you've done before, but you have to come up with some surprise, so that when you get back to that last familiar strain it's almost like falling into something.

Donald Fagen (Steely Dan)

Sometimes the more chords you use, it stops the forward motion, even over the exact rhythmic base. Which is why – aside from ignorance and so on – other people don't use too many chords. It's easier to keep it going.

'Miami' Steve Van Zandt (Bruce Springsteen)

By '72, pretty much everything had shifted to the songs. By '72, pretty much everything that could be done with a guitar had been done, with the exception of Eddie Van Halen, who had yet to come. What were you gonna do that Clapton, Beck, Page, and Hendrix hadn't done? … The emphasis had to shift to songs. However good a guitar player you were at that point, you had now to work within the context of a song: our guitar playing was gonna come in handy and be useful, but not so much to just go off on long solos to impress somebody anymore.

Jack White (White Stripes)

I've always wanted to write songs that people could at least sing on their way to work and stuff like that. That kind of really melodic poppiness.

Songwriting is storytelling, melody, and rhythm, those three components. If you break it down but you keep the three components, then you have what songwriting really is, without excess and overthinking.

Angus Young (AC/DC)

Sometimes when you write a song, you know it's a good idea but it still don't sound like you. So you take it a stage further until it does or you say, no, this ain't working, and you leave it.

Katie Melua

The best test of a song is for me to just sing it and play it on guitar alone and see if it works. They all have to pass that quirky little test. You can always tell quite easily which ones work and which don't.

Ian Anderson (Jethro Tull)

I sat there sometimes with that writer's block, staring at the wall, unable to come up with anything; it would happen. But I learned very, very early on, in the summer of '68, necessity is the mother of invention. You've got a recording schedule and you've got to turn up to work with some ideas.

Suzanne Vega

I love songwriting. To me, there's all these elements that are mixed into it, of magic, spells, and prayers … children's games … science. I like to bring all these things together so it's all one. You can draw from any source.

Robbie Robertson (The Band)

It would be nice to abandon the verse-chorus-bridge structure completely, and make it so none of these things are definable. You could just call those sections whatever you would call them … make up new names for them.

Burt Bacharach

I compose everything on piano and in my head. I go back and forth between a keyboard and the couch. I kind of get it bar by bar; for me I don't get a total perspective of where it's going straight away. They're never easy because, you know, it's one of those things; every hole is important, there's no filler time. You've got a limited period of time with a pop song. I always used to think of them as four-minute movies with high and lows.

David Wilcox

I used to think I couldn't write a song without a new tuning, and that's often the case, but I think there are more songs than tunings.

Grasshopper (Mercury Rev)

A lot of the time it's intuition – you don't really analyse it, just stay true to yourself and go with the flow. But when you finish a record you have to take time out to reflect where you're at. You have to look back and say, 'OK, what happened there? What does that mean?'

Nick Hodgson (Kaiser Chiefs)

I've always been writing songs … I look back at some of the early ones and I think, actually they're pretty rubbish. But what I did notice was that each of the songs had good parts in them. They had one good bit but the songs as a whole weren't very good. It just takes time practising and learning how to write songs. You actually get to a level where they're proper songs like 'I Predict A Riot'. That's fully formed. There are no spare bits.

SECTION 16

RECOMMENDED ALBUMS FOR SONGWRITERS

This list is not meant to be the greatest albums of all time, though some of these records would be included on such a list. Inclusion here is not primarily about great performances, profundity, commercial success, influence, or the ability to evoke a period. I'm not attempting to present a perfect cross-section of popular music since 1960, nor are all musical genres represented.

Instead, these albums show different directions in which the popular song has been taken. Careful listening to them will teach you an immeasurable amount about the song, what it is capable of, and what an elastic form it is. Lyrics, melodies, rhythms, hooks, song structures, arrangements, vocal and instrumental performances – they're all here, albeit in differing mixtures. If you can get your head round the songs on all these albums, then you're doing pretty well in songwriting awareness.

The Beach Boys: *Pet Sounds* (1966)
The pop song as 'pocket symphony'. Check out the box set *The Pet Sounds Sessions* for real archaeological detail.

Bob Dylan: *Blonde On Blonde* (1966)
Get tangled up in imagery as Dylan's folk muse dons a pair of cool shades and goes acid-rock.

Love: *Forever Changes* (1967)
Quirky, innovative lyrics and arrangements that juxtapose strings with 12-string guitars. Extraordinary titles, and songs that are expressive and unpredictable.

The Band: *The Band* (1969)
Seasoned as a barrel of vintage whisky – an unforgettable 'take' on country rock.

Various Artists: *Motown Chartbusters*, Vols. I-V (1969-71)
Okay, it's a cheat: five albums' worth of Hitsville USA classics from the company that charged rental space in the *Billboard* Top 100 during the 1960s. Great songs you can also dance to.

Led Zeppelin: *Led Zeppelin IV* (1971)
If you want to write heavy rock, this is how you do it. Great guitar riffs and disciplined ensemble playing. 'Stairway'

is a seamless venture into the longer structure, but don't miss the epic 'When The Levee Breaks', an object lesson in hard-hitting repetition, and the truly mysterious 'Battle Of Evermore'.

Simon & Garfunkel: *Greatest Hits* (1972)
Probably the best deployment of two voices and acoustic guitars since the Everly Brothers.

The Beatles: *1962–66/1967–70* (1973)
Yes, their albums were great. But this is how the Fab Four reinvented the 45, from mop-top pop to hippie dreams and beyond.

Bruce Springsteen: *The Wild, The Innocent And The E Street Shuffle* (1973)
Bruce's second album may not be as focused and popularist as its two successors, but it shares the same interest in long-scale song structures, haunting arrangements, and lyrics that teem with characters and local colour. A unique rock-soul fusion.

The Carpenters: *The Singles 1969–73* (1974)
If MOR songwriting is your aim, these people wrote the textbook.

Queen: *Queen II* (1974)
The second album shows the progressive champs of multi-track overdubbing madness getting into their stride and stretching song structures. The level of arrangement detail on this record is astonishing. Who else but Freddie Mercury could have made so quintessentially English a rock song as 'The Fairy Feller's Master Stroke', named after a Victorian painting?

Joni Mitchell: *Hejira* (1976)
Classic singer-songwriting with fine lyrics set to open-tuned guitars and the fretless bass of Jaco Pastorius.

Fleetwood Mac: *Rumours* (1977)
Multi-platinum AOR, light and breezy, with a few bitter undertones concealed like daggers under black lace. Listen for melodic guitar work, vocal harmonies, and tight song structures.

Siouxsie & The Banshees: *Ju Ju* (1981)
A punk band re-invents itself as African Gothic. This album is a lexicon of unusual musical approaches, from the weird spidery guitar lines to the tribal drumming, and, of course, a host of dark emotions.

Bob Marley: *Legend* (1984)
Marley's songwriting shows how reggae could reach a wider audience by combining religious and political themes with commercial melodies.

R.E.M.: *Life's Rich Pageant* (1986)
Classic 1980s alternative/'college' rock. The early R.E.M. blueprint of obscure lyrics, odd melodies, unconventional dual voices, and jangle guitar is polished and reaches maturity on this record. Few rock bands have so deserved the adjective 'poetic'.

Kate Bush: *The Sensual World* (1989)
A warmer album than its more popular predecessor, *Hounds Of Love*, this record is astonishing for the emotional depth of the songs and the amazing arrangements. Who else but Bush would have pitted rock guitar against Bulgarian harmony singing?

Madonna: *The Immaculate Conception* (1990)
Not even two double-albums could now gather up all of Madonna's chartbusters. Love her or loathe her, she and Patrick Leonard knew how to put a hit single together and maintained a remarkable run of success from the

mid-1980s onward. This collection has the brighter, brassier early hits.

Nirvana: *Never Mind* (1991)
Grunge's finest hour, where pop hooks and verse/chorus collide with the Big Guitar Racket.

Abba: *Gold* (1992)
Another commercial legend: mini-epics of marital tragedy that you could dance to. Take up thy handbag … and stuff your songs with hooks.

Jeff Buckley: *Grace* (1995)
The singer-songwriter strikes back for the 1990s. Highly inventive mixture of styles, tremendous range of expression, clever arrangements, altered tunings, fine lyrics, terrific vocals.

Bjork: *Post* (1995)
One example of how a female singer can find new ways forward by harnessing 1990s technology to an idiosyncratic muse.

Burt Bacharach: *The Look Of Love* (1996)
On the smoother side of things, there's nothing like a good compilation of Bacharach for an insight into melodic development and harmonic construction.

Radiohead: *OK Computer* (1996)
Perhaps lacking a little in the lyric department (though these songs cover their tracks better than their 1970s equivalents), but highly imaginative development of rock into new areas and textures.

Moby: *Play* (1999)
Innovations in the technology of music in the 90s made it possible for songwriting to become aural collage. Moby recorded the album at home, placing samples of old out-of-copyright blues singers against light beats and synth strings. Was it theft? Was it art? Was it too repetitive? It sold in millions and became the music to play in hip minimalist restaurants.

Queens Of The Stone Age: *Restricted R* (2000)
In some ways the maturing of grunge, *Restricted R* undoubtedly rocked but delivered its bursts of manic energy in highly imaginative arrangements that covered a wide musical territory. It could be dark but also funny. Forty years in, this was rock music of amazing freshness.

Radiohead: *Kid A* (2000)
In which Radiohead legendarily deconstructed the sound of *OK Computer* and created a haunting and highly inventive musical winterscape. An album full of striking sounds matched with musical twists.

The Darkness: *Permission To Land* (2003)
Their debut was seen as an entertaining re-invention of the 70s rock of Queen, with the twin lead of Thin Lizzy, but a closer look reveals that songs like 'Friday Night' and 'Holding My Own' had lyrics that were funny but unexpectedly tender, while Dan Hawkins broadened hard rock guitar's palette with touches of U2.

Fleet Foxes: *Fleet Foxes* (2008)
Uneven in execution and production, and with a worrying tendency to drift sometimes into solo-album mode, nevertheless the reverb-laden harmonies, mandolin, and acoustic guitars of Fleet Foxes evoke a widescreen folk Americana, as if The Beach Boys and Crosby, Stills, Nash & Young had been writing together in the Blue Ridge Mountains.

INDEX OF SONGS
INDEX OF ARTISTS
GENERAL INDEX

INDEX OF SONGS

This index lists song titles followed by the associated artist. A definite or indefinite article is not shown at the front of a title: so, for example, 'The Needle And The Damage Done' appears under N as 'Needle And The Damage Done, The', and 'A Punch-Up At A Wedding' appears under P as 'Punch-Up At A Wedding, A'.

INDEX OF ARTISTS

This index lists artist and band names. Any names beginning with a definite article have 'The' moved from the front of the name; so, for example, The Beatles appear under B as 'Beatles, The'.

GENERAL INDEX

REFERENCE SECTION | **239**

ACKNOWLEDGEMENTS

Quotations are taken from back issues of *Guitarist*, *Mojo*, *Making Music*, *Melody Maker*, *Q*, *Uncut*, *Playmusic*, *Acoustic*, *Acoustic Guitar*, *Songtalk*, *Guitar World*, and interviews conducted by the author.

For their involvement in the preparation of this book thanks to Nigel Osborne, Tony Bacon, John Morrish, Mark Brend, Paul Cooper and Simon Smith. I would also like to thank readers who have posted online reviews of this and other books in this series. My many guitar students over the past 30 years have brought new songs to my attention and sharpened my awareness of some points of songwriting discussed herein; in particular, Paul Bridges, Ella Tallyn, Hilmi Kocak, Martin Willbery, Roger Dalrymple, Pardis Sabeti, Bill Henry and Jenny Astley. For personal inspiration on the guitar when I was first learning I am indebted to Denys Stephens and Ian Jackson, and for musical instruction my music teachers at Humphry Davy Grammar, Penzance, Russell Jory and Elizabeth Duncan. Looking further back, I thank my parents Dallas and Bryan for a childhood home that was full of music, popular and classical.

AUTHOR'S NOTE

Rikky Rooksby is a guitar teacher, songwriter / composer, and writer on music. He is the author of the Backbeat titles *How To Write Songs On Guitar* (2000, revised 2009), *Inside Classic Rock Tracks* (2001), *Riffs* (2002), *The Songwriting Sourcebook* (2003), *Chord Master* (2004), *Melody* (2004), *Songwriting Secrets: Bruce Springsteen* (2005), *How To Write Songs On Keyboards* (2005), *Lyrics* (2006), and *Arranging Songs* (2007). He contributed to *Albums: 50 Years Of Great Recordings*, *Classic Guitars Of The Fifties*, *The Guitar: The Complete Guide For The Player*, and *Roadhouse Blues* (2003). He has also written *The Guitarist's Guide To The Capo* (Artemis 2003), *The Complete Guide To The Music Of Fleetwood Mac* (revised ed. 2004), *Play Great Guitar* (Infinite Ideas, 2008), 14 Fastforward guitar tutor books, and transcribed and arranged over 40 chord songbooks of music, including *The Complete Beatles*. He has written entries for a number of rock musicians in the new *Dictionary Of National Biography* (OUP), and published interviews, reviews, articles and transcriptions in magazines such as *Guitar Techniques*, *Total Guitar*, *Guitarist*, *Bassist*, *Bass Guitar Magazine*, *The Band*, *Record Collector*, *Sound On Sound*, *Shindig!*, and *Making Music*, where he wrote the monthly 'Private Pluck' guitar column. He is a member of the Guild of International Songwriters and Composers, the Society of Authors, the Sibelius Society, and the Vaughan Williams Society. Visit his website at www.rikkyrooksby.com for more information.